ALAIN ROBBE-GRILLET

Alain Robbe-Grillet

ALAIN ROBBE-GRILLET

The Body of the Text

BEN STOLTZFUS

Fairleigh Dickinson

Rutherford • Madison • Teaneck
Fairleigh Dickinson University Press
London and Toronto: Associated University Presses

Associated University Presses
440 Forsgate Drive
Cranbury, NJ 08512

Associated University Presses
25 Sicilian Avenue
London WC1A 2QH, England

Associated University Presses
2133 Royal Windsor Drive
Unit 1
Mississauga, Ontario
Canada L5J 1K5

LIBRARY OF CONGRESS CATALOGING IN PUBLICATION DATA

Stoltzfus, Ben, 1927–
  Alain Robbe-Grillet : the body of the text.

  Bibliography: p.
  Includes index.
  1. Robbe-Grillet, Alain, 1922–   —Criticism and
interpretation.   I. Title.
PQ2635.0117Z84   1985   843'.914   83-49342
ISBN 0-8386-3212-2

Printed in the United States of America

For Jacques Borel

Contents

Acknowledgments

I wish to thank my wife and children whose patience, support, and understanding throughout the writing of this book made my task a happy one. I am also grateful to my colleagues and students whose insights have added so much to my own evaluation of Alain Robbe-Grillet and the "nouveau (nouveau) roman." A special acknowledgment is due to Jacques Borel for his careful reading and insightful commentary on the text. It seems appropriate to thank all Robbe-Grillet, "nouveau (nouveau) roman," Structuralist, and Post-Structuralist scholars whose ideas I may have borrowed, either consciously or inadvertently, and whose names do not appear in the notes or in the bibliography.

Quotations from the works of Alain Robbe-Grillet are fully protected by French and international copyright and are used by permission of Les Editions de Minuit, Grove Press, Inc., and Georges Borchardt, Inc. All references to Minuit editions are from the following: *Les Gommes* (1953), *Le Voyeur* (1955), *La Jalousie* (1957), *Dans le labyrinthe* (1959), *Pour un nouveau roman* (1963), *Projet pour une révolution à New York* (1970), *Glissements progressifs du plaisir* (1974), *Topologie d'une cité fantôme* (1976), and *Souvenirs du triangle d'or* (1978). References are also made to Michel Butor, *Répertoire 3* (1968), Gilles Deleuze and Félix Guattari, *Capitalisme et schizophrénie: L'anti-Oedipe* (1972), and Jacques Leenhardt, *Lecture politique du roman: "La Jalousie" d'Alain Robbe-Grillet* (1973).

Quotations from Robbe-Grillet in English translation have been authorized by Grove Press, Inc. for the following: *The Erasers*, trans. Richard Howard (1964), *The Voyeur*, trans. Richard Howard (1958), *Jealousy*, trans. Richard Howard (1959), *In the Labyrinth*, trans. Richard Howard (1960), *Last Year at Marienbad*, trans. Richard Howard (1962), *For a New Novel*, trans. Richard Howard (1965), *Project for a Revolution in New York*, trans. Richard Howard (1972), and *Topology of a Phantom City*, (1976) trans. J. A. Underwood. Grove Press permission extends also to *The Marquis de Sade* by Simone de Beauvoir, trans. Paul Dinnage (1953). Additional quotations from Robbe-Grillet in English translation have been authorized by Georges Borchardt, Inc. for *Glissements progressifs du plaisir* (Paris: Minuit, 1974), for Michel Butor, *Répertoire 3* (Paris: Minuit, 1968), and for Jacques Leenhardt, *Lecture politique du roman: "La Jalousie" d'Alain Robbe-Grillet* (Paris: Minuit, 1973). Calder Publishing extends permission for England and dominions for quotations from *In the Labyrinth*, trans. Christine Brooke-Rose (London: Calder and Boyars, 1967). All publishers retain exclusive rights.

Permission to quote from other sources has been authorized by the following publishers in the United States: Harry N. Abrams, Inc., *Cubism and Twentieth Century Art* by Robert Rosenblum (New York, 1960); Georges Borchardt, *The Order of Things: An Archeology of the Human Sciences* by Michel Foucault, anonymous translation (London: Tavistock Publications, 1970); George Braziller, Inc., a quotation from Sartre's "Preface" to Nathalie Sarraute's *Portrait of a Man Unknown* (New York, 1958); the University of California Press, *Marxism and Literary Criticism* by Terry Eagleton (Berkeley and Los Angeles, 1976); the University of Chicago Press, *Writing and Difference* by Jacques Derrida, trans. Alan Bass (Chicago, 1978); Columbia University Press, *L'Ecriture et l'expérience des limites* by Philippe Sollers (Paris: Seuil, 1968); Cornell University Press, *Structuralist Poetics* by Jonathan Culler (Cornell, 1975); Doubleday & Company, Inc., *The Structuralists: From Marx to Lévi-Strauss* edited by Richard and Fernande de George (New York, 1972); Farrar, Straus and Giroux, Inc., *The Pleasure of the Text* by Roland Barthes, trans. Richard Miller (New York: Hill and Wang, 1975), and *Roland Barthes* by Roland Barthes, trans. Richard Howard (New York: Hill and Wang, 1977); Johns Hopkins University Press, *The Language of the Self*, Jacques Lacan, as quoted by A. G. Wilden (Baltimore, 1968), and *The Languages of Criticism and the Sciences of Man: The Structuralist Controversy*, Roland Barthes, as quoted by Richard Macksey and Eugenio Donato (Baltimore, 1970); Humanities Press, *Phenomenology of Perception* by Maurice Merleau-Ponty, trans. Colin Smith (New York, 1962); Associated Faculty Press, Inc., *From Sartre to the New Novel* by Betty Rahv (Port Washington, N.Y., 1974); New Directions, *Labyrinths: Selected Stories and Other Writings*, "The Immortal," by Jorge Louis Broges, trans. James E. Irby (New York, 1962); Philosophical Library, *Course in General Linguistics* by Ferdinand de Saussure (New York: McGraw Hill, 1966); Oxford University Press, *The French New Novel* by John Sturrock (London, 1969); Random House Inc., *The Stranger* by Albert Camus, trans. Stuart Gilbert (New

York: Knopf, 1967), and *Journals, 1889–1924* by André Gide, trans. Justin O'Brien (New York: Knopf, 1947); St. Martin's Press, Inc., *Style and Idea: Selected Writings* by Arnold Schoenberg (New York, 1975).

Permission to quote from a variety of sources has been granted by the following British publishers: Calder Publishing for a quotation from Sartre's "Preface" to Nathalie Sarraute's *Portrait of a Man Unknown*, English trans. of *Portrait d'un inconnu* (Paris: Gallimard, 1956); Longman Group Ltd., *Mazes and Labyrinths: A General Account of Their History and Developments* by William H. Matthews (London: Longmans, Green and Co., 1927); The Macmillan Press, *Roland Barthes* by Roland Barthes, trans. Richard Howard (London, 1977); Routledge and Kegan Paul Ltd., a quotation from *Oeuvres*, vol. 2 by Paul Valéry (Paris: Gallimard, 1966) and *Phenomenology of Perception* by Maurice Merleau-Ponty, trans. Colin Smith.

French copyright permissions have been granted by the following publishing houses: Editions Borderie, "*L'Eden et après:* début pour un ciné-roman" by Alain Robbe-Grillet, in *Obliques*, nos. 16–17 (Paris, 1978); Editions Louis Conard for a quotation by Charles Baudelaire from *Oeuvres posthumes*, vol. 2, "Mon Coeur mis à nu" (Paris, 1952); Editions José Corti, *Forme et signification* by Jean Rousset (Paris, 1962) and *L'Intérieur et l'extérieur* by Jean Rousset (Paris, 1968); Editions Galilée, *Glas* by Jacques Derrida (Paris, 1974); Gallimard, *L'Etranger* by Albert Camus (Paris, 1953), *Les Mots et les choses* by Michel Foucault (Paris, 1966), *Journal 1889–1939* by André Gide (Paris, 1948), *La Tête d'obsidienne* by André Malraux (Paris, 1974), *Phénoménologie de la perception* by Maurice Merleau-Ponty (Paris, 1945), *Proêmes* by Francis Ponge (Paris, 1965), "Preface" by Jean-Paul Sartre to *Portrait d'un inconnu* by Nathalie Sarraute (Paris, 1956), and *Oeuvres*, vol. 2 by Paul Valéry (Paris, 1966); Editions Grasset, *La Tentation de l'Occident* by André Malraux (Paris, 1970); Librairie Hatier, *Les Gommes: Profil d'une oeuvre* (Paris, 1973); Librairie Plon, *La Pensée sauvage* (Paris, 1962); Editions Seghers, *Alain Robbe-Grillet* by Alain Gardies (Paris, 1972); Les Editions du Seuil, *Roland Barthes* by Roland Barthes (Paris, 1975), *Le Plaisir du texte* by Roland Barthes (Paris, 1973), *Le Récit spéculaire* by Lucien Dällenbach (Paris, 1977), *L'Ecriture et la différence* by Jacques Derrida (Paris, 1967), *Figures III* by Gérard Genette (Paris, 1973), *Du Sens: Essais Sémiotiques* by A. J. Greimas (Paris, 1970), *Nouveaux Problèmes du roman* by Jean Ricardou (Paris, 1978), *Le Nouveau Roman* by Jean Ricardou (Paris, 1973), and *L'Ecriture et l'expérience des limites* by Philippe Sollers (Paris, 1968); Presses universitaires de France, *Phénoménologie de l'expérience esthétique*, vol. 1 (Paris, 1951) by Mikel Dufrenne; Union générale d'editions, *Nouveau Roman: Hier aujourd'hui*, vols. 1 and 2, ed. Jean Ricardou and Françoise van Rossum-Guyon (Paris, 1972).

Italian copyright permission has been granted by Bompiani for *Opera aperta* by Umberto Eco (Milan, 1962).

Permission to reprint modified versions of chapters one through seven has been granted by the following journals: Chapter 1 ("Generative Themes and Serial Permutations"), by *Kentucky Romance Quarterly* 29 (1982): 331–45, and by Loyola University, New Orleans, reprinted by permission of *New Orleans Review* 10 (1983), where "*Souvenirs du triangle d'or:* Robbe-Grillet's Generative Alchemy," and "*L'Eden et après:* Robbe-Grillet's Twelve Themes" first appeared. Chapter 2 ("A Partisan, Passionate, and Politic Project for a Revolution"), by *Comparative Literature Studies* 19 (1982): 365–80, and the University of Illinois Press. Chapter 3 ("The Body of the Text"), *Neophilologus*, where "The Body of Robbe-Grillet's Text: Sex, Myth, and Politics in the *Nouveau Nouveau Roman*," first appeared. Chapter 4 ("Mirror, Mirror on the Wall . . ."), from *Stanford French Review* 2 (1981): 229–45, by permission of Anma Libri, where "Inescutcheon in Art and Robbe-Grillet," first appeared. Chapter 5 ("A Dialectical Topology") by permission of *The International Fiction Review* 9 (1982): 83–92, where "Robbe-Grillet's Dialectical Topology" first appeared. Chapter 6 ("The Labyrinth"), formerly "Robbe-Grillet's Labyrinths: Structure and Meaning," is reprinted from *Contemporary Literature* 22 (1981): 293–307, by permission of the University of Wisconsin Press. Chapter 7 ("Games: Dramatized Play"), formerly "Robbe-Grillet's Games: Dramatized Play," is reprinted by permission of *Gradiva* 2 (1980–81): 61–77.

The writing of this book was made possible, in part, by research grants from the University of California. I hereby acknowledge this support.

Introduction

Throughout this study the designation New Novel ("nouveau roman") refers to Robbe-Grillet's work published between 1953 and 1959, from *Les Gommes* to *Dans le labyrinthe*. The designation New New Novel ("nouveau nouveau roman") refers to Robbe-Grillet's work published between 1965 and the present, that is, since *La Maison de rendez-vous*.

The New Novel was characterized by reflexivity, discontinuity, and achronology. In addition to these radical departures from the aesthetic conventions of classical realism, the New New Novel now emphasizes generative themes, generative numbers, paronomasia, and polysemy. The designation New (New) Novel ("nouveau [nouveau] roman") thus refers to both periods, and implies that the aesthetic of the first applies to the second, or vice versa. Robbe-Grillet, of course, is not the only New (New) Novelist, since authors such as Claude Simon, Robert Pinget, and others were also publishing their works during this time.

Robbe-Grillet's commentators, in discussing his fiction and his films, have generally taken opposite views in order to propound one of two critical preferences. Bruce Morrissette is perhaps the best known of the so-called "recuperative" critics who see meaning and chronology in Robbe-Grillet's works, whereas Jean Ricardou is an eloquent and prolific spokesman for a linguistic, nonmimetic interplay of verbal signs. The themes of Jacques Leenhardt's *Lecture politique du roman: "La Jalousie" d'Alain Robbe-Grillet* and Stephen Heath's *The Nouveau Roman* also implicitly oppose each other, the former recuperating meaning and the latter denying it.

My study reconciles the extrinsic and the intrinsic—the mimetic and the reflexive points of view. Robbe-Grillet's eleven novels, six films, one volume of short stories, four ciné-romans, eight collaborative ventures with artists and photographers, one volume of essays, and many articles and interviews justify, even require, a thematic overview, not only of the structural figures and the linguistic patterns in his works but also an evaluation of the different critical approaches to his work. The dominant reflexive modes in his writing, be they generative themes, serial permutations, or "mise en abyme" effects, define a new narrative discourse whose form, in addition to speaking of itself, also tries to subvert establishment ideology. Robbe-Grillet's works are therefore formalist and "revolutionary." His art functions simultaneously on both levels; it is a synthesis of the two. *The Body of the Text*, the subtitle of this study, thus reflects the duality within Robbe-Grillet, as well as the duality in the critical methodologies applied to his work.

However, before exploring the body of the text itself, it might be useful to remind the reader that in conventional novels time is chronological, plots are logical, and characters are more or less true to life. The use of such conventions (plausibility demands it) forces the novelist to construct a past and a present from a future he (like God) is privileged to know. He invents characters whose psychological portraits follow predictable temporal patterns. The standards of success for such novels have been and continue to be defined in terms of "flesh and blood" characters in recognizable life situations. These characteristics also define the reified novel in today's consumer society whose highest achievements are measured (monetarily) by the number of paperbacks sold to an indoctrinated and indiscriminate public.

Thus, readers weaned on the traditional novel complain that the New (New) Novel is dull because it contains no human beings and no story, whereas, in fact, though the presentation has changed, the new fiction contains both. If New (New) Novelists find it hard to tell a story, they stress the word "tell" and not "story." What has changed is that the incoherence of the plot and the problematical relationships between characters are depriving readers of the security of a mechanistic world and the consolations of an essentialist psychology.

Conventional readers, for the most part, seem unprepared to follow abrupt transitions, immersion in the present, the proliferation of names and incidents, contradictions, exaggerations, implausibilities (is this life or fiction?); in short, the deliberate flaunting of rules that used to be indispensable for the writing of good literature. "The writers of the New Novel," as John Sturrock phrases it, "are . . . anxious to expose a plot for what it is, a conspiracy; the conspirator is the novelist and the victim is reality."[1]

Whereas the traditional novel claimed to mirror life, the New Novel and its sequel the New New Novel mirror both life and art. However, New (New) Novelists work primarily with the formal qualities of language, stressing art's internal machinery: polysemy, wordplay, and specular structures, all of which weave self-referential levels that are an expression of art's self-consciousness. Nevertheless, these formal relationships between words and images also have mimetic value. The disjunction of people and things, as with cubism, in spite of or perhaps because the fragmentation distorts reality, reflects the contemporary dissolution of beliefs, the atomicity of perception, the disappearance of the depth of man, the subversion of ideology, and, last, though not least, art's revolutionary potential.

Adventuresome readers and writers welcome the New (New) Novel because it mirrors a change in our perception of reality. "This interrogative turning-in of the self," says Michel Butor, "is in answer to our altered image of the world."[2] Our awareness of a demythified world, in which man's psychosocial makeup is striving to establish new workable value systems, manifests itself in a new literary formalism that is hyperconscious of language. In his preface to Sarraute's *Portrait d'un inconnu* Sartre states that the novel is in the process of reflecting on itself. Gérard Durozoi writes that it is no longer content that matters, but the writing itself, the form.[3] "That literature in our day is fascinated by the ring of language," says Michel Foucault, "is a phenomenon whose necessity has its roots in a vast configuration in which the whole structure of our thought and our knowledge is traced."[4]

Unlike popular novelists who simplify plot and reduce relationships to stock-in-trade situations, New (New) Novelists delight in complexity and obscurity, in part for their own sake, but mainly because the world has become opaque. It is no longer transparent, let alone predictable. Hence the frustration experienced by the general reader, who, like Thesius in the labyrinth, but without Ariadne's thread to guide him, is deprived of familiar signposts. Hence also the labyrinth motif in the fiction of Kafka, Borges, and Robbe-Grillet that reflects the disorientation of modern man in a desacralized world.[5]

Since there is general agreement that man today is experiencing a crisis of values, it is normal that the new fiction, whose innovations are in no sense symptomatic of moral or spiritual decadence, should, in addition to speaking of itself, also reflect changing attitudes toward reality and human nature. The "death of man" syndrome expresses itself, in part, in the gradual disappearance of characters. In the works of Kafka, Joyce, Roussel, Faulkner, Sarraute, Robbe-Grillet, and Sollers heroes and heroines become nameless, faceless, anonymous, multiple, and nonexistent. Nathalie Sarraute dwells on the imagery of the subconversational worlds that inhabits the nether regions of characters whose names may remain vague or unknown. The nameless and faceless husband of *La Jalousie* projects a dual image of jealousy and colonialism on a landscape that denies him. Whereas New Novelists were working to subvert the accepted notions of character, the authors of the *Tel Quel* group have, since then, eliminated characters entirely. Jean Thibaudeau's *Ouverture,* Marcelin Pleynet's *Comme,* Jean-Louis Baudry's *Personnes,* and Philippe Sollers's *Drame* emphasize the adventure of a *parole* in which characters' identities are expressed as pronouns and limited to grammatical personae.

In fiction, the suppression of heroes capable of evolving in a familiar world, the destruction of character, the dissolution of privileged points of view, coincide with the ascendancy of structuralism and a decline in the influence of phenomenology and existentialism. Within a structuralist equation it is man who appears as the unknown factor. The structures of *La Jalousie* harmonize perfectly with the nameless, faceless, and quasi-empty presence of the jealous husband. He exists in a world in which he is unable to dominate the events, the objects, and the woman who determine them. It is a world in which feelings, if they exist at all, are objectified in things, reified. Herein lies an essential contradiction of the early New Novel, postulating on the one hand the determinism of external phenomena and on the other the inalienable freedom of the artist's choices and inventions. Today, each New (New) Novel exhibits itself while denouncing the codes that hamper it. Insofar as it stresses the enunciation to the exclusion of the enunciated, insofar as it favors the signifier to the signified, each New (New) Novel is a theorem on the freedom of a literature trying to escape from the strait jacket of culture or the aphasia of language. The New (New) Novel, like the quantum theory it strives so hard to emulate, is an experiment in probability, neither totally determined nor totally free—always subject to the influences of the unpredictable—the writer's language wrestling with the formidable constraints of tradition and contemporary myth.

The New (New) Novel is thus one symptom of the devaluation of the past. This desacralization, which has been furthered by discoveries in science, expresses itself today in literature, from Proust on, as achronology, whereas atomicity has its own unpredictability and discontinuity, particularly after *La Maison de rendez-vous*, a work which marks the beginning of Robbe-Grillet's

New New Novel. The New Novel was born in 1953, with the publication of *Les Gommes*, and, generally speaking, died in 1959, with the publication of *Dans le labyrinthe*. *La Maison de rendez-vous* (1965) is the first work in which Robbe-Grillet systematically disperses the identity of his characters. Edouard Manneret, the resurrected victim of innumerable "murders," is a typical example of implausible metamorphoses: he is a writer, then an actor in a play entitled *The Assassination of Edouard Manneret*, then the painter of *La Maïa*, a famous painting, then a usurer, doctor, chemist, fetischist, and secret agent. If these roles were not sufficient to nullify the realism of so outrageous a character, the similarity in sound between Manet, Man Ray, and Manneret should quickly dispel any remaining illusions about Robbe-Grillet's comic treatment or the doubts he casts on conventional fiction. Most New New Novelists, like Robbe-Grillet, use the names of people in their fiction, but they refuse to give them the priority they occupied in the past, relegating them to an accessory level where they function with varying degrees of realism. It was perhaps inevitable that someone like Claude Ollier would write a radio play entitled *La Mort du personnage*.

Language, instead of any one character, has become the protagonist of the new fiction. Instead of exploring the vicissitudes of the hero/heroine, the author now explores the capacities of language to reflect upon itself, and writing, instead of hiding its narrative devices, exposes them, deliberately. However, even before the so-called New Novel of the 1950s, Maurice Blanchot (*Thomas l'obscur*, 1932, *Aminadab*, 1942, and *Le Très haut*, 1948) was writing reflexive fiction consciously exposing its narrative devices. Queneau (*Loin de Rueuil*) was also writing novels emphasizing the texture of language or the mathematical structures of fiction. Jean Cayrol's novel *Les Corps étrangers* (1949) doubts the reality assembled by its author and his characters. Pinget's inventive and forgetful characters, like Cayrol's, dissolve before our eyes. Multiple, contradictory episodes from one text to another contest and subvert reality. Pinget's novels, like Robbe-Grillet's, are alternately constructed and destroyed, thereby devaluing conventional fiction which, normally, goes to great pains to hide its artifices in order to pretend that it is "real."

> Literary description [says Robbe-Grillet] is creative-destructive, it is not descriptive. The sentence does not report on an object which might have existed independently of it and before it. If, in the

nineteenth century, Balzacian descriptions claimed to speak about the world, modern description knows that it speaks only of itself.[6]

These claims are only partly true, however, because they conflict with other aspirations of the New (New) Novel: its subversion, its topology, its labyrinths, and its games have referential levels that often transcend the reflexive dimensions of language, which may be generative, productive, polysemous, materialistic, and riddled with specular effects. In fact, New (New) Novels always function simultaneously on the reflexive *and* the referential or "recuperated" levels. Nor is the autonomy of fiction as new as many of its proponents claim. By parodying a certain literature in vogue, Petronius, Cervantes, and Rabelais had already written antinovels that opposed and exposed "l'esprit sérieux" and the mechanisms of fiction. Charles Sorel's *Berger extravagant* had *Anti-Roman* as its subtitle as early as 1627, long before Sartre used this term in his preface to Nathalie Sarraute's *Portrait d'un inconnu*, in which he says that

> Anti-novels retain the appearance and shape of a novel; they are works of the imagination which present fictional characters and describe their lives. But they do so all the better to deceive; the intent is to have the novel contest itself and destroy itself under our eyes within the time period needed to erect it; to write the novel of a novel that does not exist, which cannot exist.[7]

Although Sartre's statement neatly defines the parameters and preoccupations of the New Novel, it does not begin to explain the complexity of the New New Novel. The latter's subversion is directed not only at itself and at literary convention but also at language and the ideology that is encoded in it. Moreover, Robbe-Grillet asserts that, as an artist, he wishes to break the grip of linguistic, ideological, and subconscious tyrannies that imprison and manipulate men everywhere. Consequently, in order to demonstrate his individual freedom, within the confines of a pervasive determinism, he plays with words and assaults the body of texts whose normative codes embody establishment values.

Since he began writing, Robbe-Grillet's attack on language and ideology has evolved simultaneously on two levels. First, the mimetic role of language is devalued in favor of its autonomous, self-reflexive characteristics, even as the new literary discourse subverts conventional standards of story, plot, and character. Second, within this new discourse, the artist's *parole*, i.e., his unique, specific, individual utterance, plays with society's *langue*, i.e., with the language we all share, in order to expose ideology's arbitrary base. If *parole* is the breach in the wall of the prison-house of *langue*, then we have an aggressive art that parodies establishment values and tortures the body of its texts. Such art elicits a sensuous and incestuous relationship with the mother tongue, but the mock violence and eroticism in Robbe-Grillet's art also satirize society's collective unconscious thereby providing a necessary catharsis to the repressed imagery of a post-Freudian era. Robbe-Grillet's interest in contemporary myth—in its sex, violence, and alienation—structures a dramatic dialogue between *langue* and *parole*, thereby providing a referential, even revolutionary, dimension to his work. This recuperated aspect of art coexists with an autonomous, self-reflexive, linguistic level whose only purpose is to enhance the sensory pleasure of the text. However, the formalism of the New (New) Novel, with its foregrounding and thickening of language, develops a poetics that is strangely at odds with the ironic gore of its content. This dualism is at the heart of Robbe-Grillet's discourse. Lest we be deceived by his self-conscious, verbal labyrinths, there is always the cry, the blood, and the body—metaphors that catapult us out of formalism into the mythic realism of everyday life.

ALAIN ROBBE-GRILLET

1

Generative Themes and Serial Permutations

> The story has not disappeared: during the course of its trial it
> has multiplied, and this plurality is now in conflict with itself.
> —Jean Ricardou

> For the text, nothing is gratuitous except its own destruction:
> not to write, not to write again, except to be eternally re-
> cuperated.
> —Roland Barthes

Once upon a time the Greeks responded to the *logos* while Chris-
tians believed that world order was determined by the word of
God. In the relatively stable metaphysical climate of the nineteenth
century, Balzac, like God, created a world that mirrored the society
of his day, chronicling among other things, the rise of the
bourgeoisie, the vicissitudes of wealth, a preoccupation with
money and what it can buy (objects, power, sex, and so on). Balzac,
like God in His world, was everywhere, but unlike Flaubert, who
wished to remain invisible, Balzac's presence is a tangible force
regulating narrative events. Until recently, the response of an artist
atuned to the implications of modern science or to recent speculations in philosophy and the human sciences was to question or to
abandon the writer's traditional role of God. In the realm of the
novel, the withdrawal of an Absolute Mind expressed itself as the
disappearance of the omniscient author. Henry James and Edith
Wharton, among others, rejected Fielding's, Balzac's, or Tolstoy's
intrusions into a narrative either to comment on the action or to
manipulate characters and events. Verisimilitude, they claimed,
was enhanced by filtering experience directly (without authorial
intervention) through the conscious mind of one or more characters. Now, near the end of a desacralized twentieth century,
writers of fiction, unconcerned about the absence of God, have
once again assumed the prerogatives of the omniscient author.

Today [says Robbe-Grillet] we have decided to assume fully the artificiality of our work: there is no natural order, either moral, political, or narrative; there are only human orders created by man, with all that that implies in terms of the provisional and the arbitrary.[1]

Whereas Henry James and Edith Wharton, like Flaubert, wanted to minimize their authorial presence by filtering reality through the narrative consciousness of a protagonist, Robbe-Grillet multiplies the points of view in order to break down verisimilitude. Whereas point of view in *La Jalousie* was essentially the husband's, *La Maison de rendez-vous* fragments the narrative and destroys the illusion of reality by drawing attention to the arbitrariness of perception that does not exclude the author's point of view. The traditional novel, with its established conventions, duplicated the order and unity of a Newtonian world, whereas the New (New) Novel, with one foot in quantum theory, multiplies disorder and discontinuity. The reader's new role is not to decipher a priori meaning, but to create meaning from multiple contradictory elements, from a *parole* that resists the reader's attempts to force it into a preestablished mold.

Writing before the "nouveau roman" made few efforts to demystify literature or to draw attention to itself. Fiction was, by and large, nonreflexive. It had its message or its story, and a certain limited foregrounding of language, but it was not interested in elaborate mirrors of consciousness. The New (New) Novel stresses formal aspects of writing that emphasize a work's "literariness." Henceforth, says Robbe-Grillet:

it is the novel itself which thinks itself, doubts itself, and judges itself; not by means of characters who indulge in idle commentaries; but by means of constant reflexion, at the readerly and the writerly level, of each element on itself; gestures, objects, or situations.[2]

Françoise van Rossum-Guyon and Claude Ollier, among others, refer to this inner autonomous functioning of the text.[3]

It is said that the goal of traditional literature is to express a pre-existing reality: this literature is the *writing of an adventure* and people oppose it to the *Nouveau Roman* which would like to be the *adventure of writing*.[4]

Mikel Dufrenne believes that aesthetic reflection, coupled with today's expansion of the arts, is experiencing a privileged historical moment. The death of art that Hegel announced, consequent to the "death of God," has signaled the resurrection of an authentic art whose purpose is to speak only of itself. Modern art has in fact produced works that are immediately perceived as aesthetic objects. Basic knowledge, with the advent of textbooks in physics or in psychology, has transformed the *De Natura* into a poem and *La Princesse de Clèves* into a novel. Christianity no longer inspires great works of art, and photography dispenses painters from imitating nature. Desacralization has freed artists from the obligation of creating referential art with a necessary message.[5]

The prototypes for self-conscious literature are probably Cervantes's *Don Quixote* and Sterne's *Tristram Shandy* in which the narrative devices, instead of being deliberately concealed, as they are in conventional novels, are bared so that the reader may understand that the subject matter is the process of storytelling itself. These novels are the forerunners of today's avant-garde fiction in which the message is devalued and in which meaning does not only come from the outside but also from the novel's speaking of its own existence. To focus on the "message" for its own sake, instead of what it says, as Roman Jakobson points out, is the "poetic" function of language.[6] Metalanguage, therefore, is the form that self-consciousness takes whenever language becomes poetic. It posits a sign system that is a vehicle for semiology's awareness of itself as a process. Novels that emphasize this "writerly" process, as Roland Barthes calls it, expose the sham and arbitrariness of literary conventions that claim to "mirror life," and by reflecting on themselves, force a higher degree of "readerly" consciousness.[7]

Finnegans Wake, as one prime example, is not necessarily about something, it itself is *something*. It is for literature what quantum physics is for science. It makes us aware of the fact that since our notion of the universe has changed, it is no longer possible to move about it in the old consecrated ways. Accordingly, Joyce invents an arbitrary, artificial world ("whorled without aimed") which is perhaps as eternal ("world without end") and aimless ("world without aim") as the whirlwind ("world" plus "whirl") of the cosmic chaos ("chaosmos"). Joyce's "whorld" order, so the theory goes, has the merit of being based on language, which is man-made, rather than on incomprehensible cosmic events. Joyce thus simultaneously desacralizes both religion and language. *Finnegans Wake*, says Umberto Eco, "is an epiphany of cosmic structure in the form of language."[8] Joyce's signifiers no longer stand for something signified.

They are objects in their own right, the subject of multiple intentions inviting different interpretations. Their complexity makes meaning not something already accomplished, waiting to be expressed, but is, instead, a horizon, a perspective of semiotic production. This dramatization of language and its productive or generative capacities, by stressing the internal reflexive activity of language and narration, is of seminal importance for the "nouveau nouveau roman."

In French literature, the closest thing to Joyce is probably Raymond Roussel, whose texts also function as generative devices. *Locus Solus* is a "game" of machines invented to create a world that is itself the product of linguistic machinery. Roussel puns on one phrase to produce another, then writes a story to unify the two: "une demoiselle à prétendants" (a girl with suitors) becomes "une demoiselle à reïtre en dents" (a paving beetle for a knight in teeth). The text displays a closed system of differences, encourages the production of meanings, and thus devalues the notion of determinate signs. Roussel's work demythifies reality as well as those literary forms that claim to mirror it. He plays on double and different identities, on time that repeats and abolishes itself, on words whose slippery meanings mean the reverse of what they seem to say—paronomastic structures that undermine the stability and predictability of a sacrosanct world.

Playing with language was, of course, a favorite game of the surrealists, who used words and colors as generative themes for images and meaning. A word such as "rubis" (ruby) leads to the word "rose," which leads to the sound for dew ("rosée"). Any of these sounds may lead to a fish called a "rouget" (in "Au beau demi-jour"), as easily as the color rose leads visually to the color red ("rouge"), or the sound "rose" to a rose window ("Rosace" in Breton's "Hôtel des étincelles," and *Le Revolver aux cheveux blancs*). Breton's verbal playfulness and inventiveness also produce "aux mollets de moelle" (calves of marrow) and "au cou d'orge . . . à la gorge . . . d'or" (neck of barley . . . to the throat . . . of gold) (in "L'Union libre"); or puns such as "la mourre" (a game of fingers and numbers) and "l'amour"; as well as "le coeur m'en dit" (the heart tells me so), and "le coeur mendie" (the heart begs), (in *Les États-généraux*).

Du côté de chez Swann, like surrealism, provides its own examples of paronomasia or wordplay that anticipate the role of "expressive metaphor" (Ricardou's term) in the works of Robbe-Grillet, Claude Simon, or Robert Pinget. The "madeleine" is both a "patisserie" and the Madeleine, a Parisian monument, "une de mes églises" [Méséglise] (one of my churches), says Proust, punning on the word "churches" thereby signifying both the village, Méséglise, and the narrative.

> To produce [says Jean Ricardou] is to work with a material. With regards to the text this material is mainly language used not as a means of expression, but as signifying matter. Within the text, these operations consist in transforming the signifying matter by organizing it according to the text.[9]

Saussure advances a memory theory about sentence construction that allows us to generate combinations and to differentiate meanings according to the richness of the language and the inventiveness of the speaker: thus language is a storehouse of sound images that manifest themselves in speaking and in writing. The ambiguity and complexity of language, to borrow philosophical arguments from Saussure and Chomsky, enable us to think of it as "generative" and "differential." Language is generative because it enables the speaker/hearer to see the (syntagmatic) constraints of any sentence; differential because it enables him to see each word against the (paradigmatic) contrasts allowed by those constraints. "Language is a system of interdependent terms in which the value of each term results solely from the simultaneous presence of the others."[10] Such a material view of language has prompted Claude Simon to define the work of the writer as a "bricolage" or assemblage in the sense of puttering (the term is from Lévi-Strauss and the Prague Circle), a labor that reminds him, he says, of a course in mathematics entitled "Arrangements, Permutations, Combinations."

> Indeed, I know of no term that better emphasizes the craftsmanlike and empirical nature of this work which consists of assembling and organizing, within that *unity* Baudelaire speaks of and in which they must *echo* and *answer each other*, all of the elements of this vast system of signs that go into a novel. This is done in a series of groping efforts: there are components which have to be smoothed . . . others which have to be "manufactured" . . . perhaps the capital revelation of this work is that these purely formal requirements, instead of becoming difficulties or obstacles, turn out to be eminently *productive*, and, in themselves engendering.[11]

In the New Novel, *Le Voyeur*, there is a piece of string rolled into a figure eight. Jean Ricardou calls it a "generative metaphor" because it is a point of departure for multiple figure eights on the island, on the jetty, on doors, in the newspaper, and so on.[12] Such imagery has an internal productive dynamism that propels the narrative forward. It authorizes the passage from one word cell or image to the next through juxtaposition without the implied metaphoric comparison and identity. Ricardou calls such a nucleus a "métaphore transitaire," although metonymy explains the slippage better. Without metaphor, says Proust, there can be no memory, but without metonymy, adds Gérard Genette, there can be no linking of memory, no narrative, no novel. If metaphor discovers the "Temps perdu" (lost Time), it is metonymy that revives it and sets it in motion. "If the initial 'droplet' of involuntary memory belongs to metaphor, 'the edifice of memory' is entirely metonymic."[13] Since metaphor is the analogic "detonator" (e.g., the figure eight of the string), it is essential to note that the first explosion is accompanied inevitably by a chain reaction which proceeds, not by analogy (as metaphor would normally do), but by metonymic contagion. Hence the compulsive proliferation of figure eights that "contaminate" *Le Voyeur* and multiply the contiguity of visual and affective associations.

The productive and generative capacities of language, to the exclusion sometimes of story, plot, and characters, are among the New (New) Novelists' primary concerns. These writers have visited the flowers (not so evil after all) of certain precursors, and to use Montaigne's image, in addition to Baudelaire's, have drawn their honey from them. To precursors such as Cervantes, Sterne, Proust, Roussel, Joyce, and Breton, we should no doubt add Kafka, Borges, Virginia Woolf, Faulkner, and Beckett, whose labyrinthine, stream-of-consciousness, achronological narratives have not gone unnoticed by the new artificers. In Faulkner's work, says Robbe-Grillet, the development of themes and their multiple associations disrupts all narrative chronology "drowning" whatever the story may have revealed. In Beckett's narratives, events and facts contradict each other thereby destroying the text's tranquility, innocence, and certitude.

The New New Novel's devaluation of conventional literary norms (plot, suspense, character) in favor of achronology, discontinuity, and reflexivity pursues the same "dehumanizing" tendencies that, from the beginning, characterized the New Novel. However, generative themes are now the ordering elements: objects, events, words, colors, numbers, images, and formal movements engender internal rhythms and patterns, giving cohesion to the apparent dispersion of the anecdotal material. "Far from disappearing," says Robbe-Grillet, "the anecdote begins to multiply; discontinuous, multiple, mobile, aleatory, stressing itself its own fictive nature, it becomes a 'game' in the strongest sense of the word."[14]

Paronomasia and polysemy have now become a game of construction designed to facilitate the semantic slippage through which a work derives its meaning: it proliferates. Language, by displaying a system of differences, allows the responsive imagination to play with ambiguity, thereby generating new meaning. Each color or image, instead of connecting with reality outside, links itself with other colors or images inside the text. This kind of generative writing ("écriture productrice") in, for example, Claude Simon's *Triptyque* (1973), multiplies the internal reflexive allusions moving us back and forth on a discontinuous horizontal axis. Signifiers, instead of signifying, refer to other signifiers whose mimetic role is undermined by mirrors, pictures, posters, postcards, and film clips to which they refer or from which they emerge. The simultaneous narration of three sexual encounters at a beach city, in a valley, and in a northern suburb, using words, images, and connotations that overlap from one setting to another, sets up resonances that come into focus whenever the spotlight, the projector, the lens, or the eye (i.e., any of these circles) illuminates the events of the novel's triadic structure. "We have evolved from the telling of a story to the proliferation of stories, which defines accurately the Nouveau Nouveau Roman" (*NRHA*, 2:341).

Robert Pinget's *Passacaille* (1969) is another example of a novel whose triadic structure ("Le calme. Le Gris. De remous àucun."— So calm. So gray. Not a ripple in view.) and rhythmic, cyclical patterning generate something from nothing. Out of the void of words such as "none," "closed," "winter," "dead garden," "no one," and "nothing"—words with which the novel begins—Pinget builds a vertical and horizontal axis whose center is the dung heap and its ubiquitous "corpse." The novel, whose title also denotes a seventeenth- and eighteenth-century musical form consisting of continuous variations on a ground bass in slow triple meter, embodies connotations from the Spanish word *passacalle: pasar* meaning "to pass" and *calle* meaning "street." Thus, the horizontal axis of the novel is the country road along which the people pass and on which the "accident" occurs. The vertical axis is provided by the upward flight of crows or magpies whose droppings and skeletal remains festoon the bushes, trees, and branches of the marsh.

The corpse, which metamorphoses from man to cow to scarecrow, establishes a "connection," as Fernand Meyer points out, between here and nowhere.[15] The cadaver, by being everywhere and nowhere, like the novel's many thematic variations and contradictions, undermines realism and reality. *Passacaille*, the dance as well as the language of the novel, moves in circles going nowhere, enjoying the pure polyphony of movement. The tension between life and death, winter and summer, creation and destruction comes to rest on the compost heap of existence—life's and art's self-generating, polysemous pile. Out of the rich dung heap of language, the author uses generative play, humor, and seriousness in order to create the body of the text—a text that is nothing and everything. A severed cow's teat, for example, is served on a plate and mistaken for a penis. The corpse's fly has been bloodied and from its opening the author removes the scroll of the manuscript. Such "play" establishes generative associations connoting relationships between the writing process, sexuality, death, castration, and so on, essential ingredients of the "nouveau nouveau roman."

The "nouveau nouveau roman," says Jean Ricardou, is the result of a patient linguistic effort whose purpose is to construct a complex network of interconnecting signs.[16] The linguistic weave or mix evolves from a number of generative themes—themes that structure the work and also give it its individual pattern. However, the word *theme* as it is used by the New Novelists refers indiscriminately to words, objects, colors, images, or ideas. Considering the fact that the word *theme* is usually employed to designate a work's central idea or thesis, the fuzziness of its new meaning is worth keeping in mind. For instance, *L'Eden et après* uses doors and fire along with other objects and images in its ten series of twelve generative themes. In *Projet pour une révolution à New York* it is not the word *red* which is the generative theme, but the color *red*, a color which arson, murder, and rape share because red is the color of blood, fire, and the revolutionary flag.[17] Robbe-Grillet, unlike Pinget, prefers colors and objects as generative themes, to the sonority of words. But he also structures serial combinations with the images of popular and classic myths. "New York is for us the perfect place—a place where there is no longer anything natural, where everything is being transformed continuously into a mythic state" (*NRHA*, 2:166).

The vocabulary used to describe the generative process is a loose one, but the structures themselves, once established, are not hard to follow. Sometimes a word, a name, or an object builds a pattern, a semantic field of correspondences whose sounds, associations, connotations, and imagery proliferate throughout the text. At other times, mythic contexts, as in *Projet, Souvenirs,* and *Topologie* lend themselves to layered thematic excavations. "In *Topologie,* for instance, there's Greek mythology and Hamilton. For me it's the same thing. That is, I don't believe that popular culture is different from high culture. In reality they deal with the same themes."[18] The theme of the "raped virgin," for instance, is one of the main themes of *Topologie:* a virgin is exposed to Zeus's shower of gold, or to the deadly showers of warriors' arrows, or to the sharp stylet of the author's "hand" stabbing the vulva of a woman on an engraving of burnished copper. In fact, the cry of the mythical virgin sets *Topologie* in motion, even as the naked women of the five male progenitors (Delvaux, Hamilton, Magritte, Rauschenberg, and Robbe-Grillet) "play" their roles in the prison, in the theater, in the house, and in the landscape of the author's imagination—an imagination that encompasses all phantom topologies and is the fifth privileged space, the "generative cell"—the mind that engenders. This cell is a secret room, a "chambre secrète" (the title of an early short story), from which these fictions emerge.

The five spaces featured in *Topologie* are like a cell's DNA. The number five generates not only the novel's *topoy* but also the five bars on the cell's five windows, the five fingers on the hand holding the stylet-pen, the five male generators, and so on. The number five, like the color red for *Projet,* orders a system within a system, engendering combinations and permutations based on nine "themes." Like the twelve themes of *L'Eden et après,* these nine themes form serial patterns within *Projet, Topologie,* and *Souvenirs,* patterns that seem to signify nothing but themselves. Yet the novels do signify; they are not pure reflexive surfaces. Each novel transcends the autonomy of its parts, the adventure of writing, its own internal patterning. If the randomness and atomicity of generative play mirror the great cosmic game that Kostas Axelos speaks of, then such fiction belies its formalism.[19] Generative play, which is spontaneous, humorous, free, and self-ordering, may in fact create something out of nothing, thus communicating feelings and attitudes that have ontic significance. Sexual fantasies, says Robbe-Grillet, are signified unmistakenly by the images of the black thief, fire, and the subway;[20] it is these fantasies, he says, that have been used as generative themes in his most recent books (*NRHA,* 2:141).

It hardly matters, however, whether the color red in *Projet* generates arson, murder, and rape, or whether these three themes, in turn, generate the scenes, events, and images that follow. Red is the symbolic color of the Revolution even if it is only linguistic. But such use of the color red is also an example of man's mythmaking tendency. Verbal and artistic tracings, man's symbolic activity, as Ernst Cassirer has pointed out, are the odyssey of the mind.[21] Thus, Revolution as a concept, even in a novel such as *Projet*, which Ricardou and others claim to be nonrecuperable and non-symbolic, culminates in symbolic expression. However, since the revolution in *Projet* is linguistic and affective rather than political, its impact derives not from the coherence of its ideological doctrine, which is secondary and minimal, but from its assault on the norms of art, ideology, and of established good taste. Indeed, when it was first published, the novel succeeded in offending practically everybody. Girls are tortured, raped, and injected with fluids, while black revolutionaries burn, pillage, and terrorize, even as other masked individuals act out a variety of maddeningly con-tradictory roles. Although these activities correspond to revolu-tionary stereotypes, the author's real, though covert attack, like Roland Barthes's subversions, is on *langue, doxa,* and *myth.* Says Robbe-Grillet:

> I am not one of those who believes that the secretion of myth by cultures derives exclusively from the alienation of man in capitalist society or in bureaucratic socialism. I would ally myself instead with this phrase that Roland Barthes pronounced one day: "As long as death exists, there will be myth." (*NRHA,* 2:161)

Whereas *Projet* deals with New York as a city in which contempo-rary myths are inflated and distorted, *Souvenirs du triangle d'or* blends alchemy and writing into a work of fiction that assumes mythic proportions in its own right. The analysis that follows fo-cuses on the text's generative alchemy.

Generative Alchemy: *Souvenirs du triangle d'or*[22]

In the novel *Souvenirs du triangle d'or,* the prime generative theme is a golden triangle, an image composed of two ideograms: gold and triangle. From this shape and this color the author generates all the subsidiary themes and the mythology of the novel. It is perhaps interesting to note that its first title was *Propriétés secrètes du triangle,* a provocative use of the adjective *secrètes,* considering Robbe-

Grillet's former "attacks" on the use of metaphor, symbol, and depth. Whereas, in the past, Robbe-Grillet claimed to eschew all a priori symbolism, he now says that the triangle is a "divine symbolic form."[23] Tongue in cheek and symbology aside (Robbe-Grillet seems to enjoy toying with his readers and his critics), the shape of an inverted triangle ($\triangledown$) and the atomic number for gold (79) do allow him to generate numerical, geometric, mythological, and carnal forms. Accordingly, the atomic number for gold manifests itself as a "play" on two numbers: seven and nine. Both are incorporated into the nine rings of the archery target whose center is called "the gold" because it is so colored.

"La Cible" (The Target), is Robbe-Grillet's title for this particular section of *Souvenirs*—a passage that was first published as a preface to the Jasper Johns catalog for the 1978 exhibition at the Centre Pompidou in Paris. The target-text centers around and is generated by Jasper Johns's paintings of a broken target, a white target, green targets, targets with faces, and targets numbered in color and in black and gray. The number nine that Robbe-Grillet uses in his text comes from Johns's picture series entitled *Numbers*. The objects in Robbe-Grillet's nine circles are also objects chosen from Johns's art. "La Cible" begins with the number nine in the outer circle, and, in reverse order, moves toward one—the center of the target. Eight is a piece of rope, seven is a twisted coat hanger, six is a spoon, five is a handprint, four is an overturned chair, three is a half-eaten apple, two is a shoe, and one is a ruler. The narrator in his cell throws a beer can (remember Johns's Ballantine ale cans) at the "targette"—French for door-bolt—and hits the door squarely in the center. It seems clear that Johns's targets and objects have generated this piece of fiction that doubles also as a preface.

The beer can as well as the metal grill around a sidewalk tree, like the target, also have nine concentric circles (*STO*, p. 136). Number two, the woman's shoe, as a recurrent object and fetish, is associated with the number seven (*STO*, p. 137). Of all the numbers referred to (pp. 132–37), nine and seven are given the greatest prominence. An inverted 2, we are told, looks like a 7. The woman's shoe ("il est . . . pratiquement neuf—it is practically new/nine" [p. 28]), which was caught in the perforation of the grill's second circle, also looks like a 7. "Consequently, a few cursory modifications in the text should suffice in order to insert the shoe in the seventh rank where it belongs" (*STO*, p. 137). The shoe though demythified is reminiscent of Claudel's *Soulier de satin*. It also has a reciprocal signifying relationship with the triangle:

> Carolina bends down to pick up another piece of flotsam: her second blue shoe, whose mirrored ornament has been torn out with pincers, leaving a wide open wound in the tender leather. The wound extends from the upper center as far as the tip of the triangle that shapes its front section. It forms a kind of mouth, splitting the toe of the shoe along its longitudinal axis. There is blood flowing from between the two open lips; the thick liquid seems black under the funereal rays of the moon. (STO, p. 194)

In the novel's many mirrors, objects such as the shoe, the triangle, and the lips, and colors such as blue, gold, and red reflect each other continuously. Nor is the shoe the only item generated by the inverted triangle: the green apple, the rose, the fur, the beggar-girl named Temple all issue from the slit vertical orifice (either eye or lips) contained within the triangle. One image slips into another as "contaminated" associations pass in and out of the cell of the author's playful imagination—an eye that sees reality but speaks it surreally: "the red-haired tuft of the sacred triangle" (STO, p. 107) is the shoe that is also referred to as a "sacred object," is also the *Golden Fleece* that is being performed at the Opera, is also Temple's "blond triangular fleece" (STO, p. 59), is the curly mane of the wild beast, perhaps the extinct *aurochs*, a bisonlike animal that once roamed the northern plains of Europe, but which now, if we are to believe the text, is to be found in Uruguay.

Aurochs: Au is the Latin symbol for gold. The sound *aur* resembles the French word *or* (gold). The word *rochs* or *roc* (anticipating the novel's alchemy and search for the philosopher's stone) is also associated with the meteorite that appeared in *Un Régicide*, reappeared in *Topologie*, *La Belle Captive*, and now, once again, in *Souvenirs du triangle d'or*. It has a V imprint on it—an imprint that seemingly connotes "the ancient divinity of pleasure appearing doubly as Vanadis Victorious and Vanadis Vanquished" (STO, p. 77):

> The stereotype of woman in our society is double; hence it is also double in my books and films. The stereotype of woman is, on the one hand, the slavewoman, the woman made servile, tortured, dominated, and, on the other hand, the stereotype which is just as important in our whole culture is the symbol of freedom. Freedom, the image of freedom in all of painting, in all of literature, is always a woman.[24]

The V of the inverted triangle (signifying and generating the concept *woman*) contains a circle and is contained within a circle:

Ⓥ (*STO*, p. 58). The apple, the metal grill, the target, the light bulb, the flashlight lens, the top of the beer can, the eye, the hole, and the egg are all circular objects, some such as the egg and the light bulb verging on the elliptical. The bald Doctor Morgan (another round surface), who performs experiments on Angelica/ Carolina/Christine, inserts an oval object, like a small hard-boiled egg without a shell, into her vagina in order to study her responses and the egg's programmed effects (*STO*, p. 202). These round objects are all associated with the mysterious globe that makes its appearance in the narrator's prison cell and which seems to have its own autonomous existence. The globe, in turn, generates images of pleasure, syntagmas of a waking dream that slip in and out of the cell, through passageways, along the beach, or into the forest where young girls, like quarry, are pursued by hunters and dogs, to be captured and killed. *Le Triangle d'or* is, among other things, a secret society that allows such "games."

Le Triangle d'or is also the "Opera House" (notice the circle of the O) where the *Golden Fleece* is being performed, where a father (the author) masturbates his daughter (the text). *Le Triangle d'or* is also the temple of a religious society, symbolized by the girl whose name is Temple. The burning bush is a phoenix, the *femme-oiseau*, a mythical bird alluded to frequently. Thus, the sexual, mythical, visual, textual, geometric, and numerical connotations generated by the title ultimately converge on that one spot in the "golden center" of the circles and of the triangle: "the inner bisectors of the three angles intersect in the center of this second circle" (*STO*, p. 58).

The body of the text is consumed by fire. Its destruction is gratuitous, although like the phoenix, is eternally recuperated. The author, like an alchemist distilling gold, exploits the colors of the alchemical process: black, white, gray, red, green, and blue. In order to transmute base metals into gold, the metals are broken down into their separate component parts through the action of fire, purified, blended, and finally fixed at the appropriate stage. Fire is important, and the burning text is essential to the process— in this case, literary alchemy. Black, white, and red are the three main colors because black indicates dissolution and putrefaction, a sign that the experiment is going well. The locked door of the "sanctuary" is black, as are the narrator's Cadillac, the student's notebook (entitled *Propriétés secrètes du triangle*—the novel's original title), the leather thongs binding the girl, the narrator's right glove, the long coats of the bowler-hatted men, the lace stockings of the naked girls walking through the palace of illusions, the distant point of the beach known as *Le Cap Noir* (Black Point), the coat hanger in the narrator's cell, and so on. (Doctor Morgan's jacket, like the girl's deerskin boots) is the color of purification. The experiment must be proceeding well because the floor, ceiling, and walls of the narrator's prison cell—the generative cell—are white. The gray of the door signifies the passage from black to white, and on the wall is the red imprint of the narrator's hand. Red, in alchemy, is the color of complete success. The fact that it is associated with the five fingers of the hand is even more significant since, in *Topology*, five was a generative number and the hand was the sign of authorial power and presence—the "signature."

There are intermediary colors, such as yellow (the ruler), green (the apple), and blue (the shoe), which are associated with the seven stages that produce the gold. There is no evidence, however, that Robbe-Grillet pays much attention to the alchemy of calcination, putrefaction, solution, distillation, sublimation, conjunction, and fixation. Even his use of metals such as bronze, copper, tin, and steel is vague. The color scale, however, is exploited completely and gives satisfactory alchemical results. The cell door is gray, like quicksilver, the metal with which the alchemical process begins. The sand on the beach is gray, and one of the crocodiles has gray skin. In *The Book of Lambsprinck* there is a picture of an alchemist holding a huge salamander in the fire.[25] In *Souvenirs*, hunters have tied a young girl to a stake as bait in order to capture a crocodile. Angelica's blue shoe is made of crocodile skin. However, the crocodile metamorphoses into a violin, and it is no doubt the reader who takes the sexy bait:

> It is not a question for me of trying to rid myself once and for all of the mythological elements around me, but on the contrary to *speak them*, i.e., to exercise over them the power of my freedom, instead of giving in to them as though they were *traps* [my emphasis] with a fatal, preset mechanism. (*NRHA*, 2:161)

Many of the scenes in *Souvenirs* are borrowed from Angelica's books of childhood mythology, scenes that Robbe-Grillet uses as examples of the contemporary, ongoing, sadoerotic myth. The blood flowing from "the lips of the shoe" (in the surrealist passage already quoted) is black because at night, as a result of the "Purkinje effect," red is perceived as black. In alchemy care must be taken that the solution not return to black, for then the experi-

menter will have to begin all over again. Nevertheless, the text
continues to evolve. A beach ball has a rose, salmon-colored hue.
Angelica's name is Salomon, and either she or someone else like her
works at the salmon factory where each tin (signifying no doubt
both the metal and the container) of salmon displays the emblem of
a siren. . . . We are getting closer. . . . The green apple contains an
electronic device that opens the "sanctuary's" black door (*STO*,
p. 25). The sanctuary is where Doctor Morgan's "sexual" and "textual experiments" take place (*STO*, p. 155). The sanctuary is the
secret room, the generative cell of fiction, the alchemist's laboratory
where objects, e.g., base metals, like Rimbaud's "Voyelles," are
transmuted into gold. Alchemy, as a metaphor for art, is not new,
and the writer who transforms prosaic reality into poetry is per-
forming functions that are not unlike the alchemist's:

> the imprint of the hand was red, the shoe blue, the ruler yellow. . . .
> By combining the ruler and the shoe one should get the bright green
> of the apple. There must be the hope of a solution in that. . . . The
> ruler with the hand should produce an orange, which will not fail to
> appear. . . . The strong hand on the delicate woman's shoe should
> produce the verb violate. (*STO*, p. 149)

Alchemists believed that with sulphur (i.e., *la règle jaune*—the
yellow rule) they could purify copper (Doctor Morgan's trunk,
appropriately, has corners reinforced with copper), eliminating its
reddish hue to produce gold, the noblest metal and their ultimate
goal. The reader's role in this textual game is obviously to find the
combination or the code that will open the black door to the text—
to crack the electronic code of the green apple that will enable him
to get inside where the experiments occur and insight begins. The
sanctuary is the text, and Temple is a girl on whom the author
leaves his red mark, whose body he sometimes paints with red
paint so that breasts, thighs, and hands will leave red smears on a
white wall, as they do, for example, in *L'Eden et après* and *Glissements
progressifs du plaisir*. Since the hand's five fingers were also the
generative themes of *Topologie, Souvenirs's* intertextual nod is unmistakable. Unmistakable also is Robbe-Grillet's nod to Yves Klein's
"body painting" on white walls.

The yellow color of the ruler, when mixed with the blue of the
shoe, produces green, e.g., the apple. Mixing yellow (the ruler)
with red (the hand) produces orange. Red (the hand) and blue (the
shoe) produce violet, a play on the French verb *violer*. Since the

purpose of the novel is to violate Temple, to penetrate the sanctuary, i.e., the golden triangle, the ambiguity of the words *violet-
violer* is in line with the text's thematic thrust. The specular effects
of words, colors, and things, like the intertextual allusions to *Temple
aux miroirs*, a book of "erotic" photographs by Irina Ionesco and
Robbe-Grillet (with accompanying text), are contributing, generative aspects of the overall transmutation. If the shoe signifies Temple (i.e., *langue*) and the hand signifies narrator (i.e., *parole*), then
the statement "strong hand on the delicate woman's shoe" equals
the verb to violate. In its metonymic precision this equation leads to
the following solution:

1. red and blue equal *violet*
2. hand on shoe makes *violate*
3. narrator violates Temple (the color violet is proof of that)
4. therefore *parole* violates *langue*
5. the author is free (since the narrator leaves the cell)
6. creation, i.e., free play, is art
7. art transmutes objects into gold
8. the author is therefore a magician
9. the reader opens the door, i.e., penetrates the text

With the aid of the "philosopher's stone," the alchemists try to
transmute gray lead into gold. Each color represents a stage in the
process, indicating the likelihood of ultimate success. The green
apple opens the bronze door that is lacquered in black, thereby
providing access to the ordering process of the writer's imagination
and the beach girls who have golden hair and golden skin. Pay dirt
is inside the Temple, and gold is the name of the game. The golden
triangle is thus both the generative theme and the answer to the
puzzle of the text. The objects, colors, combinations, permutations, and slippages from one level to another, once decoded, trig-
ger the secret mechanism, opening the door to the inside. Once
inside the cell, the pearls, the light bulb, the globe, the circle, and
the ovum perform their magic. Parthenogenesis occurs as the narrator and his twin Angelica give birth to fiction by means of the
unfertilized egg that Doctor Morgan has slipped into her vagina: "I
take in my hands my poor head without hair which is also like an
egg. No, I am not mad" (*STO*, p. 162).
This "globe," like the reader, is now "inside" generating its own
imagery *(parole)* whose abrupt, seemingly implausible transitions
between the inside of the cell and the world outside structure
Robbe-Grillet's dialectical topology. There is one long, continuous

co-mingling of the inside and the outside, of *parole* with *langue*, of the self with the other. The objective and the subjective meet at that mythic center in the golden triangle whose imagined memories generate the present fiction. Robbe-Grillet's stock-in-trade images are an emotional trap—crocodile bait—the girl trap he sets for the reader whose expectations are conventional and who is inevitably lured into recuperating the sexual signifiers in traditional ways. Accordingly, the nine key objects or stages of "Piège à fourrure," as they did in *Topologie*, form the combinations of the target's nine rings in whose center is the gold. The numbered objects of each ring appear and disappear as Robbe-Grillet continues to play with an imagery that is allegedly deprived of depth, but which, in fact, has all the symbology of traditional art.

Hemingway used to say that hunting and writing had much in common because neither hunter nor writer knew exactly what kind of game he would bring home. Robbe-Grillet's hunters, his personae, while tracking girls, are always also after gold—the noblest metal and fiction's highest reward. The "sanctuary" is therefore the "golden temple" where the quest, the hunt, and the adventure of writing occur. Robbe-Grillet's Temple is thus curiously reminiscent of Temple Drake in Faulkner's *Sanctuary*, and the narrator's incarceration reminds us of Popeye's. Temple may thus signify the place, the person, or the golden triangle of Everyman's mythic quest. Such "recuperation" of a reflexive novel, in which the usual specular reflections (pictures, posters, mirrors, and so on) undermine realism and reality, can nevertheless be demonstrated by the alchemical signs the author posts along the way—signs that remind us of the "golden fleece" while undermining Jason's mythic quest.

A remarkable passage that appears early in the novel adumbrates the idea that to write is to hunt for gold. Prior to the hunter's shot and the girl's sharp and piercing cry for help, Robbe-Grillet describes the naked adolescent riding her horse bareback into the sea:

> the long blue-black mane and the supple tail with its firebrand hairs of gold prance and caper in the warm morning breeze, while the girl, without stirrups or spurs, tries to guide her blond steed further into the sea that is jetting in all directions under the restive hooves, mingling with the bright laughter of the amazon whose slender body, sprayed by the sheaves of foam, glistens like the shiny metal, suddenly, in the rising light. (*STO*, p. 11)

The golden sheaves of foam reflect the dawn brilliantly. The color of the dawn ("aurore": aur + or + e), containing the French sounds and word for gold, according to the *Petit Larousse*, is a "golden yellow." Thus, the golden image of the equestrienne riding into the sea moments before she is shot exploits the title's generative potential and anticipates the novel's alchemical quest.

The similarities between writing and hunting gain further credence when the narrator closes the black book *(Propriétés secrètes du triangle)* and the two halves come together with the sound of a shot. Hunter and writer are now one as the girl's cry blends with the flesh-colored phoenix, *L'Immortelle*, always vulnerable and always resurrected. The ascent of the phoenix rises inevitably to challenge the falling of the stone: "Once again the falling stone" *(STO*, p. 237), which is where the novel ends.

Such imagery implies that spontaneous "regeneration" challenges gravity, that quantum physics challenges Newtonian mathematics, that atomicity and discontinuity challenge predictability. A new order opposes a priori values as this New New Novel challenges the conventions of the traditional novel. All this and more are implied in the rising phoenix and the descending stone. To deny this "depth," by limiting the reading of a New (New) Novel to its formal and reflexive characteristics, as do the advocates of nonrecuperative fiction, is indeed not only to limit the creative role of the reader but also to eliminate the text's mythical dimension.

Whereas polysemy and the play of generative themes have formal qualities and relationships, they also, fortunately, as *Souvenirs* demonstrates, have a potential for magic that transmutes the reflexive significance of a work into personal experience signifying more than the mechanical interaction of its parts. To ignore this dimension is to remain within the prison of language, unable to break down its walls by means of free, spontaneous, generative acts. Artistic play does not only mirror the randomness of the great cosmic game; *Souvenirs* also demonstrates authorial purpose. The alchemy of this novel is not random, and its "bricolage" has direction. Even "writing as an adventure," as opposed to "the adventures in writing," a contrast that Ricardou and others have so often stressed, generates extrinsic experiences by communicating insights about the creative process. To create is to be free. Robbe-Grillet's art—an art that explores this free space—thereby engenders something in the reader which transcends the mechanisms of language. A metaphor, for instance, if it is not a cliché, in spite of Robbe-Grillet's railings against it in the past, demonstrates the freedom of the artist to generate fresh connections. Robbe-Grillet's metaphors and metonymy do as much; he himself admits this and he uses their magical and transforming powers:

> When you said that the twin Vanessa devours the bird of fire at the end of the spectacle, what did you mean by that?
> It is probably a sexual metaphor, once again, like everything else. (*STO*, p. 78)

Robbe-Grillet's overriding need to assert his freedom as an artist challenges even his ingenuity, prompting him, as in *Le Jeu avec le feu* and in *Souvenirs*, to play with Christian imagery. Whereas alleged offenses against religion, tradition, and convention are perceived and defined by the "moral" public as outrageous and blasphemous, their shock value demonstrates, at least, that Robbe-Grillet is bound by no system other than his own. His purpose is to undermine convention and to demythify tradition. However, in order to achieve this end, he must, inevitably, deal with the myths themselves: religion, Nature, censorship, colonialism, virginity, violence, male superiority, and so on. His fiction "speaks" these public and private myths, whereas his essays address the arbitrariness of all codes and value systems:

> The material which I use in organizing narratives, novels, and films is ideological; that is, it is cut from the discourses that society addresses to me. . . . I cut out fragments, and it is these fragments which serve to create my speech, to develop my own *discours*.[26]

His art, says Robbe-Grillet, does *not speak about* these stereotypes; it is an art composed of social clichés—a collage of stereotypes, images of fear, violence, and eroticism—an assemblage that will expose these platitudes. Robbe-Grillet strives to arrange such images in patterns that will defy ideology, believing that it is useful to demonstrate the nature of society's arbitrary systems. Thus art's "artificiality" simultaneously asserts the author's freedom and its opposition to the "natural" (*SCP*, p. 48).

Although Robbe-Grillet would affirm that his artistic discourse has no avowed moral purpose, it can be argued that its mere existence constitutes a moral presence. Gide once said that society's "counterfeiters" were the great immoralists because they did more harm than anybody else. In *Les Faux-monnayeurs* it is the counterfeit values of a bourgeois order that are blamed for Boris's "suicide," and in his indictment of this rule Gide blames selfishness, ignorance, inauthenticity (Sartre's "bad faith"), and Puritan morality for the lies, insensitivity, and indifference which characterize human relationships. Whereas certain formal aspects of Gide's art, such as inescutcheon and reflexivity, are now much in vogue when speaking of the "nouveau roman," Robbe-Grillet's criticism of bourgeois conventions also has some of the flavor ("Familles, je vous hais"—Families, I hate you) of Gide's moral indignation:

> in Nazi Germany, which was a really mad society, there were theoreticians who presented as quite natural the "fact" that the so-called Aryan race would dominate all other races. This was "natural." This is what Marx called ideology. In sum, ideology is established order which masquerades as natural order, which pretends not to be a creation of society but, on the contrary, a sort of divine law dictated, so to speak, by God, exactly as God dictated the ten commandments to Moses. Every society pretends that its laws are natural and tries to make them endure. Tries, I say, and succeeds rather well thanks to the purveyors of ideology—our schools, our universities, and the like. . . . My discourse is not that of society, it is even opposed to society's discourse. (*ODFF*, pp. 4, 11)

The formal interaction of generative themes can give rise to considerations that, in themselves, are neither linguistic, nor grammatical, nor syntactic. If Robbe-Grillet's generative interplay enables him to incorporate ideology into his discourse, i.e., to assemble fragments of society's myths, in order to oppose them, then his New (New) Novel is introducing disorder into the previous "order" of the social system. To the degree that it disrupts the system, its aim is "revolutionary," though its immediate revolutionary impact is probably minimal. How many people read or even like the "nouveau roman?" Still, on an artistic and philosophical level, the alleged "disorder" imposed by generative themes represents new ways of structuring art and reality. The previous analysis of *Souvenirs* demonstrates some of the ways in which this new order functions.

Robbe-Grillet believes that there are two different kinds of artists: the first kind accepts the world as it is, whereas the second kind, by means of an artistic *parole*, tries to create a world that does not yet exist (*NRHA*, 2:51). Robbe-Grillet's art, which belongs to the second category, is no longer the *langue* of the system, even though his *parole* uses fragments of its discourse. If Robbe-Grillet introduces modules of organized disorder into the system, he increases the information potential because the amount of information contained in a message is determined by the degree of its organization. Information is a determinant of order. Disorder, or entropy, is the opposite of information.[27]

The order of the New New Novel, i.e., its structure based on the organizing principle of generative themes, is perceived as disorder by those readers who look for and expect to find the conventional readerly patterns of plot, suspense, character, and chronology. The conventions of the traditional novel are defined as order, whereas variations from the established norm, using generative themes based on an arbitrary "assemblage" of serial units, are perceived as disorder.

To illustrate this point, Umberto Eco, in *L'Oeuvre ouverte* (The Open Work), traces the development of the tonal system in music from Bach through Beethoven and Wagner to Schoenberg's dodecaphonic music. Bach, says Eco, formalized tonal music according to a scale of twelve tones organized in a hierarchy. Beethoven, when he adopted this system, introduced dissonances and intervals that did not exist in Bach's hierarchies. A listener, therefore, could no longer say with confidence that any one note was dominant or tonic or subdominant. Harmonies had become dissonances. Wagner, who came after Beethoven, moved even farther away from Bach's tonal system by refusing to resolve cadences, an innovation that resulted in immense, continuous dissonances. With Wagner one always hears what he called "vague harmonies." These vague harmonies were generalized even further when Schoenberg reasoned that in order to abolish the hierarchy between all the notes, each note should be repeated as often as every other. Thus were born Schoenberg's "serial arrangements" in which a work was fragmented into a certain number of pieces: the twelve notes of the "scale" could be repeated in different orders, but no note was repeated until the other eleven had been used (*ODFF*, pp. 12–13).

Whereas Schoenberg's "serial arrangements" are generally comparable to Robbe-Grillet's generative themes, the comparison is a loose one and must not be pushed too far. There is a degree of similarity, however, as the repetitive use of the nine themes of "Piège à fourrure" in *Topologie* and *Souvenirs* demonstrates. Schoenberg's "atonal" system has no inherent meaning, except that it disrupts the order of tonal music. The serial arrangement of generative themes in fiction, insofar as it resembles seriality in music, would also seem to have no meaning, other than "disorder," were it not for the fact that these generative fragments, be they objects, images, or whole paragraphs, are borrowed from the mythic panoply of man's conscious and unconscious desires. Thus, *penetration*, "Piège à four-rure's" sixth "note" or category, connotes eroticism, violence, and mystery. The hunter in the forest of *Souvenirs* who stabs the young girl after the dogs have caught her, while signifying the code stereotype of erotic violence on the "readerly" level, connotes the opening of the text on the "writerly" level. The violation of young girls is, on the one hand, the author's manhandling of *langue* and, on the other, his manipulation of the text. To make sense out of serial disorder, the reader must "penetrate" the text. In *Souvenirs*, the text is simultaneously Christine, Temple, and the "sanctuary." Their penetration is linked directly, in Barthian terms, with "bliss," since in literature pleasure is also associated with insight and understanding. The Freudian key opens the door of the text, so to speak, and by playing with its serial arrangements, allows the reader to re-create the author's narrative patterns. The reader can now generate order out of the initial disorder. Even after the code has been cracked, the linguistic and imagistic combinations within each New New Novel seem inexhaustible, every reading thus generating fresh, pleasurable, and blissful encounters.

Twelve Themes: Serialism in *L'Eden et après*

Another typical example of the use of serialism in art is the film *L'Eden et après* (1970), a film that Roy Armes believes is one of the most original works of modern cinema.[28] The film uses a complex series of generative themes that Robbe-Grillet has compared to Schoenberg's "atonal" system.

> *Eden* was constructed, not with a binary structure, reality/imagination as mentioned by some critics, but on the basis of twelve themes, each one reproduced in ten series (five large series and five small ones within the large) somewhat like the twelve tone scale [i.e., system] of dodecaphonic music.[29]

In his book *Style and Idea*, Schoenberg emphasizes a possible link between sound and image by relating tones to objects:

> Just as our mind always recognizes, for instance, a knife, a bottle or a watch, regardless of its position, and can reproduce it in the imagination in every possible position, even so a musical creator's mind can operate subconsciously with a row of tones, regardless of their direction, regardless of the way in which a mirror might show the mutual relations, which remain a given quality.[30]

In music, a tone has pitch, quality, and duration. In film, an object has size, color, and duration. Although it is prudent not to push synesthesia too far, the high pitch of a tone may be compared to the small size of a cherry, just as the cherry's red color may be compared to or may, in the listener/viewer's mind, elicit the timbre of a musical instrument. Finally, a filmed object, like sound, may be of long or short duration.

If tones are comparable to objects, then themes must be something else, since ideas in music and film are constructed from syntagmas of sounds, words, and images. In music, as in film, by convention, the word *theme* is most frequently used to designate a work's central idea or thesis. Although Robbe-Grillet uses objects and images as thematic generators, their number is not limited to twelve. It may also be confusing to have Robbe-Grillet refer to objects as "themes." Even more disconcerting than this semantic difficulty is the actual enumeration of twelve themes that contain signifiers (such as the stolen picture—a thing), motifs (such as the labyrinth), and concepts (such as death).

The difficulty then, with Robbe-Grillet's twelve themes, as he lists them, is that he mixes themes with motifs with objects. Objects generate themes and ideas generate objects. Sensing this problem, Robbe-Grillet has said that it is perhaps impossible for a viewer to reconstruct the film's twelve generative themes. However, if we keep Schoenberg's original comparison in mind, it may be possible to structure analogies between *L'Eden* and a musical system based not on objects but on categories. The sheer number of people, images, and places precludes a meaningful comparison between them and the twelve tones of dodecaphonic music. But if we start at the other end, i.e., with the more abstract concepts signified by groupings of objects, images, and places, we can reconstruct a twelve-theme system. In the table that follows, the list on the right corresponds generally to Robbe-Grillet's. The essential difference between the two is that my list does not mix apples (themes) with oranges (objects).

Robbe-Grillet's List of Generative Themes[31]	*My List*
1. Picture (object)	1. Art (theme)
2. Labyrinth (motif)	2. Alienation (theme)
3. Imagination (theme)	3. Freedom (theme)
4. The dance (motif)	4. Play (theme)
5. Sperm (viscous material)	5. Eroticism (theme)
6. Doors (objects)	6. Exoticism (theme)
7. Male sex (theme)	7. Superman (theme)

8. Prison (place)	8. Captive woman (theme)
9. Blood (liquid)	9. Violence (theme)
10. Death (theme)	10. Death (theme)
11. The double (theme)	11. Fear (theme)
12. Water (liquid)	12. Purification (theme)

A shot of a painting on the wall of Violette's room, entitled *Composition #234*, a semiabstract rendition in white and blue of Houmt Souk, gives us the *art theme* (1). The *theme of alienation* (2) is rendered as the students' estrangement from their studies. Their boredom and indifference is shot as a large mathematics lecture hall in which Violette sees flowers on the blackboard instead of equations. The prestidigitations of the handsome stranger connote the *theme of freedom* (3). The student games in the Eden Café connote the *play theme* (4). The *theme of eroticism* (5) is shot as a girl eating a raw egg. A travel poster of Tunisia on the wall of the Eden Café connotes *exoticism* (6). Duchemin, the tall, blond, blue-eyed, handsome stranger connotes the *superman theme* (7). The *captive woman theme* (8) is rendered by shots of Violette in the Eden Café, which looks like a labyrinth-prison. The "shooting" of a student and the "rape" of another signify *violence* (9). A ritual death ceremony with candles is *death* (10), whereas the *fear theme* (11) is stated literally with "fear powder" that Violette licks off Duchemin's hand. Her paranoid reactions, like musical tones, engender a rapid succession of images and sounds. The *theme of purification* (12) is stated with water: Violette drinks a glass of water as an antidote to the "fear powder" and recovers.

The chosen "row" of themes, like Schoenberg's twelve tones, thus forms the basis for the cinematic narrative (which is melody in music), its space (which is rhythm in music), and its metonymy (which is harmony). As with Schoenberg's system, the mutual relation of tonal signifiers is shot separately as successive slow scenes, or as fast, disparate, contiguous images—a relationship that regulates the succession of intervals as well as their association into "harmonies." In *L'Eden*, as in a serial composition, the order of the images and tones is sometimes transposed, inverted, or read backward. No "theme" or tone returns unless it is separated by the other intermediate eleven, thus ensuring an equal distribution of emphasis on all twelve. The chosen "row" of twelve forms the basis of the film's diegesis and the music's melody.

Although musical harmony may have its visual counterpart in metonymy, the students' mood at the Eden Café is anything but harmonious. Disenchantment with reality pervades the Café, the university lecture halls, a room where the students smoke pot and in which Violette makes love. This feeling of ennui, this sense of alienation that communicates itself to the spectators, is in fact the students' reality and constitutes one of the themes of the film. Thus, the theme of alienation (no. 2) has its signs: students dramatizing ritual games of rape, murder, and death in a café that is a labyrinth.

L'Éden et après opens with a voice saying "subjective, objective, injective, superjective, bijective," beginning with actual words and ending with absurd, nonexistent ones. This comical devaluation of reality is followed by images of the neon sign of the Eden Café, followed by other "signs" (i.e., object-images) such as eyes and pipes that are accompanied on the sound track by piano music. These effects evolve into disparate, dissonant, nonmusical sounds. We hear next a voice saying "objects, images, imagination, fantasies, phantoms, deforming mirrors, reality, my life." We see a girl being "raped" on a table in the Eden Café. A voice says "the image of a sum is the sum of the images." We see shots of the Tunisian landscape. Violette's voice says: "In our useless and studious life nothing really ever happens."

The rapid succession of frames in this "overture," and the series of objects contained within them, adumbrate the twelve themes of the film. To reflect on these themes at all is to discern a pattern of death, violence, eroticism, and alienation. Other themes, such as exoticism, the superman stereotype, the captive woman stereotype, and freedom correspond to additional exaggerated social codes. Still other themes, such as art, play, and purification are figures of intentionality, an assertion of authorial identity.

Robbe-Grillet assembles the images of contemporary myths, exaggerating and deforming an iconography drawn either from high culture (Duchamp's *Nude Descending a Staircase*) or from low culture (the comics, junkyards, sex magazines). In short, the themes with which Robbe-Grillet builds his system are fragments of our collective psyche:

As you know, sadistic imagery, with an ever increasing insistence, is appearing in certain popular areas: the jackets of novels sold in stations, cartoons, film publicity, etc. The difference is that in [my film] the sadistic imagery is emphasized without any moralizing alibi. . . . Our society has images of rape, torture, woman-as-thing, or of spilled blood already in its head; what I am doing is to expose them to the light of day, showing them as platitudinous images now in vogue. (*SCP*, p. 48)

Roy Armes believes that the exploration of such a world in which cultural stereotypes become dream and in which advertising images acquire a future dimension is ideally suited to the cinema in general and to Robbe-Grillet's work in particular ("R-G in Africa," p. 108).

Violette, the heroine of the film, plays games of chance, rape, murder, and death—games that mime the cultural stereotypes they dramatize. Each exaggeration, like a giant Campbell soup can in a series of pop art posters, or as in a Rauschenberg "combine," is a sign, connoting one or more of the twelve themes. The twelve themes, like the twelve tones of Schoenberg's system, appear as rapid, discontinuous images that will be repeated "thematically" in the café, in the factory, and in North Africa—the three places (Robbe-Grillet has organized them into five) where the ten series help to construct the twelve themes.

Most, if not all, of these themes overlap, since it may not be possible to produce art without freedom or to think of death without love. Things in the film, such as a stolen painting, or events, such as student games in the Eden Café, or relationships, such as the one between Violette and the stranger, Duchemin, depending on the particular "blend" of associations, will signify one or more themes. For illustrative purposes, suppose we use theme eleven, fear, symbolized by Violette's licking "fear powder" off the back of the stranger's hand (Duchemin). Violette's instant panic evokes a succession of images: chains, hooks, a scorpion, cages, fire, blood, broken glass, spikes, the rack, the dead stranger, a bloodied photograph—things and scenes that, through synecdochic contiguity, construct or shape the concept "fear."

Robbe-Grillet has fragmented this idea of fear into objects and images that are then juxtaposed in order to construct the picture of the whole. He has selected images whose discourse illustrates the twelve themes.[32] Anecdotal meaning, says Robbe-Grillet, may emerge from a juxtaposition of two or more images:

> If you bring together the theme [i.e., image] fire and the theme death you produce a narrative fragment: the mortal fire. I have organized an adventure, not in the traditional narrative sense as the critics define it, but have, on the contrary produced anecdotic sense through the serial juxtaposition of twelve more or less arbitrary themes [i.e., ideas] chosen in advance. (*NRHA*, 1:205)

For instance, there is a Tunisian sequence of a nude descending a staircase, perhaps Robbe-Grillet's nod to Duchamp's famous painting in the Philadelphia Art Museum. In addition to signifying the art theme, the frame contains allusions to at least six other themes. The scene depicts a nude woman descending a spiral staircase whose metal banister resembles prison bars. When the woman reaches the bottom of the circular staircase, she is seen standing in profile, back arched, left arm over her eyes, her abdomen opposite the tip of a giant, old-fashioned plow that is pointing directly at her. The themes of art, love, death, superman, captive woman, and fear, through metonymy, synechdoche, overlapping, and "contamination" of signifiers are contained in that brief sequence. This synchronic activity of images can thus, effectively, be compared to chords in music.

Allusion to a famous painting connotes "art," whereas the naked woman, iron banister, and plow connote "captive woman subject to male, aggressive love." Robbe-Grillet's hieroglyph, like the dreamwork of Freud's analyses, contains the pictogram whose objects, i.e., signifiers, express the content of the total image. But the audience viewing the scene of the nude descending the staircase generally laughs at the playful elements it contains—perhaps the incongruity of the outsized plow (though why this should be perceived as funny would require a separate, lengthy analysis).

Sadoerotic signifiers (no. 5 and no. 9) merge with the death theme (no. 10) and with art (no. 1). Dutchman's (a comic variant no doubt of Duchamp's name) nude model is seen lying "dead" in a bathtub in blood-stained water. Mock violence is everywhere, and the film contains a variety of deaths by attack, poisoning, and drowning. In a Djerba prison, a woman's body is seen several times on a rack, or next to giant spikes, like those of an inverted harrow. Do harrow and plow in a sadoerotic context "read" as perverse variants of an earth goddess fertility motif? Robbe-Grillet himself suggests this possibility when he states that "woman, as a mythical object, maintains a secret rapport with Nature (lunar cycles, pregnancy, maternal instinct)."[33] We could also say that Violette has undergone a "harrowing" experience, that she has been "racked" with fear and distress. Since film, as Christian Metz points out, is language without *langue*, i.e., a unit of *parole* that transcends English, French, German, or Russian, its universal puns are translatable into English regardless of the fact that the film was conceived in French. Film language short-circuits *langue* going directly from frame, objects, and images (the artist's *parole*) to theme. Puns,

therefore, as disguised signifiers, invite translation from a precon-
scious imagery into conscious, i.e., rational categories. Without
such translation, the twelve themes would be arbitrary and
meaningless.

The captive woman theme (no. 8) is developed not only on the
narrative level, with Violette's imprisonment and torture, but also
on the affective level, with images of nude women in cages, as
though these women were rare birds to be admired or wild animals
to be tamed or merchandise ready for shipment to the brothels of
the world. The caging of an erotic object, like a naked woman, with
its white-slave-traffic overtones, anticipates sadoerotic scenes of
torture and murder, the end product of another cultural
stereotype—male aggression and the theme of violence. The superman theme (no. 7) is thus linkd to violence (no. 9) as much as the
captive woman theme (no. 8) is linked to fear (no. 11). If the freedom of the male contrasts with the bondage of the female (none of
the males is imprisoned or tortured), then fear seems to be the
corollary of woman's subservience. Fear is the film's most consistent theme and obvious signifiers, like the fear powder—things
(shall we say tones?) that point directly to fear or are associated
with it—are frequent. A partial listing would include *pistol, abduction, prison, nude*, poison, scorpion, knife, fear powder, factory,
corpses, darkness, blindfold.

If with fear signifiers (or tones) we list erotic signifiers (no. 5)
such as *pistol, abduction, prison, nudes* in cages, sperm (glue, paint),
key, plow, eggs, chains, spikes, the rack, pipes, a handbag, and so
on, we see that signs such as *pistol, abduction, prison*, and *nude* belong
to both themes and are present in both categories. We can say,
therefore, that because of a pairing of objects, signifiers may connote simultaneous themes—themes that may triple or quadruple
depending on how the spectator is "reading" the film.

In film, as in music, certain narrative solutions or thematic reso-
lutions probably occur as a result of cultural conventions and historical expectations. Forms that a conservative public may find
shocking may be commonplace to the avant-garde. In fact, all too
frequently what seems acceptable or unacceptable depends on social patterns, background, education, and experience—types of exposure conditioned by a natural, historical, or social milieu. Accordingly, for those unfamiliar with serialism in art, a Schoenberg
composition, or a film such as *L'Eden* will appear dissonant and
disorderly. A tonal system, for example, corresponds to probabilities that the auditor knows will occur and he probably derives

pleasure from that knowledge and the fulfillment of his expectations. The apparent disorder of a dodecaphonic system disrupts this auditor's pleasure, unless he knows that "atonal" music is nothing more than another different system of probabilities. Like a composer, the *auteur* of a serial film chooses and orders a constellation of images that lend themselves to multiple relations which are synchronic and diachronic and can be assembled forward and backward on a vertical as well as on a horizontal axis. Serial art, says Umberto Eco, has destroyed one sequence of probabilities in order to introduce new meaning and a new type of discourse. The higher level of apparent disorder is accompanied by higher levels of information. What characterizes a poetics of this kind is that the possibilities for message proliferation multiply, thus engendering contradictory meanings (*OO*, pp. 89–90).

Contradiction leads to defamiliarization, which, in *L'Eden*, corresponds in some ways to the ennui in Kafka's works. Violette, like K. in *The Trial*, is "arrested" for unknown crimes. She is held captive for her alleged complicity in the theft of her own painting. Finally, through guile and after many episodes she frees herself from her tormentors, escapes to the roof of the prison, steps over dead menaces such as the shark (what is a shark doing on a prison roof?), and walks alone along the sandy beach. She soon tires, her steps falter, and she falls, crawling in the sand on her hands and knees.

The theme of alienation (no. 2) manifests itself as a schizoid double—an almost identical Violette—young, blonde, short-haired, slim, dressed in a black-and-white print minidress and knee-high boots, who lifts Violette number one up from the sand, takes her back into town, gives her water and fresh clothes identical to hers, restores her calm, brings her back to herself, and then once more vanishes into the sea. But contrary to what we might expect, the splitting of the self acts as a healing experience: it is the theme of purification (no. 12). It is as though Violette's sojourn in Djerba and her "vision" of the double had endowed *her* with magical powers enabling *her* to rival those of the enchanted stranger. It is as though Violette's newly found freedom had, in the end, endowed her with strength. Subsequently she finds the painting for which so many had "died." She is now a liberated woman, equal to the "superman."

Paronomasia (no. 4) helps us decode the film's incongruities. As in a dream, mystery (the infrastructure) has its own internal logic. Thus Duchemin, seen dead in a European canal, is no more "dead" than Dutchman at the foot of a jetty stairs in Tunisia. Violette, who finds Duchemin "dead," goes for help and returns. But Duchemin has vanished and in his place she finds her handbag. Why the handbag? Why is Duchemin gone? Such anachronisms devalue the logic of conventional film narrative, but they also connote dreamlike incoherence on its most elemental level, because most of the things, places, and events in this film are substitute signs, i.e., hieroglyphs. The "fact" that Violette finds the stolen painting after her "liberation," which comes after her "trip" to North Africa, which ensues from the events triggered by the stolen "key" and the like invites speculative and "recuperative" interpretations. The imagery of Violette's waking dream resembles the linguistic puns, compression, and distortion of experience that Freud describes in "The Interpretation of Dreams."[34]

Erich Fromm maintains that dreams are a language. Jacques Lacan affirms that a dream, like any language, also has sentence structures which appear in the form of a rebus. A child's dream represents the primordial ideography of such "writing," whereas an adult reproduces the simultaneously phonetic and symbolic use of signifying elements. The hieroglyphs of ancient Egypt and the ideograms of Chinese writing would be examples of this syntactic "simultaneity":

> The important part [says Lacan] begins with the translation of the text, the important part which Freud tells us is given in the [verbal] elaboration of the dream—in other words, in its rhetoric. Ellipsis and pleonasm, hyperbaton or syllepsis, regression, repetition, apposition—these are the syntactical displacements; metaphor, catechresis, antonomasis, allegory, metonymy, and synechdoche—these are the semantic condensations in which Freud teaches us to read the intentions—ostentatious or demonstrative, dissimulating or persuasive, retaliatory or seductive—out of which the subject modulates his oneiric discourse.[35]

The link between key and phallic symbol is probably necessary and inevitable. We may be inclined to dismiss the fact that someone in *L'Eden* takes Violette's key and steals a picture from her room. But when the key reappears on the piano keyboard at the Eden Café, the juxtaposition is startling. Thus, the object "key," in association with the keyboard, emerges as the probable code for Schoenberg's twelve-tone system and the "key" to the film. The key, the painting, the stranger, and a documentary film on Tunisia send Violette's imagination spinning off into associative fantasies in which the students assume double identities as bad guys, natives, artists' models, and victims. Duchemin, the stranger, becomes Dutchman, the artist; Frantz, the waiter at the Eden Café, becomes a "shady" rug merchant, Violette finds a twin, and so on, as the theme of exoticism (no. 6) and its corollaries of evasion and of the double come into focus.

In this context, Violette's inquisitive, fantasy wanderings through Djerba in search of the stolen painting correspond to her "flight" from an uneventful life as a student: sadoerotic encounters, prison tortures, abduction by Bedouins galloping on horseback compose a stereotyped romantic fantasy that contrasts effectively with, yet is an extension of, the games played in the Eden Café. Her mind "plays" inventively with this new reality that is a "departure" from the previous boring dramatizations of her peers. Nevertheless, Violette's alienation, fantasy, and imagination subsume two other themes: art (no. 1) and freedom (no. 3). Whereas her estrangement prompted submissive behavior and fear of the semen-like material in the "menacing" factory, by the time her North African sojourn ends, she is gleefully smearing her arms, face, and body with a gluelike sperm, daring to slap Dutchman who is now in bed with her. This "trip" is her deliverance; her newly found freedom, which contrasts with her previous subservience and diffidence, allows her, in due course, to escape from her "prison." The North African "reality" is Violette's, since her voice narrates the elaborate, contradictory sequences of events. Nevertheless, her concluding remarks at the end of the Tunisian sequence subvert the screen's referential realism:

> I am once again alone in my room. Nothing has happened yet. In a while I will go out to rejoin my friends at the Eden.
>
> All of them will have the tired expressions of people returning from distant places. . . . To relieve our boredom we will play hide-and-seek or blind-man's buff.
>
> Toward the end of the evening, when play will have reached its high point, everything will suddenly be silent.
>
> Slowly, one by one, we will turn our heads toward the glass doors. Behind the transparent partition, we will see the stranger who has just arrived, who is looking at us with his pale eyes, who is already opening the door. . . .

The interpretation of sexual symbols such as a key, a handbag, glue, and so on cannot proceed "innocently" or "spontaneously" because Robbe-Grillet has read Freud and deliberately uses Freudian symbols. Robbe-Grillet's most recent films and novels are, in fact, a form of Freudian pop art. Their role is to expose "ideology" as well as to subvert its unconscious social codes.

> In my last books [and films] phantasms have been used as generative themes; they no longer function as the hidden phantasms of post-Freudian works. From the moment that the mechanisms of the psyche were taken apart by Freud, they became part of a cultural, even popular material, since they are now used in advertising, in brochures, in widely disseminated books. Such phantasms are no more than images cast as the platitudinous objects of the assembly line. Inevitably, from the very moment that psychoanalysis exposed the depths of man, those depths disappeared. (*NRHA*, 2:141)

Robbe-Grillet's serial art, by virtue of its arbitrary, antinatural, and defamiliarizing effects tends to devalue conventional forms. Kandinsky used to say that abstract art had "discredited" the object, whereas Schoenberg claimed that serial music had "emancipated" dissonance. Schoenberg used this expression to characterize the release of dominant seventh and other dissonant chords from their tonal "obligations" to resolve according to convention.[36] When these conventions are devalued, when the artist opposes the normative cultural code, then he is "en avant," simultaneously conscious of and ahead of the destabilizing forces that are undermining the historical, social, and religious heritage:

> We have often been asked [says Robbe-Grillet] why we preferred our system of generative [themes] to the traditional narrative sequence. The answer is that, for the first time, a mode of [artistic] production has manifest itself as anti-natural; and that in itself seems to me extremely important, because the myth of the natural, as you know, was used by a social, moral, and political system in order to establish and prolong itself." (*NRHA*, 2:159)

Neither Schoenberg nor Robbe-Grillet, however, considers these innovations or the accompanying desacralization to be artistically irresponsible. Schoenberg believed that dissonances were "emancipated" when sounds which had once been incomprehensible had been understood and assimilated. Likewise, it can be deduced from Robbe-Grillet's work, particularly *Souvenirs du triangle d'or*, that a triangle and two circles need not necessarily represent certain objects described within the novel. They should be viewed rather as dynamic systems capable of generating different objects from one context to another. Thus, in *Souvenirs du triangle d'or* (1978), the novel's alchemical theme emerges from the color gold, the numerical theme from Jasper Johns's *Numbers* and targets, the carnal theme from the shape of the inverted triangle, and the mythological theme from the word *souvenirs*. These are the generators that produce the structure, images, slippages, specular effects, polysemy, paronomasia, and, hopefully, the pleasure that the reader experiences in reordering the themes.

L'Eden's circular time scheme, its incongruities, and narrative contradictions, like music, mean everything and nothing. *L'Eden* invites the active participation and re-creation by the viewer who is the missing link in the film's diegesis. This emancipation from conventional forms asserts the superiority of a system in which contradiction, opposition, and play—a deliberate structural dialectic—are perceived as valuable because they open new channels of information and insight.

In spite of the film's atomicity, the stolen picture of Djerba is still a picture of a town. The town through which Violette wanders is still a labyrinth. *L'Eden* itself is a labyrinth. The audience is held captive in the labyrinth of Violette's romantic fantasy—a fantasy that is an extension of Robbe-Grillet's art. The building up and tearing down of the film's twelve themes provide a way out of the prison of cultural stereotypes that govern our modes of thinking. Escape from these molds leads to freedom. Free behavior, in turn, depends on the bringing into consciousness of the repressed imagery of our subconscious—those fantasy images and cultural stereotypes that correspond to and define the film's twelve themes. Escape from the repressed stereotypes of taboo and social imperative, as well as the reenactment of a corresponding though previously repressed imagery, is catharsis. But catharsis is freedom—a *purification*—the film's twelfth theme.

> Reading is a "catharsis," the spectacle a purgation. Those moralists who wish to interdict the showing of sex and blood are the ones we find behind the most repressive societies: Naziism was Puritan, Hitler chided Goebbels for his mistresses, persecuted homosexuals, burned the books he deemed immoral. (*SCP*, p. 48)

L'Eden et après, like the Judeo-Christian emblem that it is, unifies the film's twelve themes by demonstrating that life "after Eden" is indeed composed of fear, death, freedom, eroticism, bondage, and the like—twelve themes that can be stated, combined, and recombined in any order, at any time, in any place, with anyone willing to invent, take a chance, and play.

> today we [the artists] are ready to fully underwrite the artificiality of our work: there is no natural, moral political, or narrative order; there are only human orders created by man, with all that that implies concerning the provisional and arbitrary. (*NRHA*, 2:160)

We have seen how Robbe-Grillet's generative themes in his fiction and his films structure an ongoing, serial autonomy of the text. However, in view of the fact that Robbe-Grillet's art is simultaneously reflexive and mimetic, the next chapter analyzes not only his theoretical pronouncements but also focuses on the extrinsic referents within a Marxist context. This will make it possible to dramatize the "revolutionary" potential of a "recuperated" text outside a closed system.

2

A Partisan, Passionate, and Politic Project for a Revolution

> True civilization . . . is not to be found in gas, or in steam, or in levitation. It comes from a reduction in the traces of original sin.
>
> —Baudelaire

The achronology, discontinuity, and atomicity of astronomy, physics, and probability theory have become formal, recognizable features of the New (New) Novel and the New Cinema. The randomness of the "cosmic game" has been incorporated into serial art as a semiology of play. Heidegger's "time and being" and Merleau-Ponty's "intentionality" of the body have been "dramatized." Marx and Freud have also been assimilated, digested, and spewed forth not without a heavy linguistic dose of Saussure's "arbitrariness."

Readers who believe that the "nouveau roman" is a nonpartisan, self-reflexive, and nonreferential art form will not only disagree with this evaluation but will also think it presumptuous to stress its current subversion of "ideology," i.e., to emphasize its revolutionary potential.

Nevertheless, the novel *Projet pour une révolution à New York* (1970) and the film *Glissements progressifs du plaisir* (1974) are characteristic examples of Robbe-Grillet's "revolutionary" *écriture*, both fictional and cinematic. However, since neither work is rooted in socialist realism nor displays any of the customary rhetoric, zealots are bound to be disappointed and even critical of an enterprise whose formalism seems to promise such meager revolutionary fare.

Although *Projet* and *Glissements* manifests some of the reifying tendencies dear to Lucien Goldmann, neither possesses the kind of redeeming social content advocated by Georg Lukács. The author of *Realism in Our Time* believed that a "correct" aesthetic understanding of social and historical reality was a precondition for real-

ism; that the characters in a work of art should reflect this "understanding"; that the socialist realist writer should have
"concreteness," i.e., an awareness of the development, structure,
and goal of society as a whole; that the socialist realist writer could,
therefore, contribute to the downfall of the bourgeoisie and the
liberation of the proletariat.[1] In short, the socialist realist writer
could influence and predict the outcome of history.

Terry Eagleton, in *Marxism and Literary Criticism*, reminds us
that "Marxism is the scientific theory of human societies and of the
practice of transforming them; . . . that the narrative Marxism has
to deliver is the story of the struggles of men and women to free
themselves from certain forms of exploitation and oppression."
Eagleton insists that the aim of Marxism in politics, literature, and
criticism is to transform human societies.[2]

In this same vein, Georges Bataille, like Marxists generally,
views the world as a place to be changed, and communism itself as
action personified. The writer's role is to actively participate in the
necessary and inevitable overthrow of "corrupt" societies.[3] "Any
authentic reflection of reality in literature," says Lukács, "must
point to this movement" (*ROT*, p. 55). Accordingly, Lukács rejects
the Sisyphian lives of the characters in *La Peste* because they "are
without direction, without motivation, without development." In
view of Camus's outspoken stance against all dehumanizing forces,
Lukács's example is indeed interesting and revealing. *La Peste*, says
Lukács, is the reality of a human existence in which terror has no
beginning and no end (*ROT*, p. 59). Instead of terror, Lukács advocates an aesthetic of the novel blending the epic and the tragic. The
dialectic of this mature form, says Goldmann, stresses the radical
opposition between man and the world, between the individual and
society.[4] Socialist realism thus clearly defines the parameters of the
novel and explains Lukács's and Goldmann's inordinate admiration
of Thomas Mann and André Malraux who, like Balzac and Tolstoy, were able to "grasp and portray trends and phenomena truth-
fully in their historical development." A priori, then, socialist realist critics must reject writers such as Kafka and Beckett whose
angst, nihilism, and subjective notions of time mark them as de-
cadent wordsmiths who are incapable of understanding the true
movement and direction of history. There is an intimate connection, says Lukács, between a writer's ability to create lasting human
types and his allegiance to an ideology that allows for a belief in
social development. This "static immobilism" of Kafka's and Beckett's works, he says, reduces the significance and universality of

their typology and denies the dynamic movement of history (*ROT*, pp. 42–92). Sartre, in a colloquium speech on the social function of the writer, stated that because the physical needs of oppressed people were so great, he could not read Robbe-Grillet in a third-world country.[5] Robbe-Grillet was, for him, another case of "static immobilism."

The class struggle is indeed real, as is the rise and fall of nations. Whether art should contribute to this historical process, or whether it should content itself to mirror dialectical realism, or whether it can mirror anything at all depends on one's aesthetic and/or sociopolitical preferences. Rather than debate that issue here, I focus instead on conditions that can be defined as repressive or oppressive in order to show how *Projet* and *Glissements*, two works that are clearly derivative of Kafka and Beckett, can be "revolutionary." However, Robbe-Grillet's critique of "ideology"—the ideas, values, and feelings by which men experience their societies at various times—is neither Right nor Left: although Robbe-Grillet believes in the overthrow of bourgeois values, he rejects any a priori definition of history.

> The idea of an absolute and definitive truth is perhaps the one which has done us the most harm. It has also engendered bureaucratic socialism. Couldn't we dream instead of a revolution which would take place according to perpetually changing systems which would never claim to construct "the" truth?[6]

Robbe-Grillet's views, in opposition to Lukács's and Goldmann's, have affinities with Walter Benjamin's "shock montage" and Brecht's "alienation effect." The discontinuity, atomicity, and metonymy of Robbe-Grillet's work (Benjamin calls it "montage") reflect the fragmentary, discontinuous, and demythified sensations of modern urban life. Robbe-Grillet's technique of connecting dissimilars (not as extreme as the surrealists' juxtapositions, but startling nevertheless) to shock an audience into insight corresponds to Benjamin's "principle" for artistic production in a technological age.[7]

However, instead of pushing a revolutionary message through existing media, as proposed by Lukács, Robbe-Grillet, like Benjamin, is interested in revolutionizing the media itself. "Commitment," then, is less a matter of presenting "correct" political opinions in one's art, as it is of reconstructing the artistic forms themselves. These forms will not be reflections *of*, but reflections *on* social and psychological reality. The purpose of such art, as Brecht maintained, is to communicate experience in an unfamiliar light by forcing the audience to question values and behavior that were previously taken for granted. The intent of this "alienation" is not to conceal the processes or seams of the artistic experience, but to expose them, to reveal the fact that art, like society itself, is a constructed entity. Thus, a bourgeois audience, which was once a passive consumer of a finished product, is cajoled into re-creating a particular experience and is asked to participate in a creative act, which, if it has been successful—so the theory goes—will prompt individuals to apply these insights to their own lives and the society in which they live. Instead of appearing as a finished product, whose action is inexorably determined from the outset, the work, be it a play or a novel, presents itself as discontinuous, open-ended, and contradictory.[8]

Brecht's and Benjamin's aesthetic theories are, in this aspect, close to those of Umberto Eco and Robbe-Grillet, both of whom advocate "open," unfinished works requiring the active participation and collaboration of the reader/audience. The alienating and defamiliarizing tendencies of the "nouveau (nouveau) roman" are in fact comparable to Brecht's effects in his "epic" theater. The "formalism" of both Brecht and Robbe-Grillet has social reverberations; it alters not only the contents of artistic production but transforms their modes as well. Such art bears little resemblance to Lukács's nostalgia for a nineteenth-century realism that neither Brecht nor Robbe-Grillet believes is suited to the temper and complexity of the twentieth century. "Be like Balzac—only up-to-date," was Brecht's sardonic paraphrase of Lukács's position.[9]

It is no doubt significant that an allegedly Marxist Brecht and an allegedly formalist Robbe-Grillet should both reject a form which neither feels is relevant to the modern age. Lukács would have us "move forward into the nineteenth century," says an ironic Eagleton (*MLC*, p. 52).

> The bourgeois ideology [says Robbe-Grillet] is not at all limited to the capitalistic world. It is the same ideology that reigns in Moscow. Michael Sholokov's novels, for example, which are considered as the great Soviet novels at the present time, could have been written by a bourgeois writer of the bourgeois world. The communist world has exactly the same values as the capitalistic world: absence of contradiction, etc., which is part of the ideology of the two extremes East-West.[10]

Instead of removing the contradictions of society from their art, both Brecht and Robbe-Grillet exaggerate them, thereby stimulating men to abolish these contradictions in real life. Lukács, on the contrary, strives to reconcile contradiction and alienation through wholeness and harmony. The work of art, for him, should be a finished product, whereas for Brecht and Robbe-Grillet, completion is possible only through the interaction between art and the people who use it. To produce such art is to avoid being fossilized in the nineteenth century; it is being responsive to the changing conditions of the modern world. Verisimilitude in art is then no longer the mimetic process of re-creating only the textures and appearances of things. Brecht's "epic" theater and Robbe-Grillet's "nouveau (nouveau) roman" use fantasy, invention, contradiction, and alienation in order to give us a new realism capable of transforming society.

> When we speak about creating a new man, thanks to art, it is a question of creating something entirely different from the Russian revolution, which has moved from capitalism to a bureaucratic socialism. Precisely, for me, there has not been a revolution. It is the same world. The dream of a new man consists in placing in question, in a general way, the meaning of man and the meaning of his existence; whereas we have a distinct impression that meaning has not changed. (Passias, 133)

Robbe-Grillet, like Brecht, wishes to transform the world—a transformation that requires altering society's ideology: ideology, says Robbe-Grillet, "is the discourse that society gives us—a certain number of ideas that society imprints in our minds since childhood, which condition our entire life, our entire existence" (Passias, 134). In order to alter the social discourse imprinted in his mind, the artist twists, dislocates, and destroys the universe surrounding the narrator.[11] The artist deforms language and reality in order to demonstrate the arbitrary nature of the artistic construction. To reveal the seams is to parade the freedom of the artist in opposition to the tyranny of *langue* and ideology. The goal of revolutionary art is thus not to create harmonious wholes, but to incite the participant to rebel against those conditions that limit his freedom.

> Let us never forget that Hitler and Stalin were pre-eminently virtuous men, and that they made virtue (socialist, bourgeois, or Aryan—ultimately, what is the difference?) the armature of their entire political structure and the justification of their massacres. For, of course,

virtue means repression. If you believe in virtue, you must make certain virtue is respected![12]

If the function of ideology is to legitimize the "superstructure" of the ruling class in society, then an art that reveals the economic, political, psychological, or social "infrastructures" is, at the very least, subversive. This underground art threatens the legitimacy and stability of ideology. Superstructures are man-made. They are not natural. Infallibility is a sham.

> For me [says Robbe-Grillet], the notion of an ideology is related to the notion of truth. An ideology institutes a meaning which proclaims itself *the* meaning, *the* truth for ever. Modern artistic experiences have pointed out their own artificiality. They have never pretended to be virtue, equality, etc. They maintain the ideology in which they developed as a horizon. But it is only a horizon above and against which they stand apart. (Passias, 134)

Insofar as Robbe-Grillet's works are composed of fragments of the ideological superstructure, they are part of it, yet his discourse, in its critique of ideology, distances him and the reader/audience from it. Robbe-Grillet gives ideology a determinate form, and by fixing it within certain fictional limits, reveals the limitations of the ideological discourse. His art thus contributes to our deliverance from the ideological "illusion," which is precisely the thesis Pierre Macherey advances in *Pour une théorie de la production littéraire*.[13] Macherey's scientific criticism would search out the principle that relates and distances it from the ideology it opposes. To do this is to focus on a work's formal structure—a structure from which the revolutionary content emerges. A work's form, if it is revolutionary, must be alienating. Instead of coherence, such works display conflict, incoherence, contradiction, developing a meaning that, for Macherey, is "de-centered."

It is in the nature of works such as *Projet* and *Glissements* to seem incoherent, tied as they are to an ideology that silences them at certain points. Yet each work's discourse and diegesis reveal internal conflicts with ideology. Robbe-Grillet, like Macherey, believes that literature must deform rather than imitate, that artistic activity is parodic rather than mimetic. They both reject Lukács's and Lenin's epistemological theory of reflection according to which art is only the reflection of the external world in the human consciousness.[14]

If human consciousness is molded by ideology and art is no more than the reflection of this consciousness, then art reflects the ideology of the superstructure. The best-sellers in capitalist countries and works that conform to the Party line in socialist countries are the inert products of ideology, devoid of inner life, i.e., of contradiction. Instead of such lifeless products, Louis Althusser proposes a vibrant art that will let us "feel" and "perceive" the ideology from which it springs. Art can give the reader/audience an experience of a particular situation by inflating ideology and undermining it at the same time. This distancing effect allows us to "see" the nature of the ideology, moving us toward understanding, which, for Althusser, is scientific knowledge.[15]

In art, however, alienation, distancing, and contradiction are the results of experiments in form and language. In this sense, the "nouveau (nouveau) roman," insofar as it stresses the primacy of language, is much more modest in its avowed goals than the Marxist revolution. Its thrust is primarily linguistic and psychological. Ultimately, however, its reverberations, if successful, will be sociopolitical. For the moment, Robbe-Grillet, wishing to free men from the constraints of *ideology* and espousing no particular line, devalues each and every one. *Langue* is the vehicle for all ideologies and all values, be they Buddhist, Christian, capitalist, Fascist, or Marxist. Every ideology, claiming to be true, God-given, scientific, or eternal, asserts its *natural* superiority over the others by staking its own exclusive rights to men's fealty. It is this myth of the *natural* that Robbe-Grillet finds so offensive. In fact, he opposes all man-made systems that have been elevated into dogma for the manipulation and repression of the masses. "If God, like the rest of the world, is the invention of man, there is no natural order and I must establish here and now my own order—that is, constrain even more that nature whose existence is negated simply by my presence on earth" (*OD*, p. 5).

Robbe-Grillet prefers to view life as a game played according to arbitrary rules. If Marxists and capitalists can define the rules, while pretending that they are immutable, then the artist should have the same prerogative. If his *parole* offends the public, well, then, so be it. The avant-garde, by definition, is made up of those shock troops that absorb the enemy's first blows. The revolutionary goal of Robbe-Grillet's art is therefore twofold: to expose the repressed imagery of ideology and to demonstrate the arbitrary nature of the language in which this ideology is clothed. His art not only deforms literary convention, it deforms language as well. The proliferation of the text, its polysemy, the abundance of narrative

voices, pronouns, identities, and corpses, as well as the exaggerated
forms of comic and ironic gore, contribute to the defamiliarization
of the reader, the play of language, and the freedom of the artist. If
the enemy is *doxology*, then the literary game is to subvert the
enemy from within, by playing with its sacred cows, by demonstrating that it can be done.

> It is for their lack of a sense of humor that I would criticize certain
> revolutionaries. My impression today is that a revolution without
> humor would fall back automatically into a bourgeois order. The
> world I dream of is not one of a particular "established order," but a
> world in which we could play, in which we would have the right to
> play. (*SCP*, p. 49)

The pursuit of Revolution is, generally, a deadly serious enterprise that is intolerant, even afraid of "revolutionary" art. Art
thrives on freedom, not on coercion. An establishment that har-
nesses its artists to the yoke of dialectical materialism soon stifles
the overt creative ingenuity of its best talent by forcing it underground. Artists are muzzled and their works confiscated;

> the socialist Revolution [says Robbe-Grillet] is afraid of revolutionary
> Art, nor is it mistaken in its feelings. . . . from the point of view of the
> revolution, everything must contribute directly to the final goal: the
> liberation of the proletariat. . . . Everything, including literature,
> painting, etc. However, for the artist, art cannot be reduced to a
> means with which to serve a cause that transcends it, no matter how
> just, . . . an artist places nothing above his work.[16]

Hitler and Franco imposed an equally Puritan and nationalistic
form of censorship on the arts. In fact, every monolithic system,
capitalism included, shuns artists whose *parole* speaks out against
establishment ideology. "Perhaps the most grievous deception of
all," writes Ionesco, is "the tacit concurrence of the bourgeoisies of
West and East in their desire to suppress dissidence."[17]

So far, Robbe-Grillet has the distinction of having offended both
Right and Left. Nevertheless, he seems determined to pursue his
vision as an artist and it is this vision that, in spite of, or perhaps
because of, its formalism, is "revolutionary." Although *Projet* uses
some of the trappings of the class struggle, e.g., the revolt of the
economically disadvantaged blacks against exploitation by the
white establishment, the narrative itself devalues political ideology
in favor of sadoerotic themes. The novel's discourse multiplies the

chaos of a revolution that, except for the underground subway network, has already destroyed most of Manhattan. The underground—the usual metaphor for clandestine activity—is the subway system with its connecting labyrinth of tunnels and corridors in which murder, torture, and rape take place. In this novel the underground is also a metaphor for the repression of sexuality, since that is where so many illicit activities occur.

The words "Tomorrow . . . the revolution" appear on advertising posters along a corridor wall. On one of the posters, which is a picture of a woman's face with open lips, a giant phallus has been spray-painted in black. Whereas Robbe-Grillet plays with media clichés in order to expose them as images of contemporary myth, he also plays with the language on which this myth keeps rolling. His *parole* is in dialogue with the *langue* of public myth. The giant graffito deforms the composite image into its subconscious sign: desire. What was only a floating eroticism with a veiled purpose to sell lipstick becomes graphic in its intent and implications: "Buy me, desire will be satisfied!" Buying and screwing have been legitimized; they now overlap. The language of advertising exteriorizes desire, transforming it into reified acts. Language, imagery, and establishment code thus manipulate the unsuspecting public. Robbe-Grillet's art "plays" with these repressive forces in an attempt to expose and neutralize them. However, verbal play, as one of the organizing devices in his work, has premises and implications that transcend any one novel and film: creative play rejects all a priori systems while affirming the inviolate freedom of the artist. Play dramatizes the artist's *parole* in conflict with the ideology of society's *langue*. It is this collision between desire and repression that allows Robbe-Grillet to assert his subversive thrust in both *Projet* and *Glissements*. Says Robbe-Grillet:

> According to Saussure's irreconcilable opposition between *langue* and *parole*, we can say that the comedy scenes, the taste for blood, the beautiful slaves, the vampire bites, etc., do not represent the *parole* of this film [*Glissements*], but only its *langue*. Society's *parole* has been cut up into pieces in order to force it back into a state of *langue*. It is this secondary *langue* which will be used as source material to produce a new *parole*, a non-reconciled structure, my own *parole*.[18]

In *Projet*, the Revolution has already destroyed New York. Anarchy reigns above ground and in the subway system below. The city is gripped by red fear: fear of murder, fire, and rape—the three colors of the Revolution. Shady "narco-analysts" such as Doctor Morgan assault the bodies of young women forcing them to reveal the secrets of the "organization." Laura is tortured with rats, spiders, fire, and a variety of metal instruments: saws, pincers, sharp points, and pliers with which toenails and nipples are removed. But she has no secrets to tell, and the clandestine activities allegedly responsible for her "inquisition" are not so much political as they are parodies of plots of conventional thrillers. Stereotypes of sex and violence are exaggerated. They become inflated images that effectively undercut all prurience.

> For centuries [says Robbe-Grillet] generations and generations of puritanical bourgeois and puritanical socialists have waged war, side by side, against the flesh, against the body, against pleasure, and all the more intensely if pleasure has been intellectualized. (*FVT*, p. 46)

Laura, the heroine of Robbe-Grillet's "dramatic play," is a victim of the lust, desire, fornication, and pimping associated with the sex shops on Forty-second Street, where the excrescences of society's repressed libido are concentrated. Moreover, "all violence is sexual, as Marx did not say," says Robbe-Grillet (*GPP*, p. 81). The secrets of both *Projet* and *Glissements* turn out to be sexual and linguistic rather than political because the *human* "infrastructure" is psychological rather than economic. If, as the linguists maintain, language determines social, economic, and political reality, then the writer who wishes to change society must address himself first to those structures that organize perception and behavior. Robbe-Grillet writes novels and films with units of *langue*, and then with his *parole* undermines these ideological units. This subversion is of the first magnitude, an attack on the foundations of establishment order. The bodies in the text are metaphors for the norms of the superstructure as well as signifiers for the repressed desires of the infrastructure. The reader/narrator is the Freudian ego caught between the id and the superego. Consciousness or perception or intentionality or all three have to sift through conflicting narrative voices trying vainly to reconcile the contradictions in the text. The contradictions within these "open" works also reflect the contradictions in real life. Thus, the imposters in Robbe-Grillet's novels and films are actors parading imaginary selves. They are perpetually unmasking the duplicity in themselves and in others: "he takes off the bald mask of the locksmith which covered his head and face, removing progressively the layer of plastic material, slowly uncovering in its place the features of the real Ben Saïd."[19] Ben Saïd turns out to be a black double agent who is one of the narrators, who is also the author. The narrative voices nullify each other, reducing the text to a *parole* in dialogue with *langue*. The cuts ("coupures") in the text (*PRNY*, p. 203) and the splices on the tape (*PRNY*, p. 206) are the author himself ripping and assaulting the body of language. This is why bodies are violated in the white, abstract, generative cell, out of which emerges the text's dialectical topology. The social codes of the establishment outside are violated inside the cells, the rooms, and the dungeons of the author's imagination. Says Robbe-Grillet:

> All these living underground tableaux, portraying unambiguously the popular traditional imagery of the type "Tortures of the Inquisition," are in fact stereotypes for specialized magazines . . . as has already been indicated concerning the photos of the medieval prison . . . it is again a question of a certain postcard "realism" (i.e., the coded expression of ready-made meaning) which contrasts with the white abstraction of the apartment and of the cell in particular (which supposedly constitutes present reality!). (*GPP*, pp. 103–4)

In Robbe-Grillet's dialectic between pleasure and ideology, the wrong side of the law holds a preponderant place. His ritual tortures, like Sade's, are organized, methodical, detailed, and planned. Sade was forever using "the wrong side of words, the wrong side of girls, the wrong side of things" (*OD*, 5). In fact, Sade's universe is one in which all the elements are always facing the wrong way. However, the wrong side assumes meaning precisely because the right side, e.g., ideology, is securely fixed. Writing, as Roland Barthes affirms, is an intervention exercised on language—"language being a 'body of prescriptions and habits' shared by all the citizens of a country at a given time" (*OD*, 5). To bare the wrong side, e.g., to organize arson, murder, and rape as the generative themes in a work of art such as *Projet*, is to offend the habits and prescriptions of a given citizenry. Robbe-Grillet deliberately violates all Western taboos, including those on incest and religion. In *Projet*, for instance, after the ritual of a sadoerotic black mass, the communing girls are crucified:

> But in front of the twelve columns of the nave are already standing the twelve crosses to which the little girls are destined: . . . And beneath their blind gaze, the victim of the sacrifice lies in a pool of blood, her breasts torn off as well as all the flesh in the pubic area and

the upper part of her thighs. Her delicate hands, carefully washed and very white, seem to caress these lacerations, in the hollow of the dark red wound which replaces the genitals. (*PRNY*, p. 213)

Robbe-Grillet inverts the meaning of ritual, breaks the rules, disputes prohibitions, and rapes the reader, thereby affirming his freedom by remaining in a state of permanent scandal vis-à-vis his culture's ideology. His victims are continuously suffering and perishing. Tender flesh submits to terrible torments without losing its freshness. Like the architecture imposed on the words of a sentence, the constraints on the *body of* and on the *bodies in* the text become more aberrant, more violent, uncomfortable, revolting, and inadmissible. When Robbe-Grillet, like Sade, organizes language, he

> delegates its powers to narrators of the imaginary, theoreticians of unreason, historians and hagiographers of crime, legislators of injustice, scriptwriters of treason and falsehood, sculptors of living tableaux dedicated to death, stage-directors of a theatre void of dramatic action, masters of ceremonies indifferent to etiquette or rite. This language fears neither excess nor harassing repetition, neither contradiction or a humor which spoils every realistic illusion; it makes an order of disorder, of reversal, of nothing. (*OD*, 6)

In Robbe-Grillet's novels and films the encoded ideology is parodied with stereotypes of fear, sex, and violence. The work's self-reflexive construction undermines reality and realism, forcing the reader/audience to accept generative themes, forcing the reader/audience to consider the arbitrariness of all ideology. Having gone this far and having suspended previous beliefs, the reader is now ready to play with a work's serial arrangements, verbal permutations, and linguistic proliferations. Thus, the color red in *Projet* generates arson, rape, and murder. These three specific activities, in turn, are derived from the three mythic categories of fear, sex, and violence. Three times three gives us the *nine* categories Robbe-Grillet develops in "Piège à fourrure" (Fur Trap): steps, fur, opening, knife, cry, penetration, fall, flow, and stain.[20] Hitchcock thrillers, like many others of their kind, use typical *fear* conventions: the sound of male "footsteps" in the night, a creaking door "opens," a woman in bed "cries" out. *Sex* conventions may generate "fur," "opening," and "penetration." The convention of *violence* will perhaps evoke "penetration," "flow," and "stain." Any one of the prime categories may combine with any one of the nine "traps" in any order and in any sequence. These are the rules of the game, so to speak, with which Robbe-Grillet "plays" in order to expose and simultaneously devalue their conventions.

In *Glissements*, the trap is primarily sexual. Violence, however, is never far away, since Robbe-Grillet establishes a clear and definite link between the two. In this film he reveals the underside of law, order, and morality as Alice seduces each one of its representatives: the police inspector, the magistrate, the lawyer, the priest, and the nuns. Each one of these succumbs to Alice's charms, to the slippages of pleasure that she and her fantasies provide. "Thus the frame featuring the title of the film is preceded by the image of a bottle breaking on the white floor, followed by the breaking of eggs on the same floor, where their viscous contents mix with a red liquid" (*GPP*, p. 26).

The broken eggs and the spilled liquid, like the broken bottle, are the film's generative themes. They are Robbe-Grillet's signs for sex, violence, and convention, respectively. These are assembled in the generative cell—Robbe-Grillet's favorite place. Whether house, room, or dungeon, it is a recurring image in his art, the simultaneous and ambiguous symbol of creativity and bondage, of imagination and the prison of language. It contains the past as well as the future. This white cell has the purity and abstraction of things to come. In it past reality is broken. From its fragments a new reality is assembled whose images, as in *L'Eden et après*, resemble the serial music of Schoenberg's twelve-tone system.

In keeping with Robbe-Grillet's predilections, *Glissements* is set in a prison for delinquent girls whose guardians are nuns. This setting allows Robbe-Grillet's imagination free reign to play with religious, lesbian, fetishistic, and sadoerotic themes. One by one, the representatives of law and order, goaded by desire, succumb to Alice's beauty and the power of her words. It is as though each one had been lured by her siren song:

> Slithering of fish in the seaweed
> Too dense, caught in the iron bars
> Of the bed without sheets, redenned with the iron lance
> Whose tip with one jab tears the silk
> On the flesh, when the sea withdraws.
>
> (*GPP*, p. 93)

The police siren (violence) alternates with Alice's call (desire) as Robbe-Grillet weaves these two themes into the film's serial patterns. Alice's verbal fantasies generate the film's diegesis. In due course her *parole* destroys society's *langue*. Nora, her friend and lawyer, is "murdered" twice: once at the beginning and once at the end. This fantasy self-destructs along with other semblances of realism, as pleasure rises to a crescendo of violence and catharsis culminating in freedom. The syntagmas are the following: in the dungeon Sister Julia hands Alice the signifying code objects: eggs, a broken bottle, the shoe, a piece of rope, the scissors, the foot or hand of the mannikin, the shovel, the unbroken bottle containing the folded message. Alice says: "Game. Rape. Pleasure. Structure. Infraction. Sperm. Doubling." At the end of this incantatory and metonymic sequence Alice is seen standing, looking out at the sea. "This scene should be shot in a rosy, evening light and should last some time. Joyous noises of wind, sea, and seagulls: freedom" (*GPP*, p. 141).

Although Robbe-Grillet abolishes realism, his art retains a designated cultural conflict between freedom and oppression. Thus, Alice's "assassination" of convention by means of the ritualized exorcism of signs and language is like an act of terrorism whose infrastructure is sexual. Once again the *body in* and the *body of* the text are its form and its content. Robbe-Grillet annihilates ideology, but he also annihilates the text:

> every structure is mostly made up of non sense; sense, in digesting its own structural organization . . . has to annihilate it. Structure, therefore, in breaking the continuity of meaning, and in its infraction, refraction, diffraction, and infringement of serial or combinative organization, defies every attempt to recuperate it. Structure—for us— can provide only precarious and provisional meaning, slipping, always ready to collapse. (*GPP*, p. 13)

Lucien Goldmann once asked Adamov to change the fourth act of his play *Ping-pong* because it was not in line with Marx's thought, whereas the first three acts had been a faithful dramatization of *Das Kapital*.[21] It was this intervention of Goldmann's that prompted Robbe-Grillet to conclude that the revolution of the "nouveau roman" was both harder and more complex than the economic readjustment of the modes of production. Not that he opposes such a readjustment; on the contrary. But he does not believe that literature can do much to change the status quo as long as socialist and capitalist bureaucracies suppress revolution in art. Since both camps continue to reject and oppose the sexual, literary, and artistic innovations advocated by the avant-garde, they are condemned, he says, to stagnate within their repressive bourgeoisies. "Instead of operating on known political facts (colonial problems for example), the revolution which literature (or the cinema) is pursuing, is a general revolution in meaning."[22]

As for the economic and political realms to which Robbe-Grillet sometimes alludes, men do act as lawgivers and architects of world order and disorder. Since economics and the proletariat seem to determine the course of modern events, capitalists and Marxists have supplanted God as the instigators and controllers of history. The New (New) Novelists, with their newly discovered freedom, are like radical disseminators of chaos. Their works have disrupted, challenged, and undermined most of the conventions of fiction. But the chaos is more apparent than real and the disorientation of the traditional reader, whose expectations are thwarted (no characters! . . . no story!), is perhaps only temporary. The New (New) Novelists, as the title *Projet pour une révolution à New York* might suggest, like revolutionaries, are substituting a new order for the old—an order that is perceived as disorder only because readers have not yet assimilated its innovations. However, unlike revolutionaries, even though the New (New) Novelists' doctrines are terroristic, they have no power to impose them.[23] In this context Raymond Jean speaks of a *subversion* of traditional literary values and Philippe Sollers speaks of *devaluation:* "the 'nouveau roman' has announced a devaluation of the traditional economics of literature and this is what makes it profoundly political."[24] However, New Novelists are not, as hostile critics have claimed, killing the novel. They are merely changing it from within by exposing the inflation of outmoded forms. Nor is man really dead, since we all continue to eat and breathe and reproduce. What is dying are obsolete notions of human nature:

> If Man with a capital M (natural "man"), [says Robbe-Grillet] is . . . an outmoded idea, we will also have to discard our idea of History (with its capital H), because this renouned History, when it comes to politics, represents something that strongly resembles the traditional novel vis-à-vis lived experience: a narrative code woven from chronology, causality, a veritable ensemble of laws whose natural colors were instituted by the nineteenth century as a superior truth; it is also on the group level what Man represents vis-à-vis you and me: a cultural myth. (*NRHA*, 2:161–62)

In the final analysis, commitment for the writer is not political, but literary. He strives to resolve current problems, fully cognizant of the fact that literature can resolve only questions of meaning and language (*PNR*, p. 39). Nevertheless, as we have seen, the "nouveau (nouveau) roman" dramatizes the conflicts between the individual and society. Not only does it refuse to be "recuperated" by the system, it strives to subvert and eventually to overthrow establishment ideology. However, this cannot occur until society accepts the radical transformation of thought processes that are implicit in the "écriture" of the "nouveau (nouveau) roman." Says Robbe-Grillet: "we know that in the history of nations, only this curiously gratuitous art will find its place, perhaps, next to the workers' unions and the barricades" (*PNR*, p. 36).

This chapter, emphasizing the "revolutionary" potential of the New (New) Novel, provides the necessary mimetic and political antidote to the reflexive formalism discussed in Chapter 1. I have quoted at length from Robbe-Grillet's essays and interviews in order to stress his own deliberate (I hesitate to say didactic although the intention is unmistakably there), "recuperative" efforts. His fiction keeps rolling along, we could even say, gathers speed, on the *Trans-Europ-Express* of sexual politics. The texts of his New (New) Novels literally bulge with desire, parading a sexuality that barely contains itself. The bodies of these texts assert a reflexive eroticism forever striving to subvert the dominant bourgeois ideology. In the next chapter we continue to explore the sexual, mythical, and political aspirations of an insurgent "literariness."

3

The Body of the Text

> a work—whether writing, painting, or music—always and
> above all maintains a sensual relationship with the body.
> —Alain Robbe-Grillet

Conventional novels move toward climax the way intercourse
strives for orgasm. The "nouveau nouveau roman," like Roland
Barthes's *Le Plaisir du texte*, also has pleasure in mind, but it accen-
tuates the play, the texture of words, the detours, the fantasy, the
in-and-out imagery, the very sexuality of the text. Claude Simon's
Les Corps conducteurs is an apt title for other similar body texts, such
as Pinget's *Passacaille*, Ricardou's *La Prise de Constantinople*, or
Robbe-Grillet's *Souvenirs du triangle d'or*. Language in these novels,
and in others like them, is treated as a body—a body of words (is
this a metaphor or a pun?) whose corporeality and resourcefulness
are a source of pleasure and delight. Textuality and sexuality are
one. Barthes speaks of a "language lined with skin . . . the volup-
tuousness of vowels, a whole stereophony of the deep flesh." He
asks that "writing aloud" capture the "presence of the human muz-
zle" in order to throw the anonymous body of the actor into my
ear" where "it granulates, it crackles, it caresses, it grates, it cuts, it
comes; that," he says, "is bliss."[1]

Within the conventions of the New (New) Novel, the phallus
(any phallic symbol will do) is sometimes a metaphor for the creative process, whereas writing, in more ways than one, has become a
metaphor for intercourse. But even more than the sexual act,
Robbe-Grillet's texts frequently reenact violence and rape so that
the freedom of his *parole* may outrage the determinism of *langue*,
shock the conventions of the reader/audience, and expose the
stereotypes of "innocence." This organized violence committed on
ordinary speech also fulfills Jakobson's criterion for poetry, whose
function, he says, is to deform everyday language. Ideology denies

man's freedom, desire affirms it, and the "nouveau nouveau roman" joins the two. Its poetics invites the reader to explore the gap between *langue* and *parole*. The artist's pen (poetic signifier for phallus) opens up *langue* (poetic signifier for vagina), pares, thrusts, exposes, reveals, and plays—above all plays with everyday words, violates ideology, which is hidden within the folds of *langue*, whose vestments are convention, the norms of the establishment. Perceived in these terms history is desire and all revolutions are sexual: "desire does not 'want' the revolution, it is itself revolutionary," say Gilles Deleuze and Félix Guattari.[2] Robbe-Grillet's joining of *langue* and *parole*, although in itself subversive, also parallels the meeting between the reader and the text. These unions, if they are fertile, are creative: though they may shock, they engender. Even sexual "defamiliarization" can prod the reader to reassemble "reality" into new and meaningful patterns.

There is no guarantee, however, that the desired coupling between the text and the reader, or between *langue* and *parole*, will occur. The reader's defamiliarization is often extreme and his disorientation is frequently severe. The openings in the text, the deliberate "baring" of the "body's" reflexive devices, though designed to seduce, do not always ensnare. There is resistance. Only commentators who like to undress, i.e., uncover the inner structure of the text, sometimes succeed in laying bare the meaning of its sexuality. For instance, Simon's *Les Corps conducteurs* has frequent, graphically detailed descriptions of a phallus moving in and out of a vagina. In Pinget's *Passacaille*, the manuscript for the novel, rolled like a scroll, is pulled from the protagonist's fly, bloodied, as though it were a severed phallus. In Ricardou's *La Prise de Constantinople*, which is also *La Prose de Constantinople*, the city in which crusaders tarried on their way to the Holy Land is identified with a vagina whose hairy mantle becomes a flaming bush. In Robbe-Grillet's *Souvenirs du triangle d'or*, the narrator's attempts to decode the combination to the locked door of the Temple are comparable to the reader's attempts to penetrate the text (or Temple's sex). The "stylo à feutre" (felt-tip pen) in *Projet pour une révolution à New York*, as Thomas O'Donnell points out, becomes a "stylo à foutre" (screwing pen).[3]

But all this is not exactly new. Who is not familiar with the "virginity" of Mallarmé's white page as yet unsullied by the pen, or of the sexual symbolism of writing, which for Freud "consists of releasing liquid from a pen onto blank paper." Derrida, in *De la grammatologie*, analyzes in detail Rousseau's unconscious and symbolic correlation between writing and masturbation. Saussure, in veiled linguistic terms, says that everything that is active in the psychological part of a circuit (as in writing) is executive and everything that is passive is receptive.[4] Accordingly, the author of a text is the active master, the executive side speaking *(parole)*, whereas *langue* is passive, the receiver, the body that is manipulated, tortured, and sometimes raped. In *Projet*,

> a young woman who is entirely naked appears in a three-quarters view, astride a sawblade with very sharp teeth, her legs pulled wide apart by chains attached to two rings. . . . The victim, still shaken by charming contortions although already losing some of her strength, continues bleeding a little at the six points at which she has been tortured: . . . the saw has penetrated deeper and deeper at each of the patient's convulsive movements, tormenting the flesh and severing the pubic region, smeared with sperm, much higher than the top of its natural orifice.[5]

Since *langue*, like the chained lovely in the previous example, is bound by convention, it has to submit to the author's designs. Accordingly, in Robbe-Grillet's fiction modesty is flaunted, images are exaggerated, plausibility is destroyed, cultural ideology is whipped, taboos on incest are violated, social codes are sacrificed, piety is crucified, and *doxas* are burned. The traditional text is deformed, and its body is maimed, dismembered, injected, and experimented on. It is a miracle that it survives, and it does, like a phoenix rising from the ashes of its own destruction. (The phoenix is a recurrent image in *Topologie d'une cité fantôme* and *Souvenirs du triangle d'or*.)

Obviously the body of the text is not an inert assemblage of words, since language, particularly clichéd language, always resists attempts to manipulate it. The assault on the living body *(langue)* is also more than a simple metaphor, since language makes the transmission of political, religious, legal, and moral concepts possible. Robbe-Grillet's *Projet pour une révolution à New York,* which impressed many readers as trivial, turns out to be deadlier than anticipated, since it strikes at the heart, or should I say sex of our *doxal* system.[6] It is not only the language of sex or the sex of language with which Robbe-Grillet plays. If he has sex in mind it is because sex, like violence, is everywhere. In a consumer society sex is used to sell the objects that reify the individual. Sex is visible on every giant billboard, bigger than life. Violence also tends to overwhelm us: death on the freeways, in the ghetto, in the home, and in the prisons; there is death in terrorism, war, and executions. Eros and Thanatos are the twin giants running our lives. Sexuality and death, eroticism and violence, the two repressed forces claim their daily body count, and instead of opposition, there is now, as Marcuse points out, collusion.

It is this collusion that Robbe-Grillet's works portray and undermine, simultaneously:

> my generative themes have been chosen . . . from popular contemporary imagery: illustrated covers of novels sold in stations, giant publicity posters, pornographic magazines found in sex shops, the slick ads of fashion magazines, the flat figures of the funnies without perspective, in other words everything that has replaced my alleged depth, the me which has been expunged from my inner stronghold and is today exhibited in broad daylight in the showcases or even on the city walls.[7]

Robbe-Grillet says he exaggerates and thereby, simultaneously, devalues the images of the male subconscious. But readers who are accustomed to the old conventions and unfamiliar with the New New Novel, are frequently horrified by scenes in which naked girls are tortured or treated like objects. It is also conceivable that some male readers, unlike their female counterparts, will enjoy the sadoerotic violence of this fantasy world even though realism and mimesis are undercut and devalued at every turn and in every paragraph. However, for the reader to be offended or titillated signifies an egregious misreading of a text in which women's bodies, as in *La Belle Captive*, are no more than metaphors for language and, therefore, as unreal as the mannikins that Robbe-Grillet frequently substitutes for them. Although Robbe-Grillet seems to enjoy the inflated imagery of gory scenes as indices of the comedy of deflated ideology, it seems impossible, given the nature of the text, to relive it on a realistic or erotic level. The exaggerations are pure camp, something Rimbaud would have approved of, because they are also a reasoned derangement of the reader's senses. The reader who misreads is no more than a voyeur, but with insight he or she becomes a "voyant."

In *Trans-Europ-Express*, for instance, a title that connotes *Fear*, *Sex*, and *Death*, the word *Trans* slips into *transes* (meaning "fears"). *Europ*, the Paris to Antwerp train, becomes *Europe*, a girlie magazine. *Express* is simultaneously the train and the name of a news magazine, featuring "L'Homme qui est mort quatre fois" (The Man Who Died Four Times). Conventional views of reality, eroticism, and the detective story are exploded as the mock treatment of the love episodes between a make-believe drug runner and a make-believe prostitute counters the theme of "heroic" love in the accompanying music of *La Traviata*. The slippage between subsequent images of fear, eroticism, and violence generated by the words and themes of the film's title—a slippage that is transported and accelerated by the very movement of the train—links the continuously shifting associations, like the high-speed shots of the rails converging and separating, as though they too (which they are) were commenting on the narrative. This juxtaposition of thematic imagery, this metonymy (because the transitions are abrupt, without the metaphoric niceties of fade-in or fade-out) are structured by the words in the title. The "écriture productrice," generated by the themes, ambiguities, and associations, applies with equal ease to diegesis in the cinema as in the novel.

In view of the fact that advertising, like psychoanalysis, has uncovered the hidden fantasies of the human psyche, the so-called depth of man, clearly revealed as myth, makes it difficult to speak of a subconscious. The generative themes, now that they are, so to speak, in the public domain, can perhaps no longer function as unconscious, pre-Freudian images. According to Robbe-Grillet they belong to a post-Freudian era: "all that excessive psychoanalytic material that is in my books can therefore no longer belong to innocence, but on the contrary, to culture" (*NRHA*, 2:169–70).

Robbe-Grillet toys with the images of cultural myths: exposing them, rendering them visible, dissecting them, even as he dismembers the bodies of the girls and mannikins that inhabit his novels and films. Within this play of language, imagination is the torturer and the victim is reality. These dramatizations are designed to illustrate the fact that anything is possible, that people do not have to obey the constraints of ideology, although they are also free to do so if they wish. The idea of existential freedom that lurks behind all of Robbe-Grillet's texts allows him to manipulate taboos in ways that sometimes offend the reader/viewer. The New New Novel thus exhibits the author's freedom vis-à-vis the system, but more important still, from the reader's point of view, is the demonstration itself that epistemologically amounts to saying that everything is allowed. This is discussed at length in Chapters 4 and 7. Suffice it to say here that the wordplay, subversions, traps, and so on, all the generative themes and serial permutations prepared by the author, while they encourage the readers' re-creative endeavors, do not limit them to any one solution. The notion of the "open work" invites readers to play with the text as they would with reality, because art, like life, always has more than one answer to the same problem. The very act of choosing one plausible solution is, existentially speaking, an exercise in freedom, and it is this kind of insight that the new texts provide.

> If we pick up on Saussure's famous opposition [says Robbe-Grillet], I do not work on *langue* (i.e., this twentieth century French which I use just as it has come down to me) but on society's *parole* (i.e., the discourse addressed to me by the world in which I live). Except that I in turn refuse to speak this *parole*, I use it as raw material, which amounts to pushing it back into a status of *langue*, from which I develop my own discourse. (*NRHA*, 2:160–61)

Now that rape and murder, sex and violence, Eros and Thanatos, and Freud's pleasure principle and the death instinct have become cultural motifs and can be used as conscious generative themes, they are no longer "innocent" or "natural." Exposure to the light of day alters them; they can no longer bathe obscurely in their original magma. The artist's *parole* is woven from a code that the establishment would like us to think is natural, but which, if the structuralists are correct, is entirely man-made. Language may parallel reality, and the text may reflect itself, but it is not indifferent to certain repetitive patterns such as the color red, clichéd eroticism, stock situations, a cry, death—external generators with which to structure the internal machinery of the text. These texts, contrary to the beliefs of purists such as Stephen Heath and Jean Ricardou, do say something about the world. They are not exclusively reflexive and they do have referential levels. Died-in-the-wool formalists deny the presence of ideas or emotions in poetics, claiming that it is impossible to draw conclusions from a literary work. Robbe-Grillet himself is much closer to the structuralists who stress the inevitable ambiguity of texts that function on different semantic levels:

> This is the reason why fictional elements belonging to the former novel can still be found in my books. Younger writers reproach me for them, but I know I need them as long as the idea of nature has not been liquidated (and cannot perhaps be liquidated). . . . I am better able to reflect on the problems of man with respect to it; man is the only animal on earth to stand upright and is therefore in a constant state of disequilibrium, thereby erecting himself against nature. (*NRHA*, 2:171–72)

The work of a novelist like Robbe-Grillet is, therefore, a permanent demystification of nature—a nature that is forever trying to have the last word. Under such circumstances art becomes an affirmation of man, emphasizing art's artificiality and opposition to so-called "natural" processes. Robbe-Grillet opposes all "natural" myths because they are the basis on which outmoded social, moral, and political orders continue to perpetuate themselves. Bourgeois order, bourgeois morality, and bourgeois values were all thought to be "natural," he says, inscribed somewhere in a "natural" order of things, yet like narration, they are no more just, innocent, or inalterable than the men who fashion them (*NRHA*, 2:159). Even feelings and passional conduct, says Merleau-Ponty, like words, are invented. The linguistic sign unites, not a thing and a name, says Saussure, but a concept and an acoustic image ("signifié—signifiant"). The sign, whose meaning rests on social convention and acceptation, is arbitrary (*CGL*, p. 67). Since kissing is not one of the traditional customs of Japan, it is no more natural to kiss in love or to shout in anger than to call a table "a table." Everything man does is both manufactured and natural since there is not one word, not one form of behavior that does not owe something to his biological self, yet which also eludes the simplicity of animal life, thus deflecting behavior from its "pre-ordained" direction through a sort of "leakage."[8] Habit reinforces the feeling that the things and events among which we live are "natural" and permanent. Reader hostility to the "nouveau (nouveau) roman" is therefore similar to the Brechtian alienation-effect whose purpose is to make us aware that the objects and institutions we thought to be natural are in fact historical and therefore changeable. If the Brechtian alienation-effect is political, as Fredric Jameson points out,[9] then the alienation-effect of the "nouveau (nouveau) roman" is also. It would be difficult not to agree with Barthes that the historical role of today's intellectual is:

> to maintain and accentuate the decomposition of the bourgeois consciousness. . . . This means that one pretends to remain within this consciousness in order to ruin, collapse, and cave it in, in place, as one would with a piece of sugar by soaking it in water.[10]

Barthes contrasts "decomposition," which is an *internal* phenomenon, with "destruction," which is an *external* one, emphasizing that exteriority is possible only in a revolutionary situation, as in China

[Mao's China], where, he says, class consciousness is being "destroyed." A Western writer intent on "destruction" would have to use a dogmatic and immobile language *(parole)*—a language whose only characteristic would be its exteriority (*RB*, p. 68).

Robbe-Grillet's *parole* oscillates between the *internal* and the *external*, forcing the body of the text to experience the shock of transition between destruction and decomposition. The ritual sacrifice of the text (such as *Topologie d'une cité fantôme* and the young girls in it—a text constantly "slipping" from the "cellule génératrice" inside to the landscape outside—"as though the outside of the room were [on] the inside")[11] produces a "landscape with a cry" (*TCF*, p. 166), one of the thematic elements of the novel. "It is once again the same cry: a scream of terror perhaps, or of sharp pain, or maybe of fever" (*TCF*, p. 197). The external generators of the text (Delvaux, Rauschenberg, Magritte, Hamilton, and Robbe-Grillet himself) reinforce the dialogue between the active and the passive elements of language referred to by Saussure.

The artistic code provided by the five male generators meshes with the polysemy of the text's internal generators—images and objects that are identical to the nine serial signs that Robbe-Grillet describes in "Piège à fourrure" (Fur Trap).[12] The words in *Topologie:* "I am alone. I am walking at random" (p. 11) correspond to category A in "Piège": *Steps.* In due course a woman's high-heeled shoe evolves into one of several fetishes. Category B, *Fur*, blends the fetishism of fur with dream, wool, and pubic hair (or "fleece"). A woman's "fleece" is thus generator number two. In category C, *Opening*, the principal object is door. In *Topologie*, symbolic doors abound, although windows, mirrors, and keyholes also act as frequent substitutes and Freudian symbols. Category D in "Piège" is *Knife.* The surfaces on which the woman artist in *Topologie* is working are called "lames" (blades), perhaps an allusion to the cutting edge of art. Inside the cell she is engraving a large polished copper plaque with a fine stylet. In due course one young prostitute and another girl will be assassinated through the left breast with identical golden stylets. Category E, *Cry*, sets *Topologie* in motion. It is the wounded girl's cry that animates the curves imprisoned by the geometry of straight lines. Category F, *Penetration*, has sexual connotations, whereas category G, *Falling*, uses falling objects, or analogs such as a stone thrown out of a window. The following passage combines six of the seven categories already mentioned in the order in which they appear: stone, opening, cry, sharp point, penetration, fleece. The words in the text that otherwise appear "innocent" are underlined.

> Henceforth, everything happens very quickly: the *pebble* picked up by a hand from the floor with the parallel grooves receding in perspective, the hand throwing the pebble through the *aperture* with the broken grating, the *cry* of a wounded passer-by, outside, suddenly piercing the sweet calm of this late afternoon among the ruins, the *sharp point* in the engraver's hand *stabbing* the image's vulva, the model's long-drawn-out piercing cry as she moves her right hand quickly to the center of her *fleece*, abandoning her pose in the process, the guided tour with the little group stopping under the window and looking up, wide-eyed, the young woman lying on the operating table, freed, her body relaxing amid the circle of female spectators. (*TCF*, p. 37)

Category H, *Flowing*, is both substance and movement. Section Three of Space One of *Topologie*, entitled "Caillou et Stylet" (Stone and Stylet), mentions the fact that the narrator cannot see the red puddle (*TCF*, p. 36) on the floor flowing toward the round white pebble. Category J, *Viscous Stain*, associated with flowing, has a direct link, says Robbe-Grillet, with the object *door* ("Piège," p. 4). Thus door, opening, penetration, fleece, and so on—all nine generative signs (Robbe-Grillet calls them "themes") have an erotic function. "The series as a whole . . . may . . . be considered as a metaphor for sexual aggression ending in a deflowering" ("Piège," p. 5). The three themes of the phantom city (outside)—imagination, language, myth—mesh with the text (inside) in order to engender three corresponding textual myths. The nine signs of the author's imagination structure an arbitrary serial imagery generating the text's ongoing and repetitive metonymy. The author's *parole* proceeds to excavate the *langue* that is in ruins. The author's text, the raped virgin, demythifies Jupiter's rape of Danaë and focuses the reader's attention on the body of the text and the nude bodies within the text on which Robbe-Grillet performs his serial experiments.

In similar fashion, the generative pattern of *Souvenirs du triangle d'or* is the code that the reader must decrypt in order to open the black door and penetrate the body of the text. Doctor Morgan, Robbe-Grillet's persona, plays with girls' bodies, experimenting, burning, killing, canning, and injecting them with the author's *parole* (hence the strange, whimsical movements of the "globe" and of the narrative) in order to deform the *langue* of *Le Globe*, the establishment newspaper. Christine is crucified, burned, and resurrected as a phoenix. Her torture, death, and metamorphosis, which challenge the sanctity of the Crucifixion, assert the author's freedom to violate all conventions, even Christianity, the most sacred convention in the Western world. But Robbe-Grillet's imagery, which ravishes the Christian sacraments, signifies nothing more than the author playing with the body of language, forcing it to give up its secrets. Writing, once again, is a sexual act, playing with language is orgasmic, and remembrance of the golden triangle is an experience of fire. "Je brûle" (I'm on fire), says Christine, echoing the priestess's words in *Salammbô*.[13]

The eroticism of this "*fiction flamboyante*" (flaming fiction), as Ricardou calls it, sets fire to the text which consumes itself in orgasmic bliss. In *Souvenirs*, Doctor Morgan violates Christine by forcing lit candles up her vagina. Finally, in a mock wake, "naked and adorned, Christine rests on a bed of roses, surrounded by twelve candles" (*STO*, p. 214). One of the candles falls over setting fire to the casket, the flowers, and Christine's pubic hair: "The flames spread quickly, from one spot to another, moving up the groove between the thighs, as far as the pubis which, in turn, catches fire" (*STO*, p. 215). The text is simultaneously Christine, Temple, and the "sanctuary" whose name is the "golden triangle" (shades of Faulkner). Their penetration is linked directly, in Barthian terms, to "the pleasure of the text," since in literature pleasure is also associated with insight and understanding. The Freudian key opens the door of the text, the secret door to the Golden Temple, and by playing with the generative themes contained within, allows the reader to re-create the author's narrative patterns.

The generative cell inside the text always communicates with the outside through doors, windows, keyholes, corridors, and passageways, thus establishing a necessary reversibility between the two. This reversibility and ambiguity of the *inner* and the *outer* contributes to the decomposition of our "idées reçues" which cry out in pain with each new violation. If the raped virgin is the central theme of *Topologie* and also a cultural archetype relating to the fantasy world of the male, then Robbe-Grillet's private imagery duplicates (as the mirrors and the photos of the novel seem to imply) the public mythology and its stereotypes: prison cells, naked women, rape, murder—the imagery of the *inside* and of the *outside*.

Encratic language, the language of the *outside* which becomes the language of the *inside* (because all language and the ideology for which it stands precedes each man's birth), is produced and spread under the protection of the establishment. It is statutorily a language of cliché and perpetrated by repetition by its official institutions: the schools, sports, advertising, television, popular songs. These institutions all say essentially the same thing, often using the same words. Such stereotype, says Barthes, "is a political fact, the major figure of ideology" (*PT*, pp. 40–41). Hence "the cry" within a literature dedicated to a *parole* whose wish and purpose, while speaking of finitude, is to challenge encratic language, its banalization of feeling, and its codification of the "natural."

What emerges from this challenge, says Foucault, is that man, by reaching the summit of all possible speech, arrives at the brink of that which limits him, "where death prowls, where thought is extinguished, where the promise of the origin interminably recedes, (*SMLS*, p. 281). It was perhaps inevitable that this new ontology in literature should have been revealed in the works of Artaud, Roussel, and the New (New) Novelists. In Artaud's work, language having been rejected as discourse and reapprehended in the plastic violence of "cruelty," is referred back to the *cry*, to the *tortured body*, to the flesh of the text, the materiality of thought. In Roussel's work, language having been pulverized by a systematically fabricated chance, speaks endlessly of death and "the enigma of divided origins" (*SFML*, p. 281).

The cry emanates from a consciousness of the self split by its allegiance and affinity to nature on the one hand, and on the other, at having created the unnatural. Language reflects this duality, first in the artificiality of its discourse, which does violence to nature whenever it transmits information or knowledge from one person to another for intentional reasons; and second, when poetics rejects discourse in order to apprehend sensation as "cruelty." Nevertheless, whether used for discourse or poetry, language retains its artificial quality. As Merleau-Ponty points out, the arbitrary sign is never reducible to the natural one because all signs are man-made. Hence Artaud's rejection of Cartesian discourse in favor of the Balinese dance whose meaning is inseparable from it and whose *langue* is uncommunicative of anything other than itself. "We need . . . to seek the first attempts at language in the emotional gesticulation whereby man superimposes on the given world the world according to man" (*PP*, p. 188).

A particularly important principle with regard to literature is that language cannot be considered as a utilitarian or decorative instrument of thought. If evolution in man is the rise of consciousness, and if consciousness (at least for man) is inseparable from language, then language teaches the definition of man. "Man does not exist prior to language, whether as a species or as an individual,"[14] says Roland Barthes. Nor is there a state in which man is separated from language that he himself creates in order to "express" what is taking place within him. What distinguishes human beings from the lower animals is not their power to speak, but their ability to create signs. The doctrine of the arbitrariness of the sign should, once and for all, eliminate the myth of a natural language, whether it be the dance, music, gastronomy, or fashion. If it is now possible to anticipate the creation of a single unified science of culture as language, then literature as a product and discipline of that culture, as *S/Z* demonstrates, inevitably reflects the society from which it emanates. This is true not only for Balzac and his time but also for New (New) Novelists like Robbe-Grillet.

Nevertheless, perhaps because Barthes prefers to think of the "nouveau nouveau roman" as devoid of content, he views its trajectory as suicidal. He does not think it possible to be simultaneously attuned to one's era and ahead of it. Whereas Goldmann sees Robbe-Grillet's and Sarraute's works as examples of reification, the logical literary end products of capitalism going from the Middle Ages to the present, Leenhardt, who is in general agreement with Goldmann, also stresses the avant-garde nature of the "nouveau roman," its innovations, its openness to new forms, and its acceptance of the aleatory and the indeterminate. The "nouveau roman" is a doubleheaded Janus looking at the past that is ending and at a future which is just beginning. The "nouveau nouveau roman" is also at the crossroads, split between an ideology that it is destroying and an ideology which it would impose. Robbe-Grillet's essay "Nouveau roman, homme nouveau" implies a correlation between the new values from which the "nouveau roman" emerged and the new image of man that is slowly being formed in its wake with the aid of the "nouveau nouveau roman." This man is not known and cloned in advance; he does not exist prior to the writing of the novel. He is born instead from the creative act, from the process of creation.

More frequently now than in the past, art makes us conscious of a creative process dramatizing the man-made, the unnatural, and the arbitrary. In the next chapter we see how specular effects function both in art and in literature in order to devalue reality and realism, thereby stressing the internal autonomy of the text. We must bear in mind, however, that this self-reflexive quality—this "mise en abyme," intertextuality, doubling and tripling of characters, and so on—always exists alongside the text's "recuperative" possibilities.

4

Mirror, Mirror on the Wall . . .

> To reflect the self is to confront being and its function.
> —Paul Valéry

Today's reflexive literature emphasizes the consciousness of the creative act, the self-awareness of the artist, the need to understand the ideological codes which influence encratic language. Structuralism has stripped the veils from thought systems in order to expose man (once clothed by language and convention) in all his moribund nudity. The shock, coupled with recent thrusts toward "hominization," has subjected man to painful experiences of desacralization and doubt. He can no longer say "I think," let alone, "I am." Like Rimbaud, he might, were he capable of it, mouth a feeble "je est un autre" (I is another), since it is not I who think, but language that thinks me, or thinks through me.

To counter this determinism, art is, once again, asking difficult though necessary questions: how does man confront being and existence and what is the relationship between the self and the other—that outer world constructed by the inner self and the inevitable interpenetration of both? Even though painting allegedly "died" soon after the turn of the century, it is obvious that artists, who nevertheless continue to create, can no longer, with integrity, "paint" like the old masters whose world vision throughout the nineteenth century was so thoroughly Newtonian. Literature, whose more conventional language (words as opposed to color and paint) imposes a greater time lag, is now duplicating stages that cubism and abstract art have already experienced.

Art historians agree, generally, that the desacralization of art, comparable to the current demythification of literature, began with Manet's *Olympia* and *Le Déjeuner sur l'herbe*. Until Manet, the evocative power of painting infused gods and dreams with life, resurrecting divinities like the *Urbino Venus* or the Virgin, whose motherhood and blue veil were painted by so many with such sacred fervor. The turning point is not the fact that Manet eliminated Venus's divinity or that he created a woman called Olympia. He achieved all this, to be sure, but he did so in order to make a picture. In *Olympia*, painting had at last discovered a purely pictorial domain, itself. And, in speaking of itself, rather than of the mystery of life or of the gods, painting became profane. At the time, the public outcry of incomprehension and condemnation was not unlike recent censure and disapprobation of the "nouveau roman."

The New Novelists' devaluation of plot and characters, in favor of the autonomy of language, like "foregrounding," is reminiscent of Maurice Denis's statement to the *Nabis* saying that "a picture before being a battle horse, a nude woman, or some anecdote, is essentially a plane surface covered with paint in a certain arrangement." In time, as with the paintings of Kandinsky, Mondrian, and Pollock, the battle horse, the nude woman, and the anecdote were eliminated. Certain novels, such as Philippe Sollers's *Nombres*, having suppressed characters and plot, are composed exclusively of white surfaces covered with words in a certain arrangement. But even before abstract art drew the spectator's attention to paintings that spoke only of themselves by means of line and color, Cézanne, Van Gogh, and Picasso were rejecting the world of appearances and substituting for it the world of creation. "What is a painting?" says Picasso, "or a sculpture? Are they . . . objects? No. What then? Let's say: thingamajigs. Yes, that will do. They are thingamajigs in which objects must encounter their own destruction. The painter takes things and he destroys them. At the same time he gives them another life."[1] This new life is the autonomy of the painted work stemming from the freedom of the artist who can no longer imitate nature. "Nature has to exist in order to be violated," says Picasso. "Yes. And painting also" (*TO*, p. 56). Cézanne, Van Gogh, and Picasso, respectively, in copying *Christ in Limbo*, *The Pietà*, and *Algerian Women* were not trying to paint better than their predecessors, Sebastiano and Delacroix, but otherwise. If they copy art rather than nature, it is in order to emphasize the painterly nature of art, since art, as a mirror of reality, had become suspect (*TO*, pp. 56–57). Cézanne had sensed this fact long before Nathalie Sarraute wrote *The Age of Suspicion* (an attack on the old conventions) in order to assert the primacy of new literary sensibilities.

With regard to representational art, Plato's passage in the *Republic*, comparing a painting with a mirror image, has influenced the

philosophy of art from his day to the present. The Greek
philosopher contrasted a painter with a carpenter. The carpenter
who makes a couch translates his idea of it into an object. The
painter who represents the carpenter's couch in one of his pictures
does not create a couch, he only copies its appearance. Thus, argued Plato, the painter is twice "removed" from the idea. With
mimetic art one can speak of "removal," but such "removal" ceases
to be a meaningful term the moment a painting is desacralized and
becomes an object in its own right. When that happens, as it does
with *Olympia*, or *Algerian Women*, or abstract art, the difference
between a painting as a made object, and a couch as a made object
(except for the specific function of each) is abolished.

Plato was no doubt right to compare representational art with a
mirror image, since both were intended to reflect nature. Stendhal
said that art was a mirror which a novelist paraded along the road of
life. However, the moment we introduce another mirror into a
painting that is already a "mirror," the signifier-signified relationship is undermined, doubt insinuates itself, and we begin to question the authority of art's referential function. When this happens,
art's mimetic role is reversed. It designates itself as the object and
slips into autorepresentation.

Today, art no longer strives to recapture the "sacred" or to paint
"beauty" or to commune with the "divine" or to mirror the "idea."
Its task, as Robbe-Grillet puts it, is much more modest, or ambi-
tious.[2] It strives to express itself. A modern painting wants first and
foremost to be a picture, to be man-made, to assert its value as art
(*TO*, p. 190). Modern art, by rejecting the past, exhibits its desacralization of gods, nature, ritual, and mystery. Modern art, like the
"nouveau roman," doubts absolutisms, even itself. A lady visiting
Matisse's studio once said: "But surely, the arm of this woman is
much too long." The artist replied: "Madame, you are mistaken.
This is not a woman, this is a picture."[3] Magritte's painting of a
pipe, entitled *Ceci n'est pas une pipe* (This Is Not a Pipe), emphasizes
the sign linking the signifier and the signified. Neither the word *pipe*
nor its picture is a pipe.

Long before the exaggerations and dislocations of color, line, and
perspective of the fauves, the cubists, or Escher, Hogarth's *False
Perspective* (1754) was a painting of an "impossible" world: the laws
of gravity do not apply, trees grow to unusual heights, and people's
arms grow to any length (*AI*, p. 244). Nevertheless, before 1900,
such violations of the laws of nature are relatively rare. It was not
until the end of the nineteenth century that painters stopped copy-

ing nature and not until the early twentieth century before they deformed it or rejected it. Cubism, beginning with Picasso's *Les Demoiselles d'Avignon*, as E. H. Gombrich observes, is a radical attempt to enforce the reading of a picture as a man-made construction (*AI*, pp. 281–83). Realism in art depends on an absence of contradiction, an interaction of clues that work together to form a consistent and coherent whole. Cubism fights such conventional illusions of reality because it introduces contrary clues that subvert its consistency. Our attempts to see a guitar or a jug or a person as a three-dimensional representation are undermined by contradictions. The figure in cubism, as R. Rosenblum points out, is assembled with fragments derived from multiple and discontinuous viewpoints. This, in turn, produces an ambiguity in time that destroys duration and instantaneity, eliciting instead "a composite time of fragmentary moments without permanence or sequential continuity."[4] The "nouveau roman" in general, and Robbe-Grillet's work in particular, especially after *La Maison de rendez-vous*, parades the discontinuity, fragmentation, and multiple points of view that cubism had explored half a century earlier.

Cubism's multifaceted reality is like a play of mirrors, each reflecting surface situated at an angle that will capture only a part of the whole—a whole which no one viewer, at any specific place, would normally be able to see. An object such as a pitcher may be constructed out of front, rear, side, top, bottom, close-up, or distant views in combination with other fragmented objects. Cubism's originality was in combining simultaneous possibilities into one seemingly incoherent yet actually cohesive vision enabling the spectator to understand the relativity of every point of view within a whole that is multiple. In keeping with the lessons of quantum physics, it annihilated conventional views of reality, teaching us that there is always distortion in perception, either because (for the sake of observation) the object has been arrested, hence denatured, or because it is in motion and therefore elusive. Yet, paradoxically, out of apparent chaos and disorder, a new order emerges that restructures perception along holistic lines.

Inevitably, such a metaphoric play of mirrors places enormous burdens on a viewer whose knowledge and conditioning may not have prepared him to understand this new language *(parole)*. Although cubism, like the "nouveau roman," desacralizes nature, art, and reality, it also emphasizes the creative act. Whenever art reflects upon itself, it raises interesting questions not only about the nature of its *langue* and *parole* but also about human freedom. In painting it is easier to break away from convention than it is in literature, because the artist has to cope mainly with the painterly tradition, whereas the writer has to fight the vicelike grip of language as well as the literary tradition with all its conventions. The degree to which he challenges both, while incorporating them into his personal style, is the mark of his creative genius and his vision.

Robbe-Grillet's specular structures, in addition to their analogies with cubism, undermine mimesis. Lucien Dällenbach, in *Le Récit spéculaire*, defines "mise en abyme" as follows: "any internal mirror reflecting the narrative whole by simple, repeated, or specious reduplication."[5] In literature, Bruce Morrissette is perhaps the first to signal Gide's influence on the "mise en abyme" cult that has developed around the works of the "nouveau roman."[6] The obvious example is *Les Faux-monnayeurs* in which Edouard is writing a novel entitled *Les Faux-monnayeurs*. Gide also published a separate work entitled *Le Journal des faux-monnayeurs*, whose title, though not the contents, reflects the other two in what Dällenbach calls a "réduplication à l'infini" (infinite reduplication; *RS*, p. 51). For Gide, the specular narrative structures a novel within a novel, or a novel about a novel, or the overlapping between fiction, his *Journal*, and his life, and, at the very least, a few reflexive sentences within a work of fiction or a play or a poem that, like a mirror in miniature, make the reader aware of the narrator's or the author's creative consciousness. *Le Traité du Narcisse* is the mythic paradigm for every work of art. Narcissus falling in love with his own reflexion is a metaphor for the artist whose work is a mirror of himself, his signature, as Derrida would say. The first-person narrative of *La Tentative amoureuse* is no more than a faint disguise for the author's persona that slips into the third-person narrative of Luc, anticipating by almost eighty years the "je-il" metamorphoses of *La Maison de rendez-vous*. *L'Immoraliste* has a circular "mise en abyme" aspect. It is a story within a story within a story in which Michel's friend tells the reader about Michel who, in turn, will tell his story. (From the beginning, Claudel criticized Gide for loving mirrors and posturing in front of them.) In his *Journal* Gide says that the best works of fiction contain autoreferential levels. The passage most frequently referred to is from his 1893 *Journal:*

> I rather like it when, in a work of art, one finds thus transposed to the scale of characters, the subject matter of the work itself. Nothing illumines it better, nor establishes more surely all of the proportions of the whole. Thus, in certain paintings of Memling and Quentin

Metzys, a small, dark, convex mirror, in turn, reflects the interior of the room in which the painted scene acts itself out. Thus, also, in the painting of *Las Meniñas* by Velasquez (though somewhat differently). Finally, in literature, in *Hamlet*, the comedy scene; and elsewhere, in many other plays.[7]

The mirror to which Gide refers and which appears in other paintings such as Van Eyck's *Portrait of the Arnolfini*, functions in literature as a metaphor for various kinds of reflecting surfaces. Specular modes, says Gérard Durozoi, devalue "truth" by de-stabilizing all realistic points of reference: "in a series of reflections it is difficult to discern the original."[8] If one mirror introduces doubt and two, as in Velasquez's *Las Meniñas* (the mirror and the invisible painting), intensify it, then the innumerable reflecting surfaces of cubist paintings destroy mimesis completely. This new, nonreferential freedom gives the artist license to mix, fuse, and confuse organic objects and physical objects: distinctions disappear. In Picasso's *Still Life with Gourd* (1909), the lines and color of the fruit, as in Cézanne's paintings, have the contours and characteristics of inorganic objects. This tendency toward abstraction (culminating in cubism and nonobjective art) that began with Cézanne's painting of nature and houses as squares, cubes, and triangles—a tendency which in time eliminated perspective, representation, and anecdote—is analogous to the absence of chronology, devaluation of plot, and desacralization of character in the "nouveau roman."

A painting entitled *La Défaite de Reichenfels* is a "mise en abyme" of the novel *Dans le labyrinthe*. Typically, Robbe-Grillet animates the figures in the picture and sets them in motion. This deliberate blurring of the real and the unreal, of the living and the dead, is pushed further in *La Maison de rendez-vous*, *Projet pour une révolution à New York*, and *Glissements progressifs du plaisir*. In *La Maison* inanimate garden dioramas at the Blue Villa, featuring hunters, wild beasts, and girls, are infused with life. In *Projet* and *Glissements*, ritual violence—rape, murder, and dismemberment—is performed indiscriminately on women's bodies and on their mannikin look-alikes. In spite of the obvious artificiality of such scenes, mimetic habits of reading are hard to extinguish. Disoriented readers tend to "recuperate" the exaggerated images of eroticism or terror, either because they miss the implied irony or because they identify involuntarily with the "repressed" imagery of their own subconscious desire. The "shock of unrecognition" is still too great and only the "happy few" reap the fruits of "defamiliarization," as Shklovsky would say.

In literary inescutcheon, the purest and best-known example of a play within a play is *Hamlet*, although there are many other examples of such internal duplication in fiction as well as in the theater. "Specular reflection," says Jean Ricardou, "multiplies whatever it imitates, or, if you prefer, emphasizes it through repetition."[9] In *La Jalousie*, A . . . and Franck are talking about a novel they are reading, an African story that, in its condensed, summarized, and broad outlines, "duplicates" the novel of which it is a part. The description of the song of the native worker renders in compressed form the structural characteristics of the narrative. Such inner repetition is always brief, schematized, and simplified. It is, as Dällenbach correctly notes, an "enclave maintaining a relation of similitude with the work which contains it" (*RS*, p. 18). But it is difficult to know what Dällenbach means when he says that the cries of the wild animals and the flight of the insects disperse the "mise en abyme" throughout the text (*RS*, p. 170). Reflexive dispersal may occur, but it is, a function of textual polysemy, the repetitive use of a word, words, or syllables in polyvalent contexts that allow for semantic shifts in meaning:

> Sometimes, in those places, it crumbles. You've got to be careful where you put your feet.
> "Don't worry on that score: she's alive!"
> *Alive.* She was. *Alive. Living.* Burned *alive.*[10]

Broadening the use of specular structures to encompass the syntagmatic microelements of polysemy, in addition to the macroelements of larger reflective enclaves, like the Indian's song in *La Jalousie*, is to disagree with Genette and Morrissette who limit the mirroring effect to simple internal duplication. Dällenbach and Derrida, however, extend its range by allowing for vocalic and semic duplication.[11] It seems impossible to deny language the reflexive characteristics that one would accord to larger enclaves when the very fabric of "nouveau roman" fiction is woven, sentence by sentence, with the thread of the artist's *parole* constantly striving to mirror its own texture and internal structures.

In painting, the classical example of specular reflection is Velasquez's *Las Meniñas*, although Van Eyck's *Portrait of the Arnolfini*, like the works by Memling or Metzys to which Gide refers, also qualify, because of a small convex mirror that duplicates the painted scene in miniature. Unlike the Arnolfini who are "present," the "absent" royal couple of *Las Meniñas* is visible by reflection only in the mirror of the painting. The picture itself is a portrait of a painter painting a portrait. The king and queen of Spain are "present" in miniature in the mirror, yet "absent" from the picture. We assume they are present on the canvas that the artist is painting even though they are not visible. There is a painted artist in the picture who draws our attention to the "real" but invisible artist who was once outside of it. The painted artist is looking at the "absent" royal couple, yet it is we, the spectators, who usurp their place. These interrelated and implied presences provide the "infinite reflection" to which Dällenbach refers—a reflection that is always infinite whenever two or more mirrors face each other. Moreover, the eyes of consciousness that peer into and out of *Las Meniñas* generate reflections and speculations on being and nothingness that go beyond purely formal considerations. The consciousness of the spectator becomes a mirror that *plays* with the to-and-fro movement of the many surfaces. The void these encounters generate is in itself dizzying, since the presence of the royal couple, except by reflection, has been denied. We are asked to reproduce it, but our presence outside the picture protests the substitution. The contradictions are insurmountable, and the painting's mimetic role is destroyed. Picasso's version of *Las Meniñas* carries this desacralization one step further by stressing not the subject matter or the outside, "absent" couple, but the painting of the painting. The picture of the picture of "absent" royalty takes the spectator on a vertiginous ride through a bottomless abyss denying certitude.

All of the painting's inner lines, as Foucault points out, focus on the "absent" couple, and, by implication, on the viewer, the person who now occupies the empty royal seat. "It is the spectator whose sight transforms the picture into an object, the pure representation of a fundamental absence."[12] The painting and the small mirror reflect a void. There is no one out there beyond the fourth wall and the spectator is not reflected in the "mirror."

Mirrors are designed to reflect "reality." Specular duplication, however, which is a reflection of a reflection (cubism is reflection to the nth power) dissolves reality, substituting for it a man-made object that reflects not nature, but consciousness. Since *consciousness* is normally not visible, an art form that can materialize it is indeed magical. It re-creates, symbolically, the "primordial emergence of organized matter, whose flood carries the living mass ever onward toward consciousness."[13]

Perhaps the neatest homologous example to *Las Meniñas* is to be found in a train compartment in the film *Trans-Europ-Express*—a scene picturing Jean-Louis Trintignant, the false drug runner, dissimulating a copy of *Europe* (a girlie magazine) within a copy of *L'Express*. To the right of Trintignant, in a glass reflection, is the head of a man who is referred to in the film as the author's publisher. On the wall above Trintignant's head is a small mirror reflecting a frontal view of Robbe-Grillet's head and shoulders. Instead of the "absent" royal couple we have, reflected, an image of the film's director. The presence of the three men gives the viewer a simultaneous triple exposure of writer, publisher, and protagonist—people without whom a novel would not exist.

The face in the mirror invites spectators, as it did in *Las Meniñas*, to substitute themselves in the empty space in front. Such a substitution is in keeping with "nouveau roman" aesthetics, which asks readers and spectators to participate in the re-creation of a novel or a film. (See Umberto Eco for a discussion of the philosophical implications of "open" works.) Suffice it here to point out that reflexive works inevitably become "open" works, i.e., works whose meaning is never absolute—works that invite *conscious* solutions provided by the reader or the spectator. The multiple reflecting surfaces of the shot from *Trans-Europ-Express*, which are not without humor, generate speculations about reality/unreality that are similar to the ones elicited by Velasquez's painting.

The mirror motif appears throughout the film in ways that reinforce the main theme. Like Manet's *Olympia*, which devalued traditional painting, *Trans-Europ-Express* devalues realistic films in general and whodunits in particular. The "mise en abyme" is omnipresent. Trintignant stays at the Hotel Miro; he walks across a street, but the scene is shot in a mirror; the mirrors in the train's washroom, as with cubism, provide three different views of the same person—a triple distancing effect. The sabotaging of reality, like the bomb that explodes at the beginning of the film, is undertaken on all levels. We have a farce within a film (more internal reflection). The drug runner on a dry run is only an actor. The prostitute who is "raped" and killed is also an actress who simulates rape and who does not die. Sugar is substituted for heroin. Blind beggars are paid informers who can see. Police agents turn out to be crooks. The author (Robbe-Grillet) riding in the train compartment is using a tape recorder for his fiction, which is not the same as the one being filmed. The film is, among other things, a pictorial exercise in sadoerotic clichés. "Empty enigmas [says Robbe-Grillet, referring to art's reflexive characteristics], arrested time, signs which refuse to signify, a giant enlargement of a minute detail, narratives which close in on themselves; we are in a *flat, discontinuous* universe in which each thing refers only to itself" (*PNR*, p. 76).

Jean Rousset believes that Robbe-Grillet's works are the beginning of a new, though different, era in the long history of mirrors, shimmering reflections, and baroque effects. "Reflection no longer reveals, as it did for the symbolists and their successors, the invisible, or a transcendence. Enigma has replaced mystery."[14] More so even than enigma, consciousness—an absolute and imperious desire to see and know—has replaced mystery. Robbe-Grillet's work, as Rousset and Christine Brooke-Rose have pointed out, is nonetheless comparable to baroque art.[15] As in baroque art, the play of mirrors and their destabilizing effects are dynamic. A constant movement in and out, the flow of arabesques, of light and shadow, discontinuity, uncertainty, metamorphoses, artistic conventions, and expectations turned upside down, are all formal aspects of a baroque aesthetic whose freedom strives to break the rules and limitations of classical art. Such art, in its pursuit of the new, devours itself voraciously. It is perpetually transforming itself and the world with it, including the reader/spectator.

Mirrors open invisible passageways from the inside out and vice versa. They communicate, allowing consciousness to exteriorize being and perceive itself as object. Reflecting surfaces unite the objective and the subjective. They, as Cocteau's mirrors demonstrate, are a point of transition. What is it that Narcissus sees mirrored on the liquid surface? Is it himself or another? What is self-love if not the inner thought rendered visible—consciousness exteriorized? Since all art speaks of the self and its reflections, specular structures are a hyperbolic form of this artistic consciousness. By *drawing* the reader/spectator into the *picture* they involve him or her more actively. The double meaning of the words *drawing* and *picture*, happily and fortuitously emphasize the flow, the in-and-out movement of the self.

Robbe-Grillet's earliest and most emphatic use of the specular mode appears in the short story collection entitled *Instantanés*. The title, meaning *snapshots*, emphasizes each story's photographic immobility whose reality runs counter to conventional expectations concerning literary realism. Each story—devoid of plot, characters, and time—is more like a picture than a short story. The first one, entitled "Trois visions réfléchies," is composed of three short narratives: "Le Mannequin," "Le Remplaçant," and "La Mauvaise Direction." The first of these is a description of a room reflected in a mirror; the second is a classroom in which the teacher and the students are absorbed by what they see on the other side of the window; the third is a landscape reflected in a pond. In the fifth "story," "Dans les couloirs du métropolitain," identical publicity posters, set at regular intervals on the platform on both sides of the subway tracks, provide a classic example of "infinite reflection."

Whereas mirrors, windows, and water are reflecting surfaces with the most privilege and status, the objective realism of Robbe-Grillet's *écriture* can and does endow the most mundane objects with powers of reflection. In *Le Voyeur* a blue cigarette wrapper floating on the waves, a piece of string rolled into a figure eight, a movie poster, a bicycle, and the like reflect a composite image, a *gestalt* of Mathias's inner desire and impending violence.[16] In *La Jalousie* the stain of a centipede, a piece of blue writing paper, and a comb passing through a woman's black hair reflect the husband's feelings. In the husband's eyes, though perhaps unconsciously, these objects signify. Like Narcissus's exteriorized and visible reflection of his self-love, the husband's innermost fears assume tangible, objective form. These objects are his jealousy. There is no enigma; the mirror image, except for one distorting imperfection in a window-pane, is in focus, perfectly.

Glass is one of the favored materials of the "nouveau roman" because mirrors, windows, and the glasslike surface of water reflect mobility and flux. Novels of objective subjectivity eschew stability and fixedness in favor of metamorphosis, contradiction, and instability. Compared to the glass marble of *Dans le labyrinthe*, the displacements of the crystal ball in *Souvenirs du triangle d'or* are, if anything, startling. Nevertheless, the marble as an intertextual prototype is a typical "mise en abyme": "in addition, the marble's surface reflects the pale, deformed, considerably reduced décor of the café."[17]

Michel Butor, before his ideological rift with the "nouveaux romanciers," refers to the special virtues of a glass window:

> The window is . . . an image dear to me. It may or may not be transparent; it may or may not allow me to see beyond it. Window or mirror . . . has its own hardness and in plunging through it I discover something else. In disclosing that something else, it reflects my image and I discover myself.[18]

The creative act, as all artists know, and as Gide has pointed out, is a process of self-discovery. Whereas the "nouveau roman" may mirror the intentions of the author, it also mirrors itself and it is the meaning of such reflexiveness that engages us in this chapter.

Mirrors, glass, paintings, posters, and mannikins, as "mise en abyme" agents are all homologous. Whereas mirrors and windows are automatic reflectors, Robbe-Grillet animates pictures, posters, and mannikins in order to give them the movement that glass surfaces normally communicate and which ordinary paintings and posters do not. In the film *L'Eden et après*, the small blue-and-white painting of a town in Djerba announces "living" romantic fantasies on this island paradise. Mannikins in *La Maison de rendez-vous* and *Projet pour une révolution à New York* assume lifelike qualities or are treated as though they had them. (Not all of Robbe-Grillet's works are equally rich in "mise en abyme" mutations.) The permutations are generally more plentiful in his later novels, particularly in *Maison* and *Topologie d'une cité fantôme*, whose "Fourth Space" is entitled: "Rêveries des mineures séquestrées entre fenêtre et miroir." Mirrors, windows, and cameras reflect, capture, and reveal David Hamilton's nymphets in varying stages of deshabille and arrested motion. Not unexpectedly there is a description of a nude, long-haired girl painting a picture. But the usual contradictions cast doubt on the narrative realism as the oil painting becomes a plaque of burnished copper and the paintbrush metamorphoses into a stylet with which to engrave a temple to the goddess Vanadé.[19]

La Maison de rendez-vous takes pleasure in multiplying the reflecting surfaces: The cover of an illustrated magazine reproduces the intrusion of the police into Lady Ava's salon. Monneret's "murder" is reenacted several times at the Blue Villa in a play entitled *L'Assassinat d'Edouard Monneret*. Other events that evening duplicate erotic scenes to be found in the gardens of the Villa or of the Tiger Balm in Hong Kong. One scene also appears in miniature form on a ring. Thus, the Blue Villa is like a prism through which things and events are refracted, animated, and accumulated.

In *L'Homme qui ment* the usual mirrors, photos, paintings, frames, and windows become reflecting spaces that "lie." They emphasize the film's title and the role of an actor who plays, i.e., acts out the ontological consequences of desacralization. Trintignant (once again) is pursued through the woods by "German" soldiers. He is shot and "killed" several times, but he does not die. He makes his way to a village claiming that he is Boris Varissa, but Varissa is dead. He says he has a message from Jean Robin, his friend in the Resistance who was "killed" by the enemy, but we see Jean Robin shoot the impostor—a Don Juan figure who has been trying to seduce three women living in a big house. The liar nar-

rates, imagines, and dreams Resistance episodes, each more implausible than the other. The narrative thickens, undermines reality, and bifurcates. Lies, doubt, and uncertainty are corollaries of
specular devices, which, by drawing attention to a picture as picture, or to a film as film, or to language as language, begin the
devaluation of reality. *L'Homme qui ment* literally tolls the news
from the church belfry that "man is dead." Fear and anxiety pursue
Trintignant, who runs stumbling through the woods, inventing
stories to protect himself from the "truth," but in the end is "shot"
(once more) in the library by his "friend" and "double," Jean
Robin. Each scene gives the spectator a semblance of truth that is
subsequently denied. "The reader or the reading is always disappointed (deceived) in his search for meaning, since the meaning
proliferates, the meaning is mirrored into a thousand reflecting
surfaces."[20]

It is perhaps not surprising that the "doubling" effect of the
mirrors should also affect the characters themselves. In his very
first novel, *Un Régicide*, Robbe-Grillet structures a "je-il" relationship that is a form of doubling. *Les Gommes* has two Duponts who
are both "murder victims." There is some confusion between the
identities of a M. Wallas and a certain V. S. In *Le Voyeur*, Robin,
the proprietor of a café, thinks he sees in Mathias a certain Mat he
might once have known. Mathias, wishing to convince Robin that
he is familiar with the region, invents an imaginary friend, Jean
Robin. The café proprietor acknowledges that there was once a
Jean Robin in the family who is now dead. In a second café Mathias
meets a sailor who may be Jean Robin, since the name appears on
the man's door, but the man is probably Pierre. In *Dans le labyrinthe*, the painting of the boy and the soldier doubles the two main
characters. At one point the soldier places his feet in each of the
boy's footprints, thinking that he too has passed that way before;
that he and the boy may be one and the same person. The author's
persona—the doctor-narrator—identifies with the lost soldier using
a "je-il" doubling similar to the one in *Un Régicide*. In *La Maison de
rendez-vous* twin sisters are both named Kim, whereas other characters are tripled: Lauren, Loraine, Laureen; Johnson, Jonstone,
Jonestone; Marchat, Marchant, Marchand.

Is such proliferation a case of one person impersonating three
others or is it three people whose names and faces resemble each
other? The answer is no doubt irrelevant since the only certain role
is the narrator's "je," which acts out all the parts. Sir Ralph is also
called Johnson, the American, even though he may be English or

even Portuguese. He says he is an agronomist, though we suspect he is a drug runner who may also be a Communist agent. Edouard Monneret, known as "le Vieux," is the presumed father of the twin Kims. His occupations range from writer, painter, and doctor, to chemist, fetishist, and political agitator. Lady Ava or Eva or Eve (perhaps also Lady Bergman and Jacqueline) is a former actress, the madam of a high-class Hong Kong brothel, president of a philanthropic organization, Communist agent, drug runner, and the like, or none of these.

The narrative destroys itself by contradiction and proliferation, as though all possible combinations needed to be tried or imagined before being discarded. Says Robbe-Grillet:

> the lines of the drawing accumulate, grow heavy, cancel one another out, shift, so that the image is jeopardized even as it is created. A few paragraphs later, when the description comes to an end, we realize that it has left nothing behind it: it has instituted a double movement of creation and effacement which, moreover, we also find in the book on all levels and in particular in its total structure—whence the *disappointment* inherent in many works of today. (*PNR*, p. 127)

It is impossible to follow or maintain a consistent or plausible idea of character because each name, each situation, and each occupation, soon after its apparition, metamorphoses into something new and different. The Protean narrator invents arbitrary combinations, plays with them, and rearranges them to suit his fancy or his sense of humor. From time to time the narrator intrudes to tell us that "this scene now no longer makes sense," or "this episode, having already taken place, no longer fits here." The author deliberately draws the reader's attention to the structures of the text, undermines the illusion of truth, casts doubt on the reality of his characters, stresses the text's imaginary dimension, and makes us aware of the work's reflexive presence. As the characters and the story self-destruct, we realize that the interest is not in *what* is being said, but in the *how*. "This applies to a symphony, a painting, or a novel: it is in their form that reality resides" (*PNR*, p. 41).

If the text can manifest a formal "consciousness," then the reader is free also to emulate its unorthodox lead in order to break away from stereotype, cliché, and convention. The examples of freedom and spontaneity that such texts provide, in addition to the pleasure itself, have no other purpose. It is impossible to build a traditional order out of the new controlled disorder. The idea of an a priori essence gives way to an essence that is in the process of creation:

this essence belongs to none other than the reader who, like the text, is free to invent himself. This subjective lesson that existentialism has so often stressed is the sine qua non of a reflexive work.

Although Proust, Joyce, Faulkner, and Beckett are not indifferent to the effects of "twin characters," when it comes to "doubling" and the resultant confusion that stems from this ambiguity, Roussel is one of the great precursors. His characters, more than any others before the "nouveau roman," lose the reader in a labyrinth of double identities. Roussel often presents twin boys or twin sisters who are in search of their identities. According to Elly Jaffé-Freem, they form "reverse images of life," since, from birth on we have a constituted couple rather than one individual (*RGPC*, pp. 125–26). Roussel also uses secondary characters who are "doubles" of the main character: a buffoon and a buffoon's doll imitate the king. When a character disappears or dies he is replaced by another person, a statue, or some device that mimes him to perfection. Thus, double identities, as specular variants, contribute to the reflexive characteristics of fiction. Roussel's language, says Foucault, "is a brilliance that cuts, unglues the cardboard surface, and announces that what it says is this double, this pure and simple double."[21]

In *Topologie d'une cité fantôme*, Robbe-Grillet, like Roussel, presents ready-made couples: twins such as David and Vanadé or Déana and David. Violette's sosie in *L'Eden et après*, although she is not identical, wears the same clothes and hairdo, performs the same gestures, and moves as though she were a mirror image. Is "the man who lies" Varissa, Robin, or someone else—someone desperately in search of a self?

Intertextuality, like twins, double names, and dual identities, extends reflection from one book or film to another.[22] A brief allusion (outside the work in which it first appears) to the voyeur's bicycle, the white Buick, doors, metal beds, prison cells, string, dismembered dolls, and the like become a "mise en abyme" for *Les Gommes, Le Voyeur, L'Immortelle, Projet pour une révolution à New York, Glissements progressifs du plaisir, Topologie d'une cité fantôme*, and others. Familiar names such as Boris, Franck, Franz, Marchat, Laura, and Jacqueline recur with the frequency of mirrors, windows, pictures, stones, and arabesques. Situations depicting or describing rape, blood, fire and aggression, like miniature mirrors in the paintings of Van Eyck, Memling, and Metzys, reflect one work into another, creating a network of interrelated images linking the different parts with the body fiction.

Specular modes, as Robbe-Grillet uses them, structure a topological dialectic between the subjective vision of the artist and the objective world in which he or she moves. "Waters and mirrors," says Jean Rousset, "dig a 'deep hole' in the ground or through the wall, thus escaping for one moment from the laws and the pull of the objective world" (*IE*, p. 197). Although Robbe-Grillet would not agree with the "myth of depth" that Rousset finds on the other side of the mirror, he does use reflection (and all its variants) to facilitate communication between the phenomenological self (inside) and the structuralist prison (outside). The "cellule génératrice" (generative cell) is therefore a double metaphor: it is both *langue* and *parole* simultaneously. It is Robbe-Grillet's point of departure for a dialogue that will, as in *Topologie d'une cité fantôme*, metamorphose into a dialectic in time and space. Time belongs to the inner, subjective dimension of perception and is hence achronological, whereas space belongs to the outer, objective dimension of the thing perceived. Since neither is possible without the other, *Topologie* becomes a synthesis of both. In keeping with this formula, the novel has five spaces which correspond to the five bars on the prison window, that correspond to the five fingers of the artist's hand (his writing tool and his signature). Part one of the "Premier espace," before moving "dehors" into part two, begins inside, "Dans la cellule génératrice." Time, as Proust's *A la recherche du temps perdu* has demonstrated, necessarily evolves in space, and Robbe-Grillet's art, like all art, works toward the reconciliation in time and space of the inside and the outside, of the self and the other, of the id and the superego. There is perhaps a level, says Mikel Dufrenne, on which dissociation between the subject and the object is no longer possible:

> a level where phenomenological reflection opens onto Hegel's absolute reflection; where one thinks of the identity of consciousness and its object—consciousness and object being two moments in the dialectic of being—as inseparable and finally identical.[23]

This artistic reconciliation of the inside and the outside, of the self and the other, manifests itself as a dialectical topology within which the properties of space and perception establish curious and reversible relationships. Doors, keyholes, windows, curtains, photographs, and paintings are frequently endowed with the gravitational pull of black holes that suck in the text and the reader transmuting them from one time-space dimension into another. In the next chapter we investigate the contradictions and reconciliations of such fictional explorations.

5
A Dialectical Topology

> We have to unite or reconcile the two presentations *(Darstel-lung)* of the inside and the outside.
> —Derrida, *Glas*

Topology is a branch of geometry that studies the qualitative rather than the quantitative properties of space. Topology investigates the kind of spatial continuity and reversibility that we find in a Möbius strip or a Klein bottle, recording the interchangeability of one surface with another. Bruce Morrissette, in applying topology to Robbe-Grillet's works, defines it as one of the "primary intellectual operations capable of revealing the modalities of surfaces, volumes, boundaries, contiguities, holes, and above all of the notions of *inside* and *outside*."[1] Vicki Mistacco gives topology an additional metaphorical dimension in which the "production" of contemporary texts depends on the continuity and contiguity of both reader and writer.[2] Topology, therefore, may refer to the spaces within a text as well as to the implied spatial relationship between the intrinsic text and the extrinsic reader—relationships that have ontological and perceptual implications.

Within the text, topology can signify the topography of a room, a house, a city, or a place. It elucidates structural relationships and configurations that may be stretched, twisted, and distorted.

> In topology [says Robbe-Grillet] there are volumes whose inside is outside. There are surfaces where one side is on the other . . . in *Projet pour une révolution* . . . the house, the street, and the keyhole . . . function as topological spaces. At times one has the impression that the whole house empties itself and that it passes entirely through the keyhole, that the whole inside of the house becomes the outside.[3]

Topology is therefore more than a branch of geometry, or geography, or medicine. It deals with art, language, and perception. It

102

is a dialectical space in which ontology and topography meet. *Dans le labyrinthe, La Jalousie, L'Immortelle, Projet pour une révolution à New York,* and *Topologie d'une cité fantôme,* following Derrida's dictum, synthesize the inside and the outside. These works, and others like them, structure a reversible and interchangeable continuity between the inside and the outside, i.e., between the subjective and the objective, the reader and the text.

While soliciting our collaboration, Robbe-Grillet's works draw our attention to those "openings" within the text that emphasize the work's reflexive characteristics. Robbe-Grillet's novels and films, while seemingly closed, labyrinthine structures, are, in fact, also "open" works that invite the reader/audience to play an active role. Within this dialectical context Lucien Dällenbach speaks of *Les Faux-monnayeurs* as one of the early examples of reflexive interplay generating meaning:

> in this case the role of the spying mirror consists less in integrating an "exterior" reality within the novel, as in abolishing the antithesis of the inside and the outside, or rather, in introducing an oscillation between the two. This is particularly evident whenever Gide's novel, by naming it, evokes Edouard's, an exercise in reversibility that sometimes takes advantage of the play of mirrors in order to obtain an even more effective short-circuit.[4]

Whether short-circuit or exchange, Robbe-Grillet's topological synthesis is an inherent dimension of his art. It is a dialectic of movement, a state of perpetual transcendence, the *Aufhebung* to which he, Hegel, and Derrida refer.[5]

On the narrative level, topological displacement may affect people, things, or places, so that characters, like rooms, experience a kind of "time warp." In *Les Gommes* there is a missing murder, in *Le Voyeur* a missing crime, and in *La Jalousie* a missing character. In *Le Voyeur,* at the end of Part I, Jacqueline disappears through the white hole of the blank page. In *Topologie d'une cité fantôme* characters fall into holes and come out on the other side completely transformed, having lost their original features and character. In *Souvenirs du triangle d'or* and *Djinn* there are narrative displacements that defy plausibility and verisimilitude. Although such shifts continue the "nouveau roman's" devaluation of conventional literature, they also emphasize the role of keyholes, windows, doors, tunnels, and the like as mediating agents between two or more spaces.

To analyze any one of Robbe-Grillet's texts is, immediately, to lay bare the structure of the topological dialogue. Morrissette and Rahv have done this nicely for *Dans le labyrinthe*, and Leenhardt, though not with topology in mind, has done it for *La Jalousie*.[6] Both novels conceal the "holes," i.e., the transition points through which the inner-outer dialectic manifests itself. Its rarefaction is an implicit if "hidden" aspect of Robbe-Grillet's early *oeuvre*.

In *Dans le labyrinthe* the narrator's imagination flows freely and effortlessly between the street outside and the room inside: "outside it is raining," . . . "outside the sun is shining," . . . "The sun does not get in here," are the second, third, and fourth sentences of the novel. At the end of the book, after the soldier's real or imaginary death, "dehors" and "ici," once more, as they did throughout the work from the very beginning, affirm the narrator's dialectic, as he, the doctor, imagines, dreams, and identifies with the soldier. The doctor's "outside" narrative moves "inside" where his consciousness merges with the soldier's quest, even as the author weaves his deceptive topological patterns in and out of rooms, streets, corridors, and stairways. The window opens on two simultaneous seasons (summer and winter), abolishing time and annihilating space. The incandescent light bulb filament inside the room "connects" with its counterpart on a lamp post in the street. The narrator's eye, with the help of the magnified shadow of a fly walking around the rim of the lampshade "hole," is projected onto the ceiling, moves across this surface, down the red curtains, and out the closed window. This description, as Morrissette has pointed out, bends consciousness around the gravitational field of a little black hole (the fly). The pattern on the ceiling traps the imagination, sucks it in, and expels it into another time-space zone. This is an example of the way Robbe-Grillet uses windows as lenses and passageways, not only to explore the self-conscious processes of writing but also to get at different levels of the phenomenological self. Glass, as Jean Rousset also points out, is "a closure and an opening, a hindrance and a freedom, a fence in the room as well as an expansion toward the outside, the unlimited within the circumscribed."[7]

As for the structure of *La Jalousie*, Leenhardt and Robbe-Grillet both stress the fact that it is based on a system of binary oppositions, using the house as a focal point for the *duel* (dual: "quelle différence?") that this novel is dramatizing.[8] The struggle for ascendancy between the antagonistic forces can be diagrammed as follows:

Binary Oppositions
Jealousy

inside . . . . *outside*
house . . . . nature
straight lines . . . . arabesques
reason . . . . instinct
order . . . . disorder
husband . . . . wife
colonial power . . . . native subservience

Other oppositions could be added, but these seven define this work's essential topology and structure. If the inside of the house is a bastion of order, reason, and colonial power (which the husband seems to wish it were), then the vegetation outside signifies not only the random disorder of natural phenomena but also the threatening potential of native anticolonial attitudes. However, this neat opposition between the straight line of male Cartesian dominance and the arabesques of female instinct and disobedience are undermined on all levels. The curved line of the centipede is inside the house, even as the geometrical banana groves order the landscape of the jungle.

It is the window blind that makes this exchange possible. The novel's title, *Jealousy*, "reconciles" the antitheses. *La Jalousie*, meaning both window blind and jealousy, is simultaneously objective and subjective. It is the point of contact for feeling and perception, for what is experienced and what is seen. The mind, inseparable from the emotions, is the house, the place, the battlefield for conflicting value systems represented by people, things, animals, colors, and actions. The husband's sense of order is in conflict with A . . . 's propensity toward disorder. Her actions (implied liaison with Franck, familiarity with the servants, nonjudgmental attitude concerning sex between blacks and whites) menace the husband's equilibrium as well as colonial stability. A dark, suspect, and, in fact, chaotic nature from outside the house has already invaded the rooms inside. The curved lines of the centipede are visible on walls, in the contours of native pottery, even in the sensuous flowing waves of A . . . 's black hair. A . . . is a source of disorder and is perhaps even in collusion with the enemy. The north side of the house, having been invaded by a profusion of arabesques, has already fallen. This is the drama with which the jealous husband is struggling—a drama fed by fear and desire: fear of losing A . . . , desire to retain a colonialist status quo.

The opposition between straight lines and arabesques signifies the ideological conflict between the characters and, by extension, between opposing value systems. The novel's images are thus its content, and its art is a synthesis by which ideas are objectified in formal ways. These characteristics give the work recuperative value, confirming, once again, the coexistence of reflexive and mimetic forms.

The white man's residence, situated in the middle of the banana plantation, is the focal point of the struggle for ascendance between the vying factions. This battle for dominion over the house has a special topography. Bachelard believes that a house used in a poetic context is a symbol of man's soul.[9] Houses, says Eliade, "are held to be at the Center of the World and, on the microcosmic scale, to reproduce the universe."[10] The house, says Bachelard, is an instrument with which to confront the cosmos. Accordingly, we sense an implied urgency in the jealous husband's gaze with which he tries to impose a linear geometry on a house that is slowly but surely giving way to the dark and untamed presence of the circle.[11] A threat to the house is a threat to the husband's colonial identity. Robbe-Grillet has thus painted the portrait of a doomed political enclave. His work is a brilliant psychological, aesthetic, and sociopolitical study of a disintegrating world. *Topoanalysis* (Bachelard's term) thus reveals the "soul" of the house. It is a *dual* image of fear and jealousy governed by the opening and closing of the venetian blind.

This house, signifying consciousness (a jealous consciousness full of "intentionality"), is the place where outside and inside meet, where feeling and perception, subjective and objective are one and the same. The centipede, signifying both the animal and the husband's emotion, represents the synthesis of two worlds that were once held in opposition, but which are now perceived as identical. Robbe-Grillet's novel demonstrates, aesthetically, the union of two opposites as the novel's dialectical topology weaves an intricate pattern exteriorizing the inside and interiorizing the outside. The husband spies on his wife (inside), imposes arithmetic patterns on the banana grove (outside), "sees" a clandestine encounter in town (outside) that is perhaps only imagined (inside his mind's eye), wanders through the empty house of his imagination as the dialectic pursues its inexorable synthesizing pattern. The centipede becomes the objective correlative, the symptom of repressed (hence unconscious) fear and desire.

The venetian blind of *La Jalousie* is used again in *L'Immortelle* to announce transitions between the inside of a room and the city outside. It also acts as an achronological time-space mediator. The blind appears in the opening scenes and reappears at appropriate intervals ordering the film's diegesis.

The dialectic is structured around Professor N., inside the room, and Leila, whose domain is the city of Istanbul, outside. The following sequence from the film's "prelude" establishes the significance of its topology. Opening scenes of Istanbul's ancient walls, shot from a moving car, are accompanied by the Oriental melody of a woman singing a Turkish song. We hear the sound of a car crash, and then see the face of Leila, the heroine (played by Françoise Brion), fill the screen. The female vocalist (not Leila) resumes her song that was interrupted by the crash. Next is a shot of a man standing in a corner of a room. The sound of a chugging engine is heard inside the room (the ferryboats plying up and down the Bosphorus will become an important motif in the film). This initial sound effect, through synecdoche, brings the city inside the room. Similar sound effects will reinforce the film's developing dialectic. In due course we learn that the man standing in the corner of the room is Professor N. (played by Jacques Doniol-Valcrose), on assignment in Istanbul. He falls in love with Leila, one of the city's beautiful prostitutes. The film establishes the fact that Leila is not free, that she is in bondage to her pimp, that she is afraid to be seen with N. in the daytime, that she is like a trained dog on a long leash who must obey her master's whistle. After meeting with N. several times Leila disappears and N., who, by now is hopelessly in love with her, spends his time (when he is not in his room) searching for her throughout the city.

This search for Leila determines the film's structure and meaning. Diegesis is achronological and reality is suspect. N. rides the ferryboats; wanders through a maze of narrow streets; knocks on doors; scrutinizes closed windows; questions mosque attendants, merchants, and the police; and stands pondering the tall cylindrical shapes of Moslem tombstones or the old city walls—the labyrinth in which he proceeds to lose himself. N. in search of Leila (who is the incarnate "body of the text"), when combined with the restoration of the walls of the labyrinth, provide an effective metaphor for the director (Robbe-Grillet) working on his film. But this fact, though in itself interesting, is not immediately relevant. What is relevant is the paradox of a real city, Istanbul, becoming a fantasy city in the mind of a love-smitten, jealous, and, in due course, fearful N. The film's diegesis evolves inside N.'s mind. The external labyrinth of Istanbul is interiorized, thus becoming an internal affective labyrinth. This interiorization explains the film's achronology that, in turn, corresponds to the protagonist's disorientation. N., in his attempt to find Leila and explain her disappearance, relives and imagines certain scenes over and over again in a vain and desperate attempt to locate the woman of his dreams. The outer reality of the city is objective, whereas the inner imaginative reality is subjective. The dialectical structure of the film moves alternately between these two poles synthesizing them along the way. Istanbul is a real city, but the events of the film are fictitious. Once again Robbe-Grillet blends mimesis and self-reflexiveness.

Insight into this process brings the topological dialectic into clear focus, explaining exaggeration, repetitions, distortions, a deliberate photographic "flatness," and clichéd sound effects. Inside N.'s memory and imagination, reality is altered and deformed by his emotions, thereby demonstrating the oneness of the object (the city) and the self (perception). The decor is not any arbitrary objective correlative, but corresponds exactly to N.'s feelings and "intentionality." He traps himself inside the room of his obsessions, and, like Leila, "dies" in a car accident outside the city walls. This is the crash we heard but did not see at the beginning of the film.

We are now ready to understand the seemingly disconnected shots with which the film opened: successive shots of Leila at the walls, on a ferryboat, in a cemetery, on a beach—serial shots that adumbrate the thematic content of the film and which are accompanied by the sound of a romantic violin—images and music together forming a clichéd picture of a tourist's dream of love in an exotic land. All this is followed by a full screen shot of Leila's face outside the venetian blind, as though she were looking in at the audience. We hear the sound of an engine, a ship's horn, and dogs barking. Where are the sounds coming from and are we, the audience, outside or inside? The ambiguity is deliberate—the dialectic is now in full swing. The venetian blind closes, followed by a shot of a man in a room who is looking out through the slats. We see a heavy-set Turk sitting on a chair on the jetty, followed by a close-up of the water and its movements. A boy from the outside looks up at the closed window. The man sitting on the jetty is also looking at the closed window. Another shot of Leila inside the room is followed by shots of the jetty, her pimp, the white Buick, the Bosphorus, trees, water, and traffic. The "prelude" is over and the narrative has begun. The conversation with Leila on the jetty carries over into the room inside. A romantic violin theme pursues N., who is once again in the corner of the room looking out through the blinds. Suddenly, he retreats from the window into the corner as though in fear, as though he does not want to be seen from the outside.

The remainder of the film elaborates the motifs of love and fear as the city labyrinth is interiorized progressively inside the room (signifying "mind") of the professor's alienation. At night, the headlights of passing cars project black shadows—the venetian blinds— on the white walls of the room—a room that has become the man's prison: "The events and oneiric landscapes are only a means with which to penetrate the opacity of more urgent phenomena pressing in on us from all sides—phenomena whose very urgency leads us astray."[12] Professor N., like the husband in *La Jalousie*, has become the prisoner of his affective labyrinth. In *La Jalousie*, the sun, shining through the blinds, casts similar shadows into the room whose alternating light and dark lines simulate the bars of a prison.

> The four walls, like those of the whole house, are covered with vertical laths two inches wide separated by a double groove. . . .
> This striped effect is reproduced on all four sides of the square bedroom. . . . The ceiling, moreover, is also covered by the same gray laths. As for the floor, it too is similarly constructed, as is evidenced by the clearly marked longitudinal interstices. . . . Thus the six interior surfaces of the cube are distinctly outlined by thin laths of constant dimensions, vertical on the four vertical surfaces, running east and west on the two horizontal surfaces.[13]

In *L'Immortelle*, the prison theme is reinforced with shots of closed and barred windows, Leila behind a metal enclosure, Leila chained to dungeon walls, Leila, like a trained animal, responding to the whistle of her master.

The venetian blind is a double metaphor. It signifies the subjective bias of perception that is conditioned by *langue*, experience, and desire, while also representing a topological cue which alerts the reader to the author's intentions. It is as though Robbe-Grillet were saying: beware the "trap of language" and desire (see, once again, "Piège à fourrure").[14] The film's grammar and syntax have a message, after all.

Within Robbe-Grillet's dialectical topology, signifiers such as the venetian blind form interesting intertextual and specular patterns. Doors, windows, mirrors, and corridors (not to mention the bicycle, the white Buick, the metal bed, proper names) bring one work into another. In *Projet pour une révolution à New York* the description of the heavy wooden door, with its curved metal design, conveys as much information to the "initiated" reader as Charles Bovary's hat. Besides alluding to and extending the linear-curvilinear dialectic of *La Jalousie* and *L'Immortelle*, it enables the reader to connect with other similar doors in *Les Gommes, Le Voyeur, Souvenirs du triangle d'or, L'Eden et après*, and others. Robbe-Grillet's doors have in fact become symbols for transitions of all kinds between reality and the imagination, between *langue* and *parole*, between social code and individual freedom, between convention and spontaneity, between a text's autonomy and its recuperative potential. One could, as with *La Jalousie*, compose a list of binary oppositions applicable to all his works. If the jealous husband and Professor N. succumb to curves and circles, the heroine of *L'Année dernière à Marienbad* loses herself in the linear Cartesian logic (inside the chateau and in the formal gardens outside, composed of straight lines and right angles) fabricated by the man who pursues her. The list of binary oppositions would consist of a geometry of law and order (the superego) whose role is to resist the continuous "subversion" and disorder of curves and circles (the id). If we think of consciousness (the ego) as a stage separating the superego from the id, then will power, imagination, and creativity (play) sometimes mediate between the two extremes. Only the intellect can reconcile the rigidity (straight lines) of the superego with the latent chaos (arabesques) of the id. Order and disorder are thus frequently contrasted on a purely formal level.

Projet pour une révolution à New York continues exploring the topological aesthetic along mythical, sociopolitical lines. The white establishment, which has law and order on its side, feels menaced by disorder, the blacks, and the Mafia. The wooden door with which the novel "opens," a door with metal arabesques, adumbrates the fears of the power elite. The novel cultivates disorder, magnifies it, and plays with it, in order to demonstrate once more that the author's *parole* can oppose the *langue* of the establishment. Doors, windows, fire escapes, and keyholes provide the necessary contact between the forbidden and the sanctioned, between the inside and the outside. They open into or lead to rooms where women's bodies *(langue)* are injected with strange fluids, where their pubic hair is set on fire, while black revolutionaries ritualize erotic plays *(parole)* on improvised platforms at strategic downtown intersections.

There is a gradual, though systematic, progression in Robbe-Grillet's works between a conservative, nonsexual imagery and an imagery that many readers and spectators now find shocking. Compare the incipient Oedipal theme in *Les Gommes* with the actual incest scenes at the opera in *Souvenirs du triangle d'or;* or the stiff, well-dressed, puppetlike actors in *L'Année dernière à Marienbad* with the women in *Le Jeu avec le feu* whose nude bodies grace a banquet table, an implied cross, or a coffin. Robbe-Grillet, like Sade, is aggressively parodying public mores, values, and religion.

Even though Robbe-Grillet insists that his art says nothing or that it has no content, the snippets of public myth with which he composes his narrative discourse do speak the ideology of the establishment. The exaggeration of this imagery, however, introduces a parodic quality that effectively undermines a clearly recognizable stereotype. Robbe-Grillet's *parole* may be formalist, but its content is revolutionary. Robbe-Grillet's works expose society's coded clichés, thereby challenging the repression of play, desire, spontaneity, and violence. His art devalues nature, convention, stasis, and the status quo. Like Gide, Robbe-Grillet is a creature of dialogue, an elusive Protean figure whose art is forever slipping from one extreme to the other. In one article or interview he will stress the purely formal interplay of language and imagery and in another he will emphasize the hopelessly old-fashioned ideology from whose fragments he derives his discourse.

The informed reader is therefore not far off the mark when he or she connects the spirals, curves, and arabesques in Robbe-Grillet's works with women, freedom, imagination, whereas straight lines, mathematical games, and rectilinear geometry tend to connote men, prison, and constraint. *L'Immortelle*, for example, contains a dramatic shot of Leila's face framed by the spiral configurations of a metal gate. There is a shot of Alice's face in *Glissements progressifs du plaisir* behind the iron spiral of a bed. In *L'Eden et après*, rectangular cages imprison naked women. There is also the celebrated sequence in *L'Eden* of a nude descending a spiral staircase. This picture appears again, with extraordinary emphasis, on the front cover of a special Robbe-Grillet issue of *Obliques* (Nos. 16–17). It is not by chance, therefore, that we find metal arabesques on the door in the opening scene of *Projet*. The spiral on the door is no more "innocent" than Charles Bovary's hat. Robbe-Grillet's art is perhaps as

meticulous as Flaubert's and his premonitory devices no less carefully wrought. For example, the opening paragraphs of *Dans le
labyrinthe*, moving back and forth between the falling snow outside
and the accumulating dust inside the room, adumbrate the topology of curves and lines:

> Across the dark asphalt of the sidewalk the wind is driving the fine
> dry crystals which after each gust form white parallel lines, forks,
> spirals that are immediately broken up, seized by the eddies driven
> along the ground, then immobilized again, recomposing new spirals,
> scrolls, forked undulations, shifting arabesques immediately broken
> up. [15]

This binary opposition between curves and straight lines is a
constant element in Robbe-Grillet's dialectic. In Part I of the "Premier Espace," of *Topologie d'une cité fantôme*, entitled "Dans la cellule
génératrice," a naked woman lies tied on a rectangular table. The
prison cell is rectangular. Another naked girl is painting a rectangular picture. There is a rectangular trap door on the floor. Several
naked girls are playing cards at a square table. The tarot cards are
rectangular. The rules of the game are written on a piece of rectangular paper. I am not gratuitously singling out rectilinear objects; the adjective "rectangular" appears in each of these descriptions. The only curves with which to break the grip of straight-line
geometry belong to the bodies of the women. It is no doubt
significant that their game takes place inside a prison cell with five
straight iron bars on the windows or that the five external
generators of the text are men: Robbe-Grillet, Delvaux, Magritte,
Rauschenberg, and David Hamilton, four artists (now that Robbe-
Grillet has become a painter) and one photographer—all of them
dealing in images.

The descriptions of women, nymphets, rooms, temples, and
landscapes in the five "spaces" of the novel are identifiable and
derivative. Delvaux's wide-eyed, bare-breasted, sleepwalkers can
be seen evolving on a landscape of ruined temples dominated by a
volcano. If we piece together the linguistic pun of Jean de Berg and
the smoking, "murmuring" volcano ("rauchen," "rauschen" and
"Berg" in German), we derive the name of the American artist. [16]
Magritte's bowler-hatted men and his gravity-defying boulder suspended over a seascape are as unmistakable as David Hamilton's
nymphets posing in front of mirrors and windows in varying stages
of deshabille. [17]

The artistic code provided by the five *external* generators of the text meshes with the polysemy of the text's internal *generators*, the nine signs generating its ongoing and repetitive metonymy. The text demythifies both language and "innocence," and since today, perhaps ever since the original "fall," man continues to experience a radical separation from nature, it seems useful to dramatize language and the systems that organize man's perceptual values. Hence perhaps the signs for "falling," which, like the white pebble, or the meteorite with the V on it, may, if we "recuperate" the novel, give it referential overtones connoting this fall from "innocence." Robbe-Grillet's annihilation of time ("It is morning, it is evening," . . . "I am here. I was there." *T*, pp. 10–11) shifts the narrative into a mythical present in which the rape of the virgin, one of *Topologie*'s main themes, is now the defloration of language— a language that was presumed to be innocent, because it was supposed to reflect mother nature and her natural processes, but which now is no longer perceived as mimetic. Hence we have the penetration inside from without; hence the emphasis on openings, all kinds of consciously manipulated Freudian openings, designed to capture meaning for the unsuspecting reader:

> I am alone, quiet, untouched. They call me Vanadé but I don't care, my real name is Suzanne. I am naked but intact. Kneeling on my prayer stool, I feel innocent and hard. My gaze is empty. It is only you examining my body with that uneasy look. (*T*, p. 126)

A similar text, with the same blank eyes, reminiscent of Magritte's painting entitled *Les Fleurs du mal*, appears at the end of *La Maison de rendez-vous*. The "open" text (inside) solicits its reader (outside). The author sets the arrested images in motion ("Maison d'arrêt," *T*, p. 25), but the reader must decode the progressive slippage between prison cell, phantom city, engraving, tarot card, and enemy assailants. The cry from the dungeon frees the bound woman lying on the rectangular table, and, as the trap door closes, the "fur trap" of latent eroticism takes over. However, the novel's myths, as Rossum-Guyon notes, are no more than "snares" whose falseness is denounced by the work's total structure.[18] Moreover, to reduce the meaning of the novel to the content of its fables is to ignore the artist's *parole*—the dialogue between determinism (rectilinear geometry) and imagination (the curves of a woman's body)—on which these myths keep rolling. The cry can be heard inside and outside the dungeon, as Robbe-Grillet's art structures the dialectic into more and more complex metonymic forms. "In the generative cell—where the motionless ritual of violence and representation still continues—the inaccessible window on the right opens onto the sea" (T, p. 43).

If windows, blinds, and doors open into the recesses of the self and also connect with the world outside, then art, which passes through both, exteriorizes one and internalizes the other. Ricardou sees the door as a perfect example of this ambiguity that the Latins called "janua," from Janus, their two-headed god looking simultaneously in opposite directions.[19] Such movement back and forth within the text, such ludification of reality, is an essential dimension of the ontological dialectic:

> When we speak of play [says Robbe-Grillet], we think also of a certain amount of play within construction components. I even said once, apropos of the writer, that he is like a door: as soon as it works, it plays back and forth. This double meaning of the word play, ludic organization on the one hand, and on the other, a deliberate built-in distance, does not displease us.[20]

In addition to the all-important rectangular door, with its wood grain and its ornate metal arabesques, *Projet pour une révolution à New York* contains a narrative "I" that changes voices and identities, shifting from one character to another. A character who at the beginning of a sentence was "he" suddenly becomes an "I," who, in turn, refers to someone else as "he," who, before you know it, has become another "I." "It is like a mobile narrative voice that sparkles throughout the play of the 'I' [à travers le jeu du 'je']."[21]

This play within the body of the text, this alternating movement between multiple narrators, enables Robbe-Grillet to resolve the apparent contradictions between the inside and the outside. However, to penetrate "the body," to "deflower" it, to provoke a flow of blood, a reader, in order to enter the text, must first pass through the door (Freud maintained that rooms signified female sexual organs and doors symbolized the genital opening).[22] "And the blood flows in a vermilion rivulet that will soon pass through the dark interstice beneath the ill-fitting door, etc" (T, p. 201). In Robbe-Grillet's fictions, blood flows frequently from beneath his doors. Although Foucault may stress the absolute dominance of "la pensée du dehors," by eliminating all notion of selfhood ("language as being appears in its own right only with the disappearance of the subject"),[23] Robbe-Grillet's synthesizing dialectic reconciles the inside and the outside, thus forcing the reader to explore the living gap between the two.

Although a work of art can be viewed as an independent entity in its own right, a novel can also act as a mediating agent between the reader and the writer (scriptor); the bodies of and in the text may also, sometimes, elicit bliss. The "holes" within such "open" texts generate a sexual topology in which the contiguity and continuity of spaces synthesize the apparently irreconcilable topological duality. Magritte's painting *The Human Condition*, like Robbe-Grillet's fiction, resolves this contradiction: the painting depicts the inside of a room where an easel with a canvas on it reproduces exactly, in its minutest detail, that portion of the landscape outside the room that is hidden by the painting. The edges of the painting blend perfectly with the trees and shrubbery. The picture is simultaneously inside and outside the room, even as the landscape itself is simultaneously outside the room and inside. The ambiguity, as with our perception of so-called natural objects, is total. When we look at a tree through a closed window, is its image outside the house or inside the mind? Magritte's rooms, like Robbe-Grillet's, become metaphors for the mind—the generative cell where imagination and creativity take place.

Robbe-Grillet's fiction, like Magritte's painting, communicates the duality and simultaneity of creative perception. My eyes are the mediating surface between the outside and the inside, while consciousness itself records the phenomenon in all its complexity (early Robbe-Grillet criticism was not wrong to label his novels as belonging to "l'école du regard"). Art, as a mediating agent, can thus be viewed as an extension of our sensory organs. And the distortions of our senses, though we may not be aware of them, as Magritte's painting of an eye entitled *The False Mirror* implies, are perhaps as acute as those of Robbe-Grillet's fiction. His rooms empty themselves through keyholes while the insides of houses become the outside. His topology, his human condition, like Magritte's, is indeed the dialectical space where ontology and topography meet. Doors, windows, and blinds, like the human eye, are the mediating agents between two seemingly opposed and irreconcilable spaces. Robbe-Grillet's art unites them both in one transcendental leap.

But the mind, "trapped" by language, sex, and ideology, and in its attempts to cope with the reality prefigured by every "intentional" synthesis, as we have seen, creates affective labyrinths within which human behavior is tragically overdetermined. However, "open art," and the dialectics of topology may offer solutions and escape routes from the prisons within which man seems to have enclosed himself. The next chapter focuses on a description of these labyrinths. Once more, Robbe-Grillet's art performs a dual function: the labyrinth of language may be reflexive, even as the figure of man within the maze may be a sign of alienation, thereby linking the text to a reality outside it.

6

The Labyrinth

By the same process whereby man spins language out of his
own being, he ensnares himself in it; and each language draws a
matic circle round the people to which it belongs, a circle from
which there is no escape save by stepping out of it into another.
—Ernst Cassirer

"As soon as a modern architect is given a project," says Robbe-
Grillet, "he draws a labyrinth: housing developments, luxurious
cities in reinforced concrete, or even the familiar environment of
the subway corridors . . . it is in fact these walls which enclose us
and crush us: fear, anguish, sadism, etc."[1]

Archeology has demonstrated that from its very beginnings in
Egyptian art the labyrinth was a place that dealt with life and
death—man's greatest mysteries. In the labyrinth men strove to
overcome death and to renew life. A dead king-god was placed
there so that his life in the afterworld might be preserved. The
living king-god renewed and strengthened his own vitality by association, in the labyrinth, with the immortal lives of his dead ancestors. The labyrinth generated emotions of joy, fear and grief—
emotions that produced ritual art in its earliest forms: music,
dancing, sculpture, and painting. As tomb and temple, the labyrinth fostered art and literature, activities which in antiquity pos-
sessed religious and lifegiving significance.[2]

If modern man, like his ancestors, continues to build labyrinths,
then contemporary labyrinthine space, in some archetypal way,
continues to reflect human structures, needs, and fears. The circular pattern of most labyrinths puts them in the category of the
Jungian mandalla—a universal symbol of central importance to the
psychic experience of man. The persistence of the image of the
labyrinth from the Egyptians to the present suggests, therefore,
that man is still looking for answers to bothersome ontological questions.

Bachelard, like Jung, believes that the figure of the labyrinth is an archetype for feelings of disorientation linked to childhood. Henri Ronse, in this connection, cites Joyce's early wanderings through the dark, dank, disquieting hallways of Clangowes Wood, stressing the fact that the anguished, oppressed, and fearful person trapped in the labyrinth experiences the illusion of walls, narrow streets, and corridors closing in on him.[3] In this respect, Borges's labyrinths illustrate a fundamental pattern:

> I had traversed a labyrinth, but the resplendent City of the Immortals was frightening and repulsive to me. A labyrinth is a house designed to confuse men; its architecture, abundant in symmetries is subordinated to that end. In the palace which I explored imperfectly, the architecture lacked purpose. Most abundant were the corridors without exit, the unreachably high windows, the elaborate doors leading to a cell or a well, incredibly inverted stairways with upside-down steps and balustrade. Other stairways, which adhered aerially to the sides of a monumental wall, died in the uppermost darkness of the turrets, leading nowhere after two or three turns.[4]

This passage, with perhaps slight modifications, also describes milieus that are not unfamiliar to Kafka's heroes. However, Kafka's labyrinths envelop his characters in a physical and metaphysical despair that is absent from Borges's. Nevertheless, Joyce's, Borges's, and Kafka's labyrinths, as metaphors for the human condition, are all places with no exit. Their space, unlike the sacred space of the Egyptian labyrinths, is profane. Their labyrinths no longer protect a dead king-god or illumine the living one. Their space menaces man.

Heinz Politzer, like many of Kafka's commentators, stresses the fact that Kafka's thinking predisposed him to adopt the labyrinth as a central image in his work, be it the intricate script of the execution machine in "In the Penal Colony," the meandering interpretations of the Law by Tintorelli and the Prison Chaplain in *The Trial*, or the tormenting complications of the labyrinth that are the animal's "Burrow."[5]

The works of Joyce, Kafka, Beckett, Borges, Sartre, and Robbe-Grillet, among many others, reflect today's alienation, disorientation, and ennui. Teilhard de Chardin, though perhaps primarily a theologian, is not the only person to have put his finger on the tender spot. He, like so many of his contemporaries, defines our malaise as the "sickness of the dead end—the anguish of feeling shut in."[6] It is useful to have a Christian like Teilhard de Chardin corroborating certain ideas of an atheist such as Sartre, whose play *Huis Clos* is in this respect so apt. As "philosophers," both men are inclined to offer solutions that artists such as Kafka and Robbe-Grillet, for instance, do not. Because art, as a rule, tends not to provide answers but to mirror the dilemmas of its time, it is noteworthy that the extreme self-conscious labyrinths of contemporary art do reflect the many levels, impasses, and frustrations of modern man.

The labyrinth may be a central image of our time. Man, as Teilhard de Chardin affirms, is perhaps moving toward "hominization," but the constant and conflicting battle of institutions has also enclosed him in dehumanizing prisons and bureaucratic towers, not the least of which is language itself. The systems and regimes that threaten and oppress man are monsters which, Gide to the contrary, also still exist outside of man, ready to devour him in the "Gulags" of political or reified exile.[7]

In addition to the bureaucratization of horror, one of the most alienating of labyrinths for Kafka is the metaphysical and psychological anguish he feels in being excluded from participation in a world in which he feels himself to be a part. This is what separates him, for example, from Borges, who seems indifferent to the world order and does not suffer from this exclusion. Nor does Robbe-Grillet, like Borges, feel any of the Judeo-Christian guilt that afflicts Kafka. Nevertheless, all three are builders of labyrinths that weave magic spells around the reader. If Kafka's labyrinths create an anguish verging on despair, Borges's labyrinths evoke fear and the mystery of being.

Through the corridors and stacks of Borges's "library of Babel" men travel, vainly searching for their justification. A gangster interned in the villa labyrinth at Triste-le-Roy experiences the world as a web of anguish. Rufus the Tribune enters and leaves the City of the Immortals through a labyrinth that, he fears, may extend into the universe, endlessly. In "The Garden of Forking Paths" Borges assembles a quadruple labyrinth mixing poetry, vagueness, and mystery—elements that help construct the ancestor's labyrinth, the cyclical novel, the plurality of destinies, and the path that leads Ts'ui Pên, the narrator, to the crime. The labyrinth through which Borges's characters wander is, as Ana Maria Barrenechea says, the double symbol of infinite mystery and world chaos.[8]

Although Robbe-Grillet's labyrinths evoke none of the mystery or fear of his predecessors, his emotional labyrinths do nevertheless explore the machinery that traps his magnificently obsessed heroes:

He finds himself at the far end of an obscure corridor, within sight of several doors. At the other extremity, the outline of stairs extending the corridor is barely visible as it rises into the blackness and is quickly lost. This long and narrow entryway also gives access to another perpendicular hall, emphasized by deeper shadows, which is on either side of the stairway, just in front of it.[9]

Specialists such as Henri Ronse and W. H. Matthews maintain that in a labyrinth there must be communication between the interior and the exterior; that traversing it inevitably leads to a center or a goal or a secret room. None of these, however, is necessarily at the labyrinth's geometric center (*CIS*, p. 36; *ML*, pp. 182–83, 189). Mircea Eliade says that with sacred space (labyrinths used to be sacred space) there is always a fixed point that enables man to orient himself away from chaos, whereas the profane experience maintains the relativity of space. In relative space there is no one fixed point and no unique ontological status. There are only neutral spaces of equal value that correspond to the fragments of a shattered universe in which no true orientation is possible.[10]

Unlike their ancient paradigms, contemporary labyrinths *seem* to have no center, offer few solutions, and provide even fewer exits. Joyce has Bloom wandering through Dublin, endlessly; Dos Passos transforms Manhattan (the metropolis as metaphor) into a labyrinth of steel, glass, and grit destroying human relationships; Kafka's and Borges's labyrinths appear to be closed. In Robbe-Grillet's novel *Dans le labyrinthe*, the protagonist is "shot" and "killed" within the confines of the city-labyrinth.[11] These heroes either die in the labyrinth or are trapped by it, unable to find a center or an exit. They wander, repeating empty gestures in a space and time that have become meaningless. "When it is desacralized," says Eliade, "cyclic time becomes terrifying; it is seen as a circle forever turning on itself, repeating itself to infinity" (*SP*, p. 107).

The circular, labyrinthine, achronological structures of Robbe-Grillet's works define them as products of a desacralized world. Mathias's and Elias's sadoeroticism (read "anger") in *Le Voyeur* and *Trans-Europ-Express* are symptomatic reactions of man to alienation and ennui. *Projet pour une révolution à New York*, which is a "nouveau nouveau roman" and belongs to Robbe-Grillet's second period (the first goes from *Un Régicide* through *Dans le labyrinthe*), exteriorizes the violence, fragments the narrative voices and the identities of characters, and multiplies the irony. Pseudo-characters parade empty selves—the "hollow men" of T. S. Eliot's "Wasteland." "Re-

ligious man thirsts for *being*," says Eliade. "His terror of the chaos
that surrounds his inhabited world corresponds to his terror of
nothingness" (*SP*, p. 64).

It is this nothingness that modern man has glimpses of and from
which he sometimes recoils in dread. Electra's "bad faith" in
Sartre's play *Les Mouches* is her refusal and inability to bear the
knowledge and burden of a desacralized world in which man is
reduced to his freedom—a freedom that, for both Sartre and
Robbe-Grillet, defines man and determines his being. Nevertheless, in spite of this inherent freedom, Teilhard de Chardin in
speaking of the human condition, and echoing Kierkegaard, describes feelings of inertia and despair experienced by men who feel
trapped in a universe that is perceived as meaningless.

> Enormity of duration—sometimes having the effect of an abyss on
> those few who are able to see it, and at other times, more usually (on
> those whose sight is poor), the despairing effect of stability and mo-
> notony. Events that follow one another in a circle, vague pathways
> which intertwine, leading nowhere. (*PM*, 226)

Modern labyrinths, generally, reflect the metaphysical ennui to
which Teilhard de Chardin alludes.

Although Robbe-Grillet's labyrinths are as intricate as those of
his predecessors, their raison d'être is no longer to generate parallel
worlds nor to frighten. His purpose, he says, is to deliver.

> I am in search of a new type of "discourse," mobile, multiple,
> uncertain, of a new way of speaking this world, which will let me
> escape from my alienation. It is therefore not a question of ignoring
> sex and violence, nor in condemning them, but to structure them
> within a "living" language [*parole*]. . . . We need to invent a discourse
> that will harness these forces, these images of fear and violence
> which, otherwise, threaten to invade us without our knowing it. To
> structure these images is to organize the space where my freedom
> always manifests itself.[12]

Robbe-Grillet's use of metonymy in the quotation of the opening
paragraph establishes an equivalence between labyrinth and sadism. To provide an exit to the labyrinth is, therefore, to offer a
solution to fear, anguish, sex, and violence—some of his favorite
themes.

While he was teaching in New York in the early 1970s, Robbe-
Grillet concluded that the city's white residents were afraid—afraid

of blacks, of fire, of adolescent assassins, of the subway, and of the revolution. Subsequently, he wrote *Projet pour une révolution à New York* in which the subterranean world of the subway system became a labyrinth of fear, madness, and death (*SCP*, p. 48). There is an inevitable contradiction here between an author who so frequently claims to write purely formal fiction, and one who, wishing to "deliver" men from their labyrinths of fear, exhibits a didacticism that is strangely at odds with everything that is usually said about him. Fortunately, Robbe-Grillet's professed contradictions are essentially rhetorical. His fiction, at its best, functions on at least two contrasting levels: it reflects the autonomy of language so dear to the structuralists while also providing referential passageways to "reality." His fiction is self-reflexive, yet it "connects" with the outside. It weaves its spell, yet it delivers. The labyrinths are linguistic—verbal constructions of the author's *parole*—yet we recognize these labyrinths—be they houses, palaces, cities, gardens, beaches, or bogs—as places in which we may also lose our way. If corridors, galleries, patios, rooms, wells, basements, attics, and winding staircases are traps for the protagonists, they are also our traps. We too wander through the streets, plazas, waterways, subways, cemeteries, islands, plantations, and marshes with which Robbe-Grillet constructs his labyrinthine world. In spite of the mazes he creates, his *play* with language, clichés, and social codes provides liberating passageways to the outside, stressing the author's freedom and the reader's option to take advantage of this opening out of the prisons of language, history, biology, geography, and time. His labyrinths are both closed and open.

The discontinuity of Robbe-Grillet's fiction, the false leads, the islands of misinformation transform his novels and films into labyrinths that in fact disorient the reader/audience. The hostility sometimes manifest toward his work indicates, in part, that he has touched a sensitive chord. Nevertheless, regardless of the reception this fiction has received, running through it is the "thread" (Ariadne's?) of creative freedom—the thread that leads the reader/audience out of the maze of fear, eroticism, jealousy, and death. The dialectic of Robbe-Grillet's endeavor transcends the reflexive level of art, blending the images of our conscious and unconscious lives, thereby providing referential dimensions that commentators such as Stephen Heath and Jean Ricardou refuse to acknowledge. Betty Rahv, among others, concludes that *Dans le labyrinthe* is "a desperate attempt of certain elements of the collective unconscious to express themselves through . . . enigmatic dead-ends, negations, twistings, and turnings of the archetypal labyrinth."[13]

The "center" that Hooke, Ronse, and Eliade refer to as the necessary focus of every labyrinth should, normally, in *Dans le labyrinthe*, everything else considered, be the street on which the soldier is to meet his dead friend's father. Every one of the soldier's efforts points toward that one goal. But *the* street has no name, the father is without a face, the time of the meeting has not been specified, and the contents of the box that the soldier is to deliver to the father are unknown to him. The soldier dies looking for the "center"—trying to perform the impossible. In primitive cultures, to penetrate to the center of the maze is to be initiated into the mysteries of religion—to learn secrets that the initiate will then use in order to help solve the dilemmas of living. But when you are trying to deliver "dead" mysteries, e.g., the contents of the shoe box, to unidentifiable places or persons, the futility is not only obvious, but necessarily meaningful.

The labyrinth, both formally and thematically, is one of the salient characteristics of Robbe-Grillet's fiction. On one level it is referential, on another, it is reflexive. A referential or "recuperated" version of *Dans le labyrinthe* will focus inevitably on the "sick" soldier. Though the soldier "dies," unable to find the "center," e.g., to deliver the shoe box, Robbe-Grillet's persona, as Betty Rahv points out, "is *already* [and always has been] *in the center of the labyrinth*" (*FSNN*, p. 142). He is in "the secret room" ("La Chambre secrète" is the title of one of Robbe-Grillet's stories in the collection *Instantanés*) from which his imagination always structures to-and-fro passageways between the inside and the outside, thereby providing answers and solutions to the seemingly futile perseverance of the soldier. The past may be dead, but something else—the artist's freedom to invent the future—is still alive. Thus, referential failure and reflexive success invite ontological speculations dealing with freedom, bondage, and the topology of being. The inside-outside dialectic of Robbe-Grillet's art explains his presence at the heart of the labyrinth, within the "cellule génératrice" (the generative cell), where creation begins and all life-giving forms take shape.[14]

Commentators inclined toward "recuperation" will perhaps also interpret the novel's sick soldier as a symbol of universal alienation, whereas still others will conclude that he represents the moribund state of contemporary art. "La Défaite de Reichenfels," the name of the nineteenth-century painting hanging on the wall, will also signify the demise of the conventions of the traditional novel. "Non-recuperative" readers, as opposed to their "innocent" cousins, will stress the text's arbitrary, autonomous, self-contained, self-reflexive, and self-regulating characteristics. For them, Robbe-Grillet's labyrinth will refer to no reality outside itself, provide no symbolic allusions, and contain no metaphysical connotations.

Whether reflexive or nonreflexive, circularity is the labyrinth's typical form. This circularity, as Pierre Astier points out, is a structural feature of Robbe-Grillet's novels.[15] *Un Régicide* is set on a round island on which the bogs and marshes are treacherous labyrinths. In *Les Gommes*, Wallas, the "detective-murderer," wanders through the streets of the city in search of the "guilty victim." The island in *Le Voyeur* is also round, like the city-labyrinth of *Les Gommes*. In *La Jalousie*, the novel begins and ends with "Now the shadow of the pillar . . . ," thus implying circularity. In *Dans le labyrinthe*, not only does the pronoun "moi" echo the beginning pronoun "je," but the novel also begins and ends with the sentence "Outside it is raining, outside people are walking in the rain with their heads bowed down." The narrative voice in *La Maison de rendez-vous*, by describing the same scenes and the same people, by using an infinite number of variations, turns round and round on itself like the soldier wandering through the streets of the besieged city.

Although it is possible to make a case for "recuperating" the soldier in *Dans le labyrinthe*, "recuperating" characters in a novel such as *La Maison de rendez-vous* is, for all practical purposes, impossible. Its atomicity, discontinuity, and contradictions undermine all attempts to make it referential. In *Projet pour une révolution à New York*, the ending of the novel, if the reader is to understand it, invites him to begin again, because it is "once more the same scene which is again unfolding."[16] New York provides stereotypical images with which Robbe-Grillet builds a labyrinth of clichés and fear. *Topologie d'une cité fantôme*, like *L'Année dernière à Marienbad*, ends with a typical code image of the labyrinth: "And I advance, once again, in front of the succession of closed doors, along the interminable empty corridor, immutably distinct and clean."[17] *Souvenirs du triangle d'or* evolves through now familiar subterranean passageways and prison cells. *Djinn* ends exactly where it began, in the circumscribed space of the hangar.

One can enumerate the same structural labyrinthine patterns in Robbe-Grillet's films, going from *L'Année dernière à Marienbad* to *La Belle Captive*.[18] In *L'Immortelle*, for example, Istanbul is a labyrinth through which Professor N. walks hopelessly looking for Leila. *Trans-Europ-Express* is a sadoerotic trap, a labyrinth of conventional clichés dealing with art, eroticism, and violence. The café, which is *L'Eden et après*, is a labyrinth of mirrors reflecting more of society's coded stereotypes. *Glissements progressifs du plaisir*, like Jean Genet's *Le Balcon*, while presenting protagonists who symbolize society's power structure (a policeman, a lawyer, a judge, a priest, a victim)—within the confines of bondage and eroticism—consciously stresses the labyrinth motif:

> The complicated passage followed by the police inspector emphasizes the structure: he seems to be turning in circles in search of a hidden center, opening many doors as he passes (of entryways or cupboards: there are even trap doors on the ceiling!), covering several times the same fragmented course, performing the same gestures, as though he were lost in a labyrinth.[19]

Unlike real mazes, which, authorities insist, cannot be closed systems and have only one solution, art's labyrinths may be open or closed. If *open*, they offer multiple solutions that each reader uses in order to find his particular "center." Furthermore, if structuralism, among other philosophies, has demystified the world, and art is full of relative spaces without a priori centers, then man, by the force of circumstance (hence the fear and the anger) is compelled to seek new answers to the age-old problems of living. The anxiety of modern man reflects the fact that he has not yet been able to adapt to the fast pace of a rapidly changing world in which the "center" of values has shifted and in which everything seems relative.

Experimental facts in the realm of quantum phenomena, for example, are effecting an even greater revolution in man's outlook than the discovery of universal gravitation by Newton. Scientists now believe that nature is intrinsically and in its elements neither understandable nor subject to law. This feature of unpredictability is one of the cornerstones in the theory of quantum mechanics in which atomicity or discontinuity are seen as the pervading characteristic of the structure of the universe. Unable to predict results with absolute accuracy, scientists work with probability. Consequently, the world is no longer a world of reason, understandable solely by the intellect of man. It acquires meaning only as man ascends from the realm of the very little (atomic physics) to the realm of the quotidian (relativity).[20] In physics, scientific investigation seems to have reached the limits of perception.

> Nineteenth-century science [says Robbe-Grillet] imagined that a
> spectator was dealing with a reality which existed outside of him and
> which he could then transcribe. Modern physics has discovered that
> the observer was an element in the observation, that observation
> modified the thing observed exactly as a reader modifies a book or a
> spectator modifies a film. (*CIS*, 109)

In linguistics, Saussure's concept of the "system" implies that
one can see only as much as one's model permits one to see. But this
starting point does more than reveal: the "system" actually creates
the object of study. Henceforth, the classical opposition between
the *true* and the *false*, between a fact and its contradiction, is no
longer the only possible instrument of knowledge.

> *The indeterminate* [says Umberto Eco] is one category of knowledge:
> within this cultural context a new poetics emerges in which the work
> of art is no longer endowed with a necessary and predictable ending:
> in which the freedom of the interpreter becomes a form of this very
> *discontinuity*, which in modern physics no longer represents failure,
> but the ineluctable basic situation, at least on the sub-atomic level.[21]

The avant-garde in the arts, in the sciences, and in the human
sciences emphasizes the cleavage between the humanistic tradition,
atomicity, and man's new awareness of a nonhuman reality. Not
only is nature unpredictable, now man discovers that his own
"mother tongue," as well as her subsumed codes and values, seems
to manipulate him in ways that, until recently, he had not imagined
possible. Although most intellectuals are aware of the process of
desacralization, not all of them welcome the trend. Mircea Eliade,
for instance, in *The Sacred and the Profane*, believes that an essential
"sacred" dimension in activities such as sex, eating, and play has
been lost. He opposes the relativity and discontinuity of profane
experience to the older, sacred rites that, for *homo religiosus*, revealed
an absolute reality in which orientation was possible:

> What we find as soon as we place ourselves in the perspective of
> religious man of the archaic societies is that *the world exists because it
> was created by the gods*, and that the existence of the world itself
> "means" something, "wants to say" something, . . . the world . . . is
> not an inert thing without purpose or significance. For religious man,
> the cosmos "lives" and "speaks." (*SP*, p. 165)

The world used to have a center around which one could situate
sacred space and sacred time. Today's profane labyrinths preclude

such absolute orientation. Primitive man used to commune with gods, whereas modern man has lost contact even with himself. Primitive man, whenever he allowed himself to be led into acts that verged on madness, depravity, and crime, believed that he was imitating his gods, whereas modern man, as Dostoevsky implies and Sartre has stated, believes that because God is dead, everything is allowed. Primitive man believed that the gods created man and the world, that culture heroes completed the Creation, and that the history of all these divine and semidivine works was preserved in myths. Modern man does not believe in gods, in culture heroes, or in myths. For primitive man the cosmos was the paradigmatic image of human existence. An Austroasiatic cultivator who used the same word, *lak*, to designate phallus and spade knew that his spade was an instrument and that tilling his field required a certain agricultural knowledge. Cosmic symbolism added value to an object or action without affecting its function. Today's mass-produced spade has no mystical overtones and, like the tractor or any other machine tool, performs only utilitarian, nonmagical functions. Its value is in its efficiency. Woman was once assimilated to the soil, seed to the *semen virile*, and agricultural work to conjugal union. A sterile queen laments: "I am like a field where nothing grows." Today, the link between Man and Nature is being severed (*SP*, pp. 28, 30, 63–64, 104, 166–68, 202).

"For the nonreligious men of the modern age," says Eliade, "the cosmos has become opaque, inert, mute; it transmits no message, it holds no cipher" (*SP*, p. 178). It is, in fact, a maze without an exit. In the presence of a tree, with its symbology of cosmic life, primitive man could experience the universal. Symbols used to awaken individual experience, transmuting it into a spiritual act, into a metaphysical comprehension of the world, whereas for modern man, this "sacred reality" is an obstacle to freedom. Profane man believes that he can become himself only when he is demysticized (*SP*, p. 203).

However, today's desacralized labyrinths may not be as menacing as Eliade maintains. Although the spaces may be relative and the objective center nonexistent, such is the nature of the modern world. If this state causes distress, man can take comfort in the fact that although no true objective center exists, he, at least, can provide a subjective focus with which to orient the relative spaces. The answer is neither in the labyrinth nor in man, but in the movement back and forth—in the relationship between the two.

This relativity that Saussure also mentions in determining the syntagmatic value of words within a sentence stresses not the meaning of a word in isolation, but each word's relationship to all the others that precede and succeed it. This emphasis on reciprocal dependence when applied to a work of art necessarily implies that meaning derives from reader rapport—a rapport that will shift whenever the work changes hands. Each reader brings a different focus to bear in determining the value of the work, which is now more often perceived as "open." Contemporary works, says Umberto Eco,

> do not constitute finished messages, forms determined once and for all. We are no longer confronted by works which have to be re-thought and relived in a given structural direction, but in front of "open" works which the interpreter completes whenever he mediates on their behalf. (*OO*, pp. 16–17)

The "open" work structures a new dialectic between art and its interpreter. *La Maison de rendez-vous*, for example, which subverts ordinary communicative codes, offers the reader, instead of a conventional story line, a description of the adventures of meaning in the text. These adventures of meaning, when they focus on an analysis of polysemy, play, generative writing ("l'écriture productrice"), and generative numbers, which in the New New Novel have usurped the role of characters and plot, invite the reader not only to re-create the text but also to complete the creative process. The work of art is, by definition, incomplete until the mediating role of the reader provides the necessary missing link. "In essence," says Eco, "the author offers the interpreter a work to *complete*" (*OO*, p. 34).

The poetics of the "open" work invites the "interpreter" to engage in acts of conscious freedom. He becomes the active center of a network of relationships out of which he elaborates a form (*OO*, p. 29). The goal of a literary work, says Roland Barthes, is not to make the reader a consumer, but a producer of the text. That is why Barthes values the *writerly* as opposed to the *readerly*. A *writerly*, i.e., "open" text, functions with the help of the reader who thus gains access to the magic of the signifier and to the pleasure of writing. A *readerly* text offers the reader only the limited choice of accepting or rejecting it.[22]

Writerly works, because they depend so much on the "play" of language, seem by their very nature, if they are to function, to generate multiple meanings. The reader re-creates the subject-object split—which is not a split, but a relationship—an inside-outside dialectic—then forms the necessary synthesis out of his aesthetic experience. A participant is needed so that the work's "intentions" may be realized. This is not to imply as Ricardou does, that all interpretations are possible or equally valid. The work will always retain a limited number of rational possibilities, more or less intended by the author, and, as Philip Pettit phrases it, subject to "reflective equilibrium."[23] It is these internal possibilities, constantly in motion, that the reader picks up and which he uses to generate meaning. The author provides the context, while the reader completes the message. "The work of art," says Eco, "is no longer an object whose fundamental beauty we contemplate, but a mystery to be discovered, a task to be accomplished, a stimulus to the imagination" (OO, p. 21).

It is presumptuous, perhaps, to suggest that the creative role of the reader is new. The reader has always been obliged, more or less, to "re-create" works of art. What seems new is the artist's awareness, Robbe-Grillet's in particular, of a dialectic between himself and the reader. Within this dialectic, the form and message of language, which Saussure compares to the front and back of a sheet of paper, are in a state of constant tension which can never be completely resolved, let alone separated. Says Robbe-Grillet:

> The nineteenth-century narrative strove to retrace a historic or pseudo-historic reality, while the modern narrative parades its power of invention. . . . Balzac's narrative considers reality closed while the modern narrative sees it in a state of continuous creative flux . . . a reality that will never be finished. . . . There are critics who have called this an "open" work, as opposed to a closed work.[24]

However, even "open" works remain closed if the reader fails to provide the creative link that will serve as the passageway between it and himself, between the inside and the outside. The "open" work remains a closed circuit, a labyrinth in which a man can get lost, until he begins to play with the text, as the author before him played with language in order to generate meaning. To play with language and its repressed imagery of sex and violence—it is the walls of the labyrinth that have repressed them, hence their persistence in our conscious and subconscious lives—is the surest way to assert one's freedom and escape from their confinement. This opening, says Eco, this play "becomes a revolutionary pedagogical instrument" (OO, p. 25). Readers familiar with the novel *Projet pour une révolution à New York* will realize that this is the meaning of the word *revolution* contained in the title, a word which colors the text with its red generators: rape, murder, fire. Every man alive, says George Sipos, invents life, and these *writerly* texts that are so deceptive, so strange, and, it would seem, unrelated to reality, may indeed have pedagogical value. "I believe that in teaching him to invent the work of art, they teach him to invent his own life, and consequently to live."[25]

To re-create the text is to play with it. (Robbe-Grillet has more than once emphasized this aspect of creation.) To play with the images of "fear, anguish, and sadism" is a form of catharsis, a liberating act. To find an exit in the labyrinth is to free oneself of these metaphorical obsessions. We know, for instance that the soldier in *Dans le labyrinthe* was "shot" by the enemy. What can we infer from this "fact?" Does it mean anything? To survive is to escape from death—physical death, perhaps, but no doubt, primarily, death of the soul—a soul oppressed by metaphysical ennui, political terrorism, ideological repression, or reified exile.

Robbe-Grillet's works are more than self-contained, autonomous, reflexive entities, because of the fact that they embody mythic elements. (Myth, says Claude Lévi-Strauss is a language in itself.) *Dans le labyrinthe* connects with all the labyrinths of the past, whereas *Projet pour une révolution à New York*, dealing with rape, murder, and arson, draws on our most powerful contemporary myths. These mythic elements, combining *langue* and *parole*, transcend the author's *parole*. They are "language functioning on an especially high level where meaning succeeds practically in 'taking off' from the linguistic ground on which it keeps on rolling," (*SMLS*, p. 174). In other words, myth is a *langue* within a *parole*, paradoxical as this may seem. Robbe-Grillet's *parole* may be reflexive, but the *parole* of a specific myth is referential; its particular context is "recuperable," because "what gives myth its operative value is that the specific pattern described is everlasting; it explains the present and the past as well as the future" (*SMLS*, p. 173).

Time in myth, as well as in Robbe-Grillet's works, is reversible, nonlinear, and nonsequential. Myth, like Robbe-Grillet's narratives, is essentially repetitive, returning again and again to the same points instead of getting on with the story. Thus, myth and narrative resist linear reading, both exhibiting a timeless structure, impressing it on the minds of the audience by repeating elements of that structure.

The timeless, circular pattern of Robbe-Grillet's fiction is thus mythical, imposing levels of meaning that are always more than purely verbal or linguistic. In addition to the "pleasure of the text," as Barthes would say, there is also the pleasure of the myth, of an old story retold. But someone might ask, if the story is demythified, as Robbe-Grillet's are, is myth relevant? Lévi-Strauss believes it is: "There is no one true version of which all the others are but copies or distortions. Every version belongs to the myth" (*SMLS*, p. 183). Even the demythified ones belong.

For Ricardou, the deciphering of Robbe-Grillet's narratives is a textual matter, leading nowhere. For Eco and Lévi-Strauss the cultural contexts of these decipherings will also always be referential; hence the possibility of "recuperating" *Dans le labyrinthe*, of situating it beyond the text, of relating it to life. The soldier may "die," "trapped by history," but the reader "escapes." The reader connects from the outside with the author's *parole* at the center of the labyrinth, and, with his imagination, transcends the barriers that would inhibit or deny his freedom. To escape from the labyrinth is to find answers to the forces (the walls) that oppress man. With insight and understanding, man navigates the passageways without being "devoured," or "shot," or "destroyed." Robbe-Grillet's topological dialectic—his imagination—moves freely between the inside and the outside of rooms, buildings, corridors, and streets, back and forth, even though the windows, doors, and cells may be closed and locked. His freedom is the key, opening vertical and horizontal exits to the confinement of the circular labyrinth.

Robbe-Grillet's labyrinths are open only if the reader works his way through the language, the imagery, and the *doxas* that obstruct his passage. The reader's acts of collaboration enable him to find a center, and having found it, there, like the king-god of antiquity, he overcomes death, renews life, and re-creates himself. He is his freedom. Myth now communes with Time, and Art, once again, has sacralized space.

Although art can provide exits to the labyrinths of language, sex, and ideology, these "open works" are effective only if the active collaboration of the reader/viewer provides the missing links, that is, if the reader/viewer plays with the text or the film in ways that generate meaningful ontological relationships. To escape from the labyrinths of fear, anguish, or sadism is already to experience a taste of freedom. In the final chapter we see how play and games further dramatize this existential freedom of the self, affirming, yet again, the referential dimensions of the reflexive text.

7

Games: Dramatized Play

> The course of the world is a playing child moving figures on a
> board.
>
> —Heraclitus

> I know of no other way of coping with great tasks, than play.
>
> —Nietzsche

The average man, the product of encratic language, the conditioned, reified, and rhetoricized mannikin of the consumer society or of the historical imperative, may have become, to use Jean
Ricardou's comic expression, a "robot-grillé." This pun of Ricardou's illustrates Robbe-Grillet's own use of ludic structures to
dramatize the conflict between the habits of robotlike men and
women and the actions of spontaneous souls who wish to free
themselves from the constraints of the stereotyped and the conventional. Within this theater of conflicting ideologies, Robbe-Grillet
uses fiction as a stage on which the play of opposing codes evolves.
Accordingly, he frequently uses generative themes drawn from
society's collective unconscious, assembles them, structures them,
and toys with them as he stages new and free ontological
tragicomedies.

The New New Novelists assert that since language is their
heroine and *parole* is in dialogue with *langue*, the repressed material
of society's unconscious imagery can be staged.[1] If, as Philippe
Sollers notes, life represses the unconscious, whereas theater ad-
dresses itself directly to it,[2] then a "theater of cruelty," as Artaud
defined it, which is neither mimetic nor naturalistic, but total,
oneiric, and hieroglyphic, is also the proscenium of the "nouveau
nouveau roman." This theater, like the plague, is capable of dra-
matically transforming a body (now it is the body of the text) from
within. The surface seems intact, but the inside has been radically
altered. Typically, the "cosmic signs" of the Balinese dance that so

enchanted Artaud are an appeal to body rhythms (now they are the rhythms of language, words, and images) that would supplant Cartesian logic and replace eviscerated conventions with a new art form.

Sollers, like Robbe-Grillet, believes that the space between the unconscious and the conscious is the stage on which thought expresses itself: "We have not understood that everything is signs and that these signs force us to think; we must, if we wish to think, act out these signs" (*EEL*, p. 92). To act these signs out is to create a language that for the "nouveau nouveau roman" is theater—a theater in which *parole*'s assault on *langue* dramatizes the freedom of the artist and the bondage of the repressed material. The nude, tortured bodies in Robbe-Grillet's recent novels and films seem to have no other function than to manifest this drama: "After the fire torture, I then move on, according to the program, to the torture with the saw and the pliers, which represents the third act."[3]

Sollers, like Robbe-Grillet, wishes to stage the corporeality of thought, touch the "black freedom" of the unconscious, and expose the words, gestures, and actions of language. " 'The theater is like a big wake at which I conduct fatality;' it is a dream eating the dream and ON BOTH SIDES OF THE DREAM I exercise my will, " (*EEL*, p. 93). Whereas Sollers, unlike Robbe-Grillet, has eliminated all characters and all anecdotal material from his fiction in order to focus on minute semic units and on the impersonal pronouns of language, the reductive process in both authors' works is the same. Sollers' cover note for *Drame* states that "we are now in the present, on the stage of language (*'parole'*)."

Michel Foucault is also concerned with space as the element in which language and thought occur. In *L'Ordre du discours* and in his essay on Deleuze, Foucault notes that in the theater events take place on a stage, each event moving with reference to every other on a number of different axes. In the "nouveau nouveau roman" this "play of events" *stages* internal, reflexive, and self-conscious processes. Robbe-Grillet capitalizes on the different meanings of the word *play* (as verb and noun), not only stressing the poetics of language but also dramatizing man's existential presence by drawing attention to art as a game—as a form of dramatized play.

> The human condition [says Robbe-Grillet paraphrasing Heidegger] is to be there. It is perhaps the theater, more than any other way of representing reality, which reproduces this situation in the most natural manner. The character in a play *is on stage*, that is his primary attribute: he is there.[4]

All of Robbe-Grillet's novels, insofar as they situate man in an existential present, exhibit this theatrical awareness. In *Les Gommes* the "patron" wipes the tabletop with "trois coups de torchon." In the French theater three sharp raps on the floor inevitably precede the rising of the curtain. The three swipes of the towel clear the stage, so to speak, for the five-act neo-Oedipal drama that will follow—a drama framed by its prologue and its epilogue. The chapters are divided into a certain number of "scenes," accompanied by stage directions such as "the only person present on the stage has not yet masked his own identity. . . . A mechanical arm sets the decor back in place. When everything is ready, the lights go on";[5] "a stage-setting determined by law (in which) the actor stops suddenly in the middle of a sentence. . . . He knows it by heart, this role he acts out every evening; but today he refuses to go any further . . . But, as every evening, the sentence once begun is completed according to prescribed form: the arm falls, the leg finishes its movement. In the pit, the orchestra continues playing with the same exhilaration" (*G,* pp. 23–24). The doctor-narrator in *Dans le labyrinthe,* who says that each of the main characters has played a role in the now completed drama, evokes similar theatrical resonances within narrative prose descriptions:

> Even though it is not easy to determine the basis for their discord, its violence is adequately suggested by the attitude of the antagonists, both of whom engage in demonstrative gesticulations, assume theatrical stances, perform exaggerated mimics . . . in order to follow the latest twists and turns which threaten to become dramatic, she covers her eyes with her hands. . . . This is followed by scenes that are even less clear, although most often mute. Their staging is less precise, less defined, more impersonal.[6]

The "theatrical" performance at the Blue Villa of *La Maison de rendez-vous* features many characters with actors' names: Lady Ava, as Jean Ricardou has pointed out, elicits Ava Gardner, Johnson suggests Van Johnson, Bergmann reminds us of Ingrid Bergman or the Swedish film director, Kim evokes Kim Novak, and Lauren may well suppose Sophia Loren or Lauren Bacall. Stage allusions are multiplied in *Projet pour une révolution à New York* where theater, play, and sadoerotic imagery produce their combined effects: "It is no doubt for this reason that I pronounce the word 'play' ['pièce']; nevertheless this particular game could well have a theatrical character and the play would then, on the contrary, be the whole representation" (*PRNY*, pp. 175–76). The word *pièce*, in the context of the game and in its poetic ambiguity, meaning both play and a chess piece, is one of many typical examples of paronomasia.

The five spaces of *Topologie d'une cité fantôme* are like five acts in the mind's collective archeology exhibiting mythical layers to be uncovered. Part VI of Space I is entitled "Entracte." There is a theatrical representation of the birth of David: "The auditorium curtain opens slowly for the three thousand seats occupied by immobile spectators";[7] "the silence and fixity of the entire scene remain absolute" (*TCF*, p. 85); "I grab my binoculars in order to verify the important staging (if not textual) detail" (*TCF*, p. 98). The archeological dig within the text reveals "sawhorses, winches, chains, and pulleys which could be the dismantled machinery of a theater for great and fantastic spectacles" (*TCF*, pp. 116–17).

Souvenirs du triangle d'or continues the "stage setting":[8] "I was never supposed to limp in this kind of scene" (*STO*, p. 52); "I wanted to enumerate some more of the ritual scenes taking place in the nocturnal palace" (*STO*, p. 78); "This last act (whose subtitle on the program is 'Un Régicide') elicits a lively response" (*STO*, p. 95); "a muffled cry is heard in the small auditorium of the theater, where, in spite of everything, nothing seems to have moved" (*STO*, p. 106); "a young woman wearing a white vaporous gown walks out with a theatrical step" (*STO*, p. 122).

Robbe-Grillet's novels are indeed a fantastic spectacle of the imagination, but his films are equally extravagant and similarly theatrical. Like Kostas Axelos, Robbe-Grillet perceives the world as a stage and the "game" itself as one enormous and minute farce.[9] *L'Année dernière à Marienbad* opens with a play. In *L'Homme qui ment*, Boris Varissa (or is it Jean Robin?) performs and takes his bows to an imaginary audience. In *L'Eden et après*, the students at the Eden Café "perform" ritual scenes of rape and death. Throughout Robbe-Grillet's novels and films there is an ongoing proliferation of actors and mannikins playing contradictory roles on imaginary stage sets. Indeed, the New Novelists behave like directors intent on focusing our attention on décor, objects, gestures, and motifs. Characters enter and exit as the novelist plays with his props, assembles them, structures serial combinations, toys with permutations, teases the reader, tortures reality, and reveals the hidden faces of desire. His audience, says Robbe-Grillet, cannot be victimized by such representations because they are rendered exactly as they appear in our subconscious, e.g., as media exaggerations of sex and violence.[10]

One of the goals of Robbe-Grillet's art is to emphasize the sovereignty of our reflective consciousness, because, as Sartre has pointed out, it is the measure of our human freedom.[11] This play of the mind gives the novelist and his audience the freedom to rearrange images without reference to experienced reality. In the "nouveau nouveau roman" the rules of the game with which the sovereign consciousness likes to cope are now the rules of language: grammar, syntax, the meaning of words—all of which determine perception and reality. A speaker, if he is to communicate, as Saussure points out, is obliged to use a *langue;* only his *parole* is free. But when we hear people speak in ways that seem programmed by commercials, rhetoric, dogma, and the codes of the establishment, we soon realize that this freedom is in constant jeopardy.

Although the freedom of language may be in jeopardy, Roland Barthes observes, not without irony, that the only object with which the writer has a pleasurable relationship is this language—this mother tongue. Moreover, in order to exercise his freedom, the New New Novelist must play with his mother's body *(langue)*, glorify it, embellish it, dismember it. Robbe-Grillet, like Barthes, only seems happy while disfiguring language (Robbe-Grillet's tortured women—the "body of the text"), a form of linguistic incest to which good taste and public opinion strenuously object.[12]

Picasso once said that art is a lie with which one tells the truth. If the painter's *parole* is comparable to the novelist's, as I think it is, then Picasso's innovations—his disfigured and dismembered women—like Robbe-Grillet's, transmit a message which transcends Nature's "code" (which is not Baudelaire's "living temple" with its implied and implicit "truth"), one that only a gratuitous act like play can give. Robbe-Grillet believes that Picasso is a great painter because he has always played with nature and with painting.[13] "Play is for us the only possible way of intervening in a world henceforth deprived of its depth."[14]

A world deprived of depth, like a deck of cards, is a world reduced to the play of its appearances. For a soothsayer there is meaning behind a queen of spades, whereas for a bridge player the card is no more than a flat surface whose value is determined by the arbitrary rules of the game *(langue)*. The beginning of a rubber is the opportunity for each player to assert his *parole* and his freedom, to play his hand, inventing a sequence that will give him the best score.

Having rejected the "myth of depth," Robbe-Grillet compares living and writing to a game of cards in which we play each card, one after the other, opposite a partner's or an adversary's, thereby instituting a personal order where, as yet, there was none.

> The game [he says] . . . assumes an even greater meaning since it is a question of playing with language rather than with cards whose rules exist before the game begins. With language, on the contrary, there are no definitive rules: the order you give to the game in your *hand* [my emphasis], the battle on the table will, simultaneously, create the rules, create the game, and assert your freedom, as well as destroy the rules, in order to clear the deck for that free man who will then be sure to follow. (*NRHA*, 1:128)

For example, *La Jalousie* begins and ends with the word *maintenant* ("now"), the word alluding simultaneously to the novel's time dimension and to the hand ("main") holding ("tenant") the pen. In this gaming context Robbe-Grillet capitalizes on the word "hand" as metaphor and pun, playing with its meaning, its ambiguities ("la paume—la pomme"), and number associations (five fingers), ordering the apparent disorder of the "hand," i.e., language, with which he is playing. Thus, in *Topologie d'une cité fantôme*, there are five spaces, five male generators (Delvaux, Magritte, Rauschenberg, David Hamilton, and Robbe-Grillet), and five bars on the cell window whose fourth bar, like the fourth finger of Robbe-Grillet's writing hand, is broken and deformed. *Les Gommes* has five acts, the name Alain has five letters in it, and so on. The author's "signature," like the "robe grillée" in *Projet pour une révolution à New York*, is everywhere, reminding us that the artist's pen is as sharp as a *stylet* (and at least as parodic as his literary *style*) or as hot as an iron. It pricks reality in the vulva of *Topologie* and it burns the dress in the pubic region of *Projet*.

Robbe-Grillet's linguistic games, some obvious, some obscure, facilitate the semantic "slippage of pleasure" within a text as well as from one text to another. This pleasure derives in part from the fact that the meaning of the signifier transcends the signified, offering itself, as Jonathan Culler observes, "as a surplus which engenders a play of meaning."[15] The meaning of implied signifiers such as "hand" and "robe grillée" (burned dress) exceeds the denoted object, connoting literary games and mirth, referring us to the author himself as a creative and inventive force. However, the message in such "open texts" requires the collaboration of the reader, who must play with the semic units, assemble the generative themes, and re-create meaning. Thus, the author's freedom is a paradigm for the freedom of the reader, who, in turn, learns how to play the game with the hand that life or the author has dealt him.

If a novel, like life or a bridge game, has no conclusive design, no one message to be recuperated, then the reader's role is to evoke the play of possible meanings to which a text gives access. A work of art, therefore, like the queen of spades, is a flat surface that can have "depth" only for soothsayers. "The absence of an ultimate meaning," says Derrida, "opens an unbounded space for the play of signification."[16] Mondrian's nonobjective art, Schoenberg's serial music, and the polysemy of the "nouveau nouveau roman" are all a "joyful Nietzschean affirmation of the play of the world and the innocence of becoming, the affirmation of a world of signs which has no truth, no origin, no nostalgic guilt, and is proffered for active interpretation."[17]

Contemporary art, which is continuously rejecting earlier models, and which by its nature posits the transience and ephemeral nature of all models, moves its readers toward independence and autonomy. What the author asks his reader to do, says Robbe-Grillet, "is not to accept any longer a ready-made world, complete, full, closed in on itself" (*PNR*, p. 134). On the contrary he would like us to participate in its creation, to reinvent the work of art and with it the world. The game begins whenever the answer to an enigma within a work of art requires re-creative play with the generative themes, the structural metaphors, and the reflexive surfaces. Only then does the reader/viewer, like the author/director, assert his freedom. Literature perceived as a game without depth or guilt is like Sartre's concept of "existence preceding essence." The acknowledged freedom of the author and the reader to choose his meaning from all the random possibilities offered to him situates the "nouveau roman" and the "nouveau nouveau roman" in an existential context, or, should I say beyond the existential context, since Robbe-Grillet, unlike Sartre or Camus, believes that the world is neither tragic nor absurd, but simply *there*.

"Play," as Eugen Fink affirms, "is an essential element of man's ontological makeup, a basic existential phenomenon."[18] Play is as primordial and autonomous as death, love, work, and the struggle for power (*OH*, p. 22). In the past, a certain theology postulated the idea of a divine, celestial game. Fourier socialists and fringe Marxists saw in future work a form of game. Marcuse, after Marx and Freud, advocated a nonrepressive society in which work and love would develop as a game. Child psychology, aesthetics, and leisure sociology have also generated insights into the nature of play. Huizinga tackled *Homo Ludens* even as the surrealists, Bataille, Caillois, and Blanchot before him toyed with language, art, reality, and the philosophy of play. Fink, after Nietzsche, Husserl, and Heidegger, delved into the importance of the cosmic and the human game. Today, the mathematical and cybernetic theory of games, in addition to information and communication games, constitutes yet another dimension of play. "The Game," says Kostas Axelos, "seems almost to open the planetary era, when beings, things and words break and fall to pieces" (*PI*, p. 8n). "Apropos of play," says Robbe-Grillet, "all my work . . . is an attempt to expose its structures" (*NRHA*, 1:127).

The "nouveau roman" reveals that in addition to the Apollonian and Dionysiac aspects of art, there is, and always has been, a ludic dimension which stresses neither solar reason, nor Bacchic fervor, but randomness, discontinuity, and improbability. Thus the "nouveau nouveau roman," insofar as it mirrors play, sheds a new light on the "cosmic game" that is different from Caillois's categories and Huizinga's definitions.[19] Whereas Caillois and Huizinga see play as a social phenomenon "outside" of ordinary life, Fink incorporates mimesis into play as ontic illusion, thereby giving it "theatrical" status. Fink believes that since the essence of the world is conceived of as play and since Being, in its totality, functions like play, man can find his true essence only in relating to that which transcends him. To play, argues Fink, is to experience the meaning of the universe (*OH*, pp. 28–30). However, within this theater of play, the actor submits to a peculiar schizophrenia: he wears a mask, assumes a role, and is subsumed by this role, existing in two spheres simultaneously (*OH*, p. 23).

The protagonist of *L'Homme qui ment* plays not a dual but a triple role. Trintignant, the actor, impersonates Boris Varissa who is not Varissa but someone else. "Varissa" describes events, each one more implausible than the other, toys with reality, acting out his disguise from one ontic level to the next. He feigns death, even membership in the Resistance, inventing a spectacular escape from the occupying forces while a distracted "German" officer reads *Pravda* (the Russian name of the newspaper means "Truth") upside down. The comic juxtapositions linked to the actor's confabulations are a tissue of lies designed, it seems, to seduce the three women living in the house on the edge of town. The actor in this tragicomedy is a Don Juan character who creates his role from one moment to the next, a character with no past and no future who is simply there, on stage, playing his imaginary identities in an existential context of free choice.

Trintignant, as a new mythical Don Juan, incarnates the same baroque characteristics that fascinated Molière: theatricality, disguise, role playing (the mask), and a taste for fun and games. A person in disguise is always a comedian. His role is one of constant metamorphosis. If Don Juan has no one identity he assumes multiple ones. His essence is in gesture and transference, and in the theatricality of change. *L'Homme qui ment* lies in order to seduce reality. He embodies the triple structure of the Don Juan situation: the inconstant lover, the female group (necessarily plural), and the dead person. But disguise perhaps more than seduction is Don Juan's real achievement. He, like art, is a lie: he is not what he seems to be. His act intensifies the artifice—a bow to implausibility and its own reflexive nature.

The house in which these events occur also functions as a metaphor for play. The stranger (Trintignant) arrives while the three women are playing a game of blind-man's buff. Even as the man's *parole* wishes to seduce the women, Robbe-Grillet's *parole* is courting the muses. *Langue*, like the blindfolded woman, encounters the actor onto whom her blind groping hands will eventually confer an identity *(parole)*. Grace, however, is neither spontaneous nor automatic as the stranger in the women's midst works very hard to fulfill an essence that might please them. He dramatizes his presence surrounded by photos, paintings, mirrors, frames, windows, and doorways, always evolving through a complex décor of specular surfaces that force us to dwell and reflect unceasingly on these self-duplicating aspects of illusion and reality.

The man who is "shot" by the occupying forces and who is miraculously resurrected is an actor who is not only hunted but haunted. His role develops around comedy, determination, and fear. While play-acting with the maid at the inn, Boris drinks from an imaginary glass, acts out imaginary seduction scenes, and takes bows to an imaginary audience. At the river with Maria, he acts out his shooting and death, falls to the ground, gets up, and takes off his "blood-stained" shirt, handing it to Maria to wash. "I am also play-acting," says Boris, "because I am already dead."

If Boris is miming the gratuitous and arbitrary nature of the cosmic game, then the "key" to freedom and temporary escape from "fear"—the key that will unlock the door to "happiness"—is contingent on connivance and collusion between the actor and the women. Indeed, as we might expect, Sylvia gives the key to the stranger who, at the appointed hour, ascends the circular staircase to the attic where the three women act out their games of bondage, communion, and decapitation amidst a décor of abandoned objects—empty frames, ropes, wheels, cross, chairs, plow, pricket, and the like—objects that connote sadoerotic, artistic, and religious contexts—objects that belong to Robbe-Grillet's stock in trade and constitute many of his generative themes. The women's game, their play-acting, in addition to the fact that they are already acting in a film, is another specular variant, stressing illusion at the expense of the work's referential level. Such effects lay heavy stress on the liberating possibilities of play. Nevertheless, even though the art of the film is reflexive, its message is referential, confirming once again the two levels on which Robbe-Grillet is playing.

Whereas Robbe-Grillet has alluded to the fragility of life, he sees the world more in terms of comedy than tragedy:

> I always have the impression of living in a world that is undermined, menaced by a cataclysm, ready to crumble.
> That's what I am struggling against. Fortunately, I have been blessed with the laughing and obstinate spirit of a Brittany farmer which prevents me from succumbing to this anguish. Besides, the best way to overcome it is to write about it, to apply a treatment to it which will create a distance between these images [fear, sex] and me. There are many distancing methods. In my first novels, I used processes which were labelled rather nastily *"object-like descriptions" ("descriptions objectales")*. Today, I am experimenting with variable structures in movement, which constantly challenge the very material they are organizing. It seems that the corrosive and therefore liberating power of humor is not to be neglected in this game, which constitutes the only possible exercise of our freedom. (*SCP*, p. 48)

These variable, moving units of language, combined with the imagery of conscious fear and repressed sexuality, structure both Robbe-Grillet's "theater" and the games he plays. What emerges from all this is that the dramatization of Robbe-Grillet's *parole* functions simultaneously on three levels: there is the drama of *langue*, the drama of *ideology* (or *myth*), and the drama of the *subconscious*. Within Robbe-Grillet's art, however, the three levels are not separable, as the author weaves his intricate linguistic and imagistic patterns in and out and through the tapestry. The "figure in the carpet" is the author's tri-dimensional signature attesting to his freedom, his playfulness, and his creativity.

The novelist may draw attention to fiction as drama, focusing on man's contingency and freedom; the artist may play with generative themes, emphasizing reflexive characteristics, or he may combine the two, stressing man's role as pawn and player in a vast cosmic game within which, to some degree, creative play modifies "natural" determinism, enabling man to "escape" temporarily from the prisons of biology, time, history, language, society, and geography. The game of Nim in *L'Année dernière à Marienbad*, like all games, is a paradigm whose mechanicsm has some "play" in it, but whose outcome, like birth and death, is predictable. The player who goes first will lose, yet, throughout the game, and within the rules, he is free to make a number of choices. He invents his future and moves unimpeded until the moment of defeat. Thus, the man who is "unlucky" at Nim, but "lucky in love" invents the cliché "last year" ("haven't we met before?") in order to seduce the woman he is pursuing. He plays with events "this year," and he, like Boris Varissa, toys with the present, with memory, and with reality. "Love is a game, poetry is a game, life should become a game (it is the only hope for our political struggles) and 'revolution itself is a game.'"[20]

If writing is a game, like everything else, then the frontispiece to Claude Simon's *Orion aveugle* is informative. His drawing of the "artist at work" denotes the tools of his trade while connoting creativity as play: a deck of cards, a picture, a pack of *Players* cigarettes, a shell (connoting perhaps the *Birth of Venus* and Art), a pen and paper—objects placed on the writer's table situated in front of an open window. Play enhances the free flow of communication between the inside and the outside, the objective and the subjective, the conscious and the unconscious, the real and the unreal, and so on.

A French window, like a door playing on its hinges, Robbe-Grillet's metaphor for the dialectical topology of self ("le jeu du je"—the play of the I), is a ludic image of the artist exploring that space inside, outside, and in-between, see "Landscape with Cry," *TCF*, p. 166), where the cry amplifies man's consciousness of solitude, his rebellion against finitude, and his will to dramatize the human comedy as freedom. If, as Sartre, Robbe-Grillet, and Foucault affirm, God, Nature, and Man are dead, then man, who should be free but is not, struts and frets compulsions, repressions, and outmoded ideologies on the stage of life, unaware of the implications of desacralization and demythification, unconscious of the labyrinths in which he has imprisoned himself. Man, however, like things, before being anything, *is there*, on stage, contingent yet free to create an essence out of his existential and phenomenal self. This awareness of unlimited choice confers on the artist a sense of freedom and joy that, for Robbe-Grillet, manifests itself as a flaunting of codes, convention, and rules. The briefest recapitulation of his artistic trajectory reveals innovations in form, chronology, and narrative point of view—all made possible by his unruly sense of humor that refuses to take dogma seriously. This rebellion against society, this *Régicide*, finds itself exacerbated by the tyranny of language, the medium he, as an artist, must inevitably bend to and use.

> It is disquieting to realise that today the only narrative discourse recognized by the majority of readers of all classes is a fossil discourse, forged at the beginning of the nineteenth century by you know what society.
> Continuous, unilinear, based on a rationalist and reassuring idea of Man, guaranteed on the Stock Market of Values by an alleged historical Truth which says nothing about creative invention, this narrative defines an order, and the name of this order is: the bourgeois order. (*SCP*, p. 48)

Because man's perception of himself and the world is determined by language and the values of the sociopolitial power structure in which he lives, the novelist who wishes to escape from the "prisonhouse" of a bourgeois order or a socialist order, or any order, but who cannot, because the *langue* he speaks inevitably, more or less, reflects the code of that system, then the novelist must invent a *parole* with which to circumvent accepted "order" by replacing it with organized "disorder." The artist plays with establishment values, thereby uncovering their arbitrary base. Such play, as one of Robbe-Grillet's novels implies, can be "revolutionary."

Robbe-Grillet's performance—his *parole*—flaunts its freedom in the most outrageous fashion. Works such as *Projet pour une révolution à New York*, *Souvenirs du triangle d'or*, and *Le Jeu avec le feu* strike out against the conventions of established good taste and accepted public morality. It is in part the "bars" of language that are bent so that the narrative voice may emerge from the generative cell. But once outside, multiple narrators parade the repressed and censored imagery of violence and desire which, according to Robbe-Grillet, inhabits our subconscious:

> the book shops on 42nd Street are not an academy of sadistic murder and "unnatural" fornication. Rather, such places are a kind of great

national theater of our passions, more or less excessive, more or less specialized, but indeed the passions of this society. And it is in such places, provided we are eighteen or over, that we can at last contemplate quite openly our hidden faces, thereby transforming into freedom, play, and pleasure what was merely alienation and risked becoming crime or madness.[21]

Robbe-Grillet plays with the forbidden lusts of our society. One of the goals of his art is to reveal our hidden faces by converting alienation into freedom, play, and pleasure. It is censored faces that Robbe-Grillet displays in his novels and films, staging oneiric dramas in that space where the conflict between illicit desire and the symbols of the establishment come together. *Glissements progressifs du plaisir* is nothing less than a triumph of the id, a victory of the pleasure principle over the representatives of law and order, the repressive types of establishment superego. Alice, imprisoned in her cell for murder, subverts the police inspector, the priest, her lawyer, and the judge, all of whom succumb to her charms, thereby preparing and facilitating the second murder. The film ends exactly where it began, illustrating, once again, Robbe-Grillet's cyclical labyrinth motif while simultaneously corrupting the narrative realism of the text. Though he overthrows conventional realism, Robbe-Grillet renders visible a new symbolic realism of the unconscious.

Whereas the corruption of justice may be a cliché, Robbe-Grillet exposes its sexual underpinnings and the ease with which "law and order" is perverted by alienation, i.e., by desire that remains either hidden or relegated to some forbidden realm, where, transformed, it manifests itself as crime or madness. Robbe-Grillet's artistic problem then is to dramatize and blend an avowed, though not to be exaggerated, didacticism with formal, poetic concerns—not always an easy matter when one is working with a text that claims to be reflexive and autonomous as well as cathartic and referential.

Since in the "nouveau nouveau roman" a woman's body may also signify the body of the text, this body is "the field of operations for the writer" ("le champ opératoire du scripteur") for whom creation is a sexual act. In *Projet pour une révolution à New York*, sexuality and textuality become one as Robbe-Grillet plays with sex and text while Doctor Morgan performs his sadoerotic operations on his animate and inanimate models. In addition to such literary foreplay, one of the many guessing games in *Projet* is to identify the three secrets concerning the narrator's identity. Question: Why does Laura, the narrator's sister, have blue eyes? Answer: She is a "chabine," that is, a blond black (in Martinique, where Robbe-Grillet once worked, a blond black is called a "chabin"). If she is his natural sister, then the narrator is also black. Besides, his name and initials, N. G. Brown would be pronounced Neg Brown in Martinique.[22] This is his first secret. His second secret is that he is a policeman and a revolutionary, therefore a double agent. He also refers to the kinky heads of the other assembled revolutionaries, who must, like him, be black. The third secret concerns the narrator's special relationship with his sister whom he has hidden inside "the room" in order to protect her from the "organization." The narrator and Laura evolve on both sides of the all-important door that structures the text's topology. Although the door itself does not open, there is communication (through the keyhole and the broken pane of glass) between the inside where she is sequestered and the outside. But if Laura is the narrator's sister and the body of the text with which the narrator is playing is his "mother tongue," then the complexities of this incestuous game devalue conventional literature as well as the incest taboo. Since the narrator is also the text, he and Laura are essentially one person. "Je suis la plaie et le couteau," said Baudelaire (I am the wound and the knife). The executioner and the victim are identical. So the person we thought was a white policeman turns out to be a black revolutionary, Laura's brother, her double.

If the narrator's identity sounds implausible, so also are the others. *Projet* is in fact a play in which the actors act and play ("ils jouent"). The characters, even the doctor, wear masks to designate their professions, but also to facilitate role changes and inversions. Finally, if they are all playing roles, and Laura's and the narrator's roles are reversible, then the novel is a trap that blocks our pursuit of a normative text. Laura's polymorphism, for example, is a humorous subversion of the educational system. In answer to Musset's question: "What do young girls dream about?" ("A quoi rêvent les jeunes filles?"—*Rêves de jeunes filles* was the title of David Hamilton's first volume of romantic photographs), Laura answers: "Of knives and blood" (Aux couteaux et au sang). In answer to Nerval's "Where are our lovers?" (Où sont nos amoureuses?), she says: "In the tomb" (Au tombeau). The structure of the text is undermined by the play in the text. All that remains finally is the door with which the work began—the author's "signature." He is thus in constant dialogue with us, his voyeur readers, outside, for whom Doctor Morgan acts out his perverse, self-distancing, and imaginary scenes. The door, says Robbe-Grillet, the heavy wooden door with its metal arabesques and Freudian keyhole, is the door to the house in which he was born (UCLA Lecture). Thus the door as "signature" demonstrates that the composition of the work is a conscious self-portrait of the writer in the act of creating the work, that the essential content of his novels is the act of writing them, that he strikes a deliberate pose, being simultaneously the mirror and the mirrored.

If writers pose, and actors assume roles, and characters wear masks, then the masks of *Projet* are perhaps also the masks of Greek tragedy. Crimes committed on stage may purge; they can be viewed as a public catharsis; they are overt representations of the subconscious:

> When I read scandalous or criminal bits and pieces in the newspaper, [says Robbe-Grillet] when I look at the display windows and the advertising posters which determine the facade of every large city, when I walk through the passageways of the subway, I find myself assaulted by a multitude of signs which, all together, constitute the mythology of the world in which I live, something like society's collective unconscious, i.e., the image it wishes to give of itself, as well as the reflection of its most haunting problems. (*AEA*, pp. 35–36)

Play, so the theory goes, subverts the intensity of repressed images, thereby providing the necessary distancing and defamiliarizing effects. However, catharsis comes into play only when the text is sufficiently ludic and all the specular structures are in place. The imagery of Robbe-Grillet's generative themes, the imagery that he subverts, is the imagery of our conscious collective unconscious. By playing with these images, he demythifies establishment norms and introduces disorder into establishment order, thereby himself becoming a rebel. His works are like cinders in the well-oiled machinery of the establishment: they make it grind and grate, they alter its rhythm, and they bring it to a halt. Robbe-Grillet and the narrator of *Projet* are thus identical. Their *parole*, their act, and their play attack *langue* and the codes for which it stands.

Robbe-Grillet's collages are yet another example of *parole's* subversion when in collision with *langue*. The illustrations in *Obliques* (nos. 16–17), featuring torn newspaper fragments under dribbles, blotches, and spots of red paint, are examples of dramatization at its most elemental level. Newsprint registers local and world happenings, current events, and human interest stories, all printed according to establishment priorities in a coded language to reflect the slant of the paper and accessible to different strata of the reading public. The newspaper is communication—reality objectified. The red paint tears this reality apart, imposing an arbitrary, playful, and subjective dimension on the impersonality of language and events. Robbe-Grillet stamps a red, individualized handprint (literally) on fragments of *Le Monde* on which one can still read "majorité," "famille," "polémique," and "tentations de la violence"— words that act as generative themes, triggering associations of images and ideas. The red paint on the newspaper cutouts is unmistakably the artist's *parole*. Paint and scissors do violence to establishment *langue* (remember Nora in *Glissements* who was "murdered" with scissors?); they rip it apart, imposing disorder on the ordered lines of the daily news. This disruptive gesture asserts different values, setting up a dialogue between the self and the other, between the subconscious (imagination) and language (the establishment), between the inside and the outside. Thus, the artist disrupts standard newspaper communication. Red paint, holes, circles, and layered openings in the text—the artist's ordered "disorder"—offer a message that runs counter to the one implied on the printed surface.

Every culture, in one way or another, communicates its values. To play with these values is also a form of communication. Thus, the distinguishing characteristic of reality is that it too is played. Consequently, any theory of information implies a theory of play as well as a game theory. In poetics, the narrator, like the narrative, is at once the subject and the object of verbal play. The pronouns I, you, and he that multiply, shift, and transfer their ambiguous presences throughout Robbe-Grillet's "nouveau nouveau roman" are the different modes of the play structure. Since the author's "signature" is the narrative, the reader experiences language as process, the adventure of the text, a text in search of itself and the meaning it generates. Thus play, like Robbe-Grillet's phenomenological topology, abolishes the subjective-objective dualism. Play articulates the text, opening and closing it through language. Hence the play of doors, windows, mirrors, reflexive surfaces, and holes which, like a Möbius strip or Klein's bottles, exteriorize the inside and vice-versa.

Robbe-Grillet's "revolutionary play" thus opposes Caillois's and Huizinga's ideas of play. Instead of playing with and thereby exposing the violence of the instincts, they would repress them, because, they claim, sadoeroticism breaks down the "fair play" of civilization that "reason, humanity, and faith" have worked so hard to establish. However, if Marcuse is right and if the repression of *Eros* and *Thanatos* has negative consequences rather than beneficial ones, then Caillois's and Huizinga's nostalgia for a "pure and innocent" society free of sex and violence forces them to reject the salutary effects of artistic play which, by its very nature, is free, spontaneous, and untrammeled. Nevertheless, Caillois and Huizinga, though unable to resolve the basic contradiction in their thinking, insist that play does have a civilizing influence. Although Robbe-Grillet agrees with their conclusion, his play, as well as his premises, differs radically: "Our ludic *parole* is not designed to protect us or to shelter us from the world, but to challenge us and the world in order to transform it by means of what might be called imagination" (*NRHA*, 1:97).

Hegel once said that play, in its indifference and frivolity, was "at the same time the most sublime seriousness and the uniquely true." Schiller observed that "man plays only when he is man in the full sense of the word and *he is totally man only when he plays.*"[23] Marx and Marcuse both urge play as an antidote to reification and the alienating effects of dehumanizing work. Marcuse says that artistic work, in addition to play, "when it is genuine, seems to grow out of a non-repressive instinctual constellation and to envisage non-repressive aims."[24] Thus, Robbe-Grillet's ludic art, as Françoise Baqué remarks, may perhaps redeem literature and society.[25] "After the bankruptcy of divine order (of bourgeois society), and of rationalist order (of bureaucatic socialism), it is important to understand that only ludic organizations are now viable" (*AEA*, p. 35).

Instead of repressing sex, violence, and fear, play will enable man to cope with their reality. To play with this reality, says Robbe-Grillet, is to reinvent it. The artist derives both his strength and his freedom from this creative role (*PNR*, p. 30). To deny art its freedom, which is its prime reason for being, he says, is to deny freedom itself. "To create," says Jean Lacroix, "is to be free. The greatness of man comes from the worlds he creates. . . . The experience of creation proves that freedom is the true destiny of man."[26] If freedom is the true destiny of man, then creative play directed at the repressive forces of society, should, like Achilles's lance, cure those who come in second contact with it. If the first exposure is disturbing, then the next time around will heal.

Oddly enough, in their own different ways, socialist and capitalist societies conspire to restrict the artist's freedom. Bourgeois pundits stress a vague humanistic idealism toward which artists should strive, whereas the advocates of socialist realism see literature as yet another instrument in the service of the socialist revolution (*PNR*, p. 40). Both, in any case, defend the artistic conventions of out-dated nineteenth-century norms. The playful element in Robbe-Grillet's works, which parodies, attacks, and mocks the assumptions of both Right and Left, comes closer, in its formalistic way, to miming the perceived role of the world as some kind of random game. There is a standard joke about the antiformalism of socialist realists. It is alleged that the sight of a zebra once prompted Zhdanov to dismiss it with the cryptic comment: "formalism."

Robbe-Grillet would surely subscribe to Francis Ponge's view in *Le Parti pris des choses* emphasizing a literature of description which allows us to "play the great game: to remake the world, with all the meanings of the word *remake*, thanks to the nature of the *word* which is simultaneously concrete and abstract, interior and ex-terior, thanks to its semantic thickness."[27] This semantic thickening of language, which until recently was the privileged domain of poetry, is being used by the practitioners of the "nouveau nouveau roman." The play of language that ignores or bypasses message, does, nevertheless, contain a message. It does not speak about the world, but like the zebra, it is the world; if it does not stand up on its own four feet, it falls. The "nouveau nouveau roman"'s mes-sage, like the unintelligible sounds uttered by Ionesco's deaf-mute orator in *Les Chaises*, may only be sound, signifying nothing. Never-theless, a writer who organizes the sounds of the alphabet and the images of life creates meaning. The poet's meaning and game, as we have seen, is always played against three opponents: language, ideology, and the subconscious. From this dramatization, as Shake-speare knew, insight emerges: the world *is* a stage and man, with no rules exterior to himself, is both the player and the played. But the world "is not *Play*," says Kostas Axelos, "it 'is' the Game" (*PI*, p. 9).

Conclusion

There is today, in all fields, an immense creative energy at work. Linguistics, the arts, the physical sciences, and the social sciences are exploding their premises in search of a new language that will incorporate previous doubts and new discoveries. Ever since Nietzsche's pronouncement on God, Nature and Man have also been "disappearing," and a new, reflexive, and doubting consciousness has replaced former absolutisms. Man has become painfully aware of bankrupt values and of his own finitude. In fact, the failure of the West's humanistic culture is one of the central problems of our times, the cause of our contemporary malaise, and the reason behind the emergence of the New (New) Novel.

The avant-garde in the arts, in the sciences, and in the human sciences has been underscoring this cleavage between the humanistic tradition, the physical world's atomicity, and man's new awareness of a nonhuman reality shaping and determining behavior and events. Both structuralism and poststructuralism have been stressing the limitations imposed on man's freedom by the autonomy of language, the pervasive influence of ideology, and the obsessive forces of the subconscious. Insofar as the language and the structures of the New (New) Novel in general and Robbe-Grillet's work in particular reflect this new consciousness, they incorporate contemporary systems of thought. Robbe-Grillet's novels and films, by devaluing the past and heightening our consciousness of these dehumanizing forces, are providing answers to man's ontological and epistemological dilemmas.

Robbe-Grillet's novels and films also incorporate fragments of today's myths and ideology into a narrative discourse in which *parole* opposes *langue*. Formalist critics are not wrong to emphasize the linguistic autonomy of the New (New) Novel, but they stop short of incorporating the *langue-parole* conflict into a complete, although distorted, frame of reference that includes mimesis. Thus, Robbe-Grillet dramatizes and exaggerates images of sex and violence, two of society's dominant forces, in order to expose, undermine, devalue, and neutralize them. The purpose of his "alienation effect" is comparable to Brecht's, and the "revolutionary" potential of Robbe-Grillet's art, although not Marxist, is directed against the oppressive ideologies of both capitalist and socialist regimes. Robbe-Grillet's discourse thus calls attention to itself as an act of linguistic and cultural signmaking. It encourages us to think not only about the nature of language but also about the culture behind it—the way of life and the forms of life encoded into ideology.

In addition to his attacks on establishment values, Robbe-Grillet's critique of Nature and her allegedly natural "correspondences" stresses a *parole* whose purpose is not to decipher meaning but to create it. In so doing the author plays with *langue*, his mother tongue, and with mother nature, explores language's sensuous and incestuous possibilities, manhandles the body of words, and violates normative codes. He assaults the body of the text, simultaneously inflating and devaluing the sadoerotic clichés of our "idées reçues." This "deflowering" of language is a permanent attack on a Nature forever trying to have the last word. Like Sade, Robbe-Grillet breaks the rules, inverts the meaning of ritual, disputes prohibitions, and rapes his "victims," thereby affirming his freedom by remaining in a state of permanent scandal vis-à-vis his culture's ideology. Under such circumstances fiction becomes an affirmation of man emphasizing art's artificiality (i.e., autonomy) and opposition to so-called natural processes. Ultimately, the sexuality of such texts becomes political as insight reveals the arbitrary nature of all systems. Robbe-Grillet hopes that in time men will invent new meaning and new lives from the ruins of "phantom cities."

Modern art, beginning with Manet's *Olympia*, wanted first and foremost to assert its independence. In time, Picasso, cubism, Kandinsky, and nonobjective art, along with the specular modes that Gide so carefully constructed, by stressing art's emancipation from Nature, also signaled new epistemological systems. Thus, mirrors, pictures, windows, polysemy, and intertextuality set up internal and cross-textual references that undermine art's mimetic role. Picasso's copy of *Las Meniñas* simultaneously devalues nature and the artistic tradition by calling attention not to the subject matter, but to the painting of a painting—to art itself. Similarly, the dispersion of the anecdotal material and the proliferation of characters in Robbe-Grillet's "nouveau nouveau roman," beginning with *La Maison de rendez-vous*, devalue conventional fiction while structuring new and different narrative systems—verbal labyrinths in which the reader can get lost.

However, Robbe-Grillet's labyrinths, unlike Kafka's and Borges', are not designed to elicit anguish or fear. Their purpose rather is to deliver man from the prisons of language and conventional clichés. The dialogue between Robbe-Grillet's *parole* and society's *langue* thus generates gaps and openings in the text which require the collaboration and recreation of the reader/audience. Such verbal constructs invite us to venture into the "secret room" where all of the sexual/textual experiments occur. This penetration, with its sexual connotations, engenders blissful insights which, in turn, provide referential passageways to the outside. Robbe-Grillet's labyrinths thereby trap and deliver simultaneously. Our participation in re-creating the "open work" of art enables us to find the center and, having found it, like the king gods of antiquity, to conquer fear, anguish, violence, and death. Such art provides a key with which to unlock meaning, assert freedom, and resacralize space.

Robbe-Grillet's works, by reconciling reflexive and referential sign systems, also resolve these two seemingly opposed aspects of his art. He blends the ideology of the establishment (outside) with the imagery of the subconscious (inside) into a narrative discourse which describes external phenomena as well as internal states of mind. The economy of such an "écriture," which appears to perform the impossible, foregrounds language as the only and inevitable synthesis and mirror of the "outer" world and our "inner" consciousness of it. Language is the point of contact for these two realities, whereas art, both as a system of signs as a form of communication, works with matter and substance, a sort of privileged magma that unites the self and the other. The most prosaic objects, seemingly devoid of depth or content are charged with subconscious meaning and mythical weight. All of Robbe-Grillet's sadoerotic metaphors, such as bodies, doors, openings, rooms, penetration, blood, flow, stains, falling, and the like, in addition to their artistic weight, also have philosophical connotations. A simple venetian blind can now reconcile the subjectivity of phenomenology with the objectivity of structuralism.

Robbe-Grillet's novels and films thus project feelings of fear, anguish, desire, and disorientation onto objects and landscapes which, in themselves, are neutral, surface phenomena devoid of symbolism, depth, or a priori meaning. It is his uncanny ability to imbue things with significance, to structure internal and external resonances, to move freely from a consciousness "inside" to a reality "outside," that gives Robbe-Grillet's art the power to resolve dilemmas that continue to divide philosophers. If language is the point of contact for the subjective and the objective and a work of art reconciles both, then any discourse that dramatizes this process performs a necessary, Herculean task. The labyrinth, both as theme and structure, subsumes not only this dialectical process but all of Robbe-Grillet's art.

Language, by displaying a system of differences, allows the responsive imagination to play with ambiguity. On the self-contained level colors, words, images, and phonemes connect with other colors, words, images, and phonemes. This kind of "écriture productrice" multiples the work's internal resonances thereby generating meaning. A word, a name, or an object builds a pattern, a semantic field of correspondences whose sounds, associations, connotations, and imagery proliferate internally throughout the text. Nevertheless this purely formal interplay also meshes with generative themes borrowed from external mythic contexts. Such unorthodox narrative techniques seem chaotic to readers accustomed to the conventions of chronology, character, and plot. Furthermore, achronology, discontinuity, paronomasia, complexity, doubt, proliferation, polysemy, and reflexivity incorporate all those "dehumanizing" tendencies that many readers find so disquieting. Nevertheless, the old order, in spite of its resistance, is being challenged by new and different narrative systems that are more attuned to the ontological, epistemological, and metaphysical realities of the modern age.

The use of generative themes inevitably gives rise to a certain formalism and serialism in film and fiction that, in some ways, resembles Schoenberg's dodecaphonic music. Serialism in art is sometimes perceived as threatening because it is construed as an attack either on convention or on the bourgeois value system. Even though the meaning of this "subversion" may not be apprehended immediately, its "arbitrariness" does devalue the "natural" order of things by drawing attention to itself rather than to its message or its subject matter. However, out of apparent disorder, the New (New) Novel constructs a new and different order that reflects not only itself, but also a world in flux.

In conclusion, all of Robbe-Grillet's art is a theater of "play" that alludes to many things: to an actor's presence on stage, to the masks worn and the roles played; to the play of language and the images language evokes, which are compared sometimes to a door swinging back and forth—playing on its hinges ("la porte qui joue"). The French verb *jouer* embodies these and other connotations. It also means to gamble—something every artist understands—thereby alluding to life itself, and to the cosmic game, whose purpose, if there is one, is opaque and whose randomness is so unnerving. If language is the new heroine of fiction, then acts and images that dramatize the body of the text are atuned not only to a discourse on how language means but also to the problems of human existence, that is, how to create meaning in an impersonal universe which seems to deny man's presence or the fantasies he spins. Out of Joyce's "chaosmos" echo Beckett's undying though perhaps not eternal words: "Imagination Dead Imagine."

Notes

Introduction

1. *The French New Novel* (London: Oxford University Press, 1969), p. 18.
2. *Répertoire 3* (Paris: Editions de Minuit, 1968), p. 18.
3. *Les Gommes: Profil d'une oeuvre* (Paris: Hatier, 1973), p. 63.
4. "The Human Sciences," in *The Structuralists: From Marx to Lévi-Strauss*, ed. Richard and Fernande de George (New York: Doubleday & Co., 1972), p. 281. Parenthetical references to this essay will appear within the text as *SMLS*.
5. "Experience of a radically desacralized nature is a recent discovery," says Mircea Eliade. "It is an experience accessible only to a minority in modern societies, especially to scientists." *The Sacred and the Profane: The Nature of Religion*, trans. Willard R. Trask (New York: Harcourt Brace and World, 1959), p. 151.
6. "Interview," *L'Express*, 1–7 April 1968, p. 46.
7. (Paris: Gallimard, 1948), p. 7.

Chapter 1. Generative Themes and Serial Permutations

1. Alain Robbe-Grillet, "Sur le choix des générateurs," *Nouveau Roman: Hier, aujourd'hui*, ed. Jean Ricardou and Françoise van Rossum-Guyon (Paris: Union générale d'éditions, 1972), 2:160. Parenthetical references will appear within the text as *NRHA*, 2.
2. "Pourquoi la mort du roman?" *L'Express*, 11 November 1955, p. 8.
3. "Conclusion et perspectives," *Nouveau Roman: Hier, aujourd'hui*, 1:414–15. "Vingt ans après," *Nouveau Roman: Hier, aujourd'hui*, 2:202.
4. Pierre and Madeleine Caminade, "Métaphore et nouveau roman," *Nouveau Roman: Hier, aujourd'hui*, 1:256.
5. *Phénoménologie de l'expérience esthétique* (Paris: Presses universitaires de France, 1951), 1:11.
6. "Linguistics and Poetics," in *The Structuralists: From Marx to Lévi-Strauss*, ed. Richard and Fernande de George (New York: Doubleday & Co., 1972), p. 93.
7. "Today the essential question is no longer that of the *writer* and the *work*," writes Philippe Sollers in *Logiques* (Paris: Editions du Seuil, 1968, pp. 237–38), "but that of writing and reading." The focus now is on writing as an institution and reading as an activity, which leads to Umberto Eco's concept of the "open work" and Roland Barthes' definitions of the "writerly" and the "readerly."
8. *L'Oeuvre ouverte*, trans. Chantal Roux de Bézieux (Paris: Editions du Seuil, 1965), p. 278.
9. *Nouveaux Problèmes du roman* (Paris: Editions du Seuil, 1978), p. 16. Claude Ollier defines a narrative system as a "self-contained organization in which each narrative figure echoes every other figure on the same level, as well as those of other levels up to the level of fictional totality. . . . we could paraphrase Hjelmslev's definition of modern linguistics and

apply it, not without a certain risk, to a whole trend in today's literature: '. . . a research ensemble based on the hypothesis according to which it is scientifically legitimate to describe fiction as *being essentially an autonomous entity of internal dependencies, in other words, a structure.*' "

"Vingt ans après," *Nouveau Roman: Hier, aujourd'hui*, ed. Jean Ricardou and Françoise van Rossum-Guyon (Paris: Union générale d'éditions, 1972), 2:204.

10. Ferdinand de Saussure, *Course in General Linguistics* (New York: McGraw Hill, 1966), p. 144.

11. "La Fiction mot à mot." *Nouveau Roman: Hier, aujourd'hui*, 2:96–97.

12. *Nouveau Roman: Hier, aujourd'hui*, ed. Jean Ricardou and Françoise van Rossum-Guyon (Paris: Union générale d'éditions, 1972); 1:281. Parenthetical references to this edition will appear within the text as *NRHA*, 1.

13. *Figures III* (Paris: Editions du Seuil, 1973), p. 57.

14. "Après *l'Eden et après*," *Le Nouvel Observateur*, no. 294 (26 June–5 July 1970), p. 34.

15. "Robert Pinget: Le Livre disséminé comme fiction, narration et objet," Ibid., p. 302.

16. *Pour une théorie du Nouveau Roman* (Paris: Editions du Seuil, 1971), pp. 25–26.

17. For an interesting discussion of the generative themes in *Projet pour une révolution à New York* see Thomas O'Donnell, "Thematic Generation in Robbe-Grillet's *Projet pour une révolution à New York*," *Twentieth-Century French Fiction* (New Brunswick, N.J.: Rutgers University Press, 1975); also Jean Ricardou, *Pour une théorie du nouveau roman*, pp. 220–21.

18. "Interview: Alain Robbe-Grillet," *Diacritics* 6 (1976): 39.

19. "An Introduction to Planetary Thought," *Yale French Studies*, Special Issue on "Game, Play, Literature" 41 (1968): 6–18.

20. "Le Sadisme contre la peur," *Le Nouvel Observateur*, no. 310, 19 October 1970, p. 48. Parenthetical references to this article will appear within the text as *SCP*.

21. *Language and Myth*, trans. Susanne K. Langer (New York: Harper and Brothers, 1946), pp. 31–32.

22. Readers interested in a broader spectrum of generative affinities between writing and painting should consult Alain Robbe-Grillet et al., *Generative Literature and Generative Art* (Fredericton, N.B.: York Press, 1983). Those interested in pursuing the connection between Jasper Johns's painting as a generative theme for portions of *Souvenirs du triangle d'or* should consult Bruce Morrissette, *Intertextual Assemblage in Robbe-Grillet from Topology to the Golden Triangle* (Fredericton, N.B.: York Press, 1979).

23. "Souvenirs du triangle d'or," *Editions de Minuit Catalogue, 1979*, p. 6. A parenthetical reference to the *Catalogue* appears within the text. *Souvenirs du triangle d'or* (Paris: Editions de Minuit, 1978). Parenthetical references to this edition will appear as *STO*.

24. "Interview: Alain Robbe-Grillet," 43.

25. See "Alchemy," *Encyclopedia Britannica*, 14th ed., 1929, p. 536.

26. Alain Robbe-Grillet, "Order and Disorder in Film and Fiction," *Critical Inquiry* 4 (1977): 10–11. Parenthetical references will appear within the text as *ODFF*.

27. Umberto Eco, *L'Oeuvre ouverte*, trans. Chantal Roux de Bézieux (Paris: Editions du Seuil, 1965), p. 76. Parenthetical references to this edition will appear within the text as *OO*.

28. "Robbe-Grillet in Africa," *London Magazine* 13 (1973): 109. A parenthetical reference to this article will appear within the text. See also André Gardies, *Alain Robbe-Grillet* (Paris: Seghers, Cinéma d'aujourd'hui, 1972), pp. 84–93. Gardies's study is structural and formalist. He makes no attempt to "explain" the cultural context or the mythic units Robbe-Grillet uses for his generative themes, i.e., nothing is "recuperated." Gardies sticks to Robbe-Grillet's original twelve themes and does not differentiate between idea generators (such as death) and object generators (such as doors).

29. *Nouveau Roman: Hier, aujourd'hui*, 1:205. *L'Eden et après*: Eastmancolor, 100 min., 35mm., Robbe-Grillet's fourth film, excluding *L'Année dernière à Marienbad* (directed by

Alain Resnais, scenario by Robbe-Grillet). Robbe-Grillet wrote and directed *L'Immortelle*, *L'Homme qui ment*, *Trans-Europ-Express*, *L'Eden et après*, *Glissements progressifs du plaisir*, *Le Jeu avec le feu*, and *La Belle Captive*.

30. *Style and Idea: Selected Writings*, ed. Leonard Stein (New York: St. Martin's Press, 1975), p. 223.

31. *Obliques*, nos. 16–17 (Paris: Editions Borderie, 1978), p. 197. Bruce Morrissette, in his study of *L'Eden*, views "themes" as "materials" to be structured, as the "reservoir" from which the author takes his subjects. See "Post-Modern Generative Fiction: Novel and Film," *Critical Inquiry* 2 (1975): 258.

32. Maria Bystrzycka, "Eisenstein as Precursor of Semantics in Film Art," *Sign, Language, Culture*, ed. A. J. Greimas et al. (The Hague, Paris: Mouton, 1970), p. 473.

33. Alain Robbe-Grillet, "*L'Eden et après*: début pour un ciné-roman," *Obliques*, nos. 16–17, p. 192.

34. *The Basic Writings of Sigmund Freud* (New York: The Modern Library, 1938), pp. 181–553.

35. Jacques Lacan, as quoted by A. G. Wilden, *The Language of the Self* (Baltimore: Johns Hopkins University Press, 1968), p. 31. See Erich Fromm, *The Forgotten Language* (New York: Rinehart and Co., Inc., 1951).

36. Stephen S. Vise, *Wassily Kandinsky and Arnold Schoenberg: Parallelism in Form and Meaning* (Ph.D. diss. Washington University, 1969); Ann Arbor, Mich.: Music, University Microfilms, 1969), p. 60.

Chapter 2. A Project for a Revolution

1. Georg Lukács, *Realism in Our Time* (New York: Harper & Row, 1964), pp. 96–97. Parenthetical references to this edition will appear withint the text as *ROT*.

2. (Berkeley and Los Angeles: The University of California Press, 1976), pp. vii–viii. Parenthetical references to this edition will appear within the text as *MLC*.

3. *La Littérature et le mal* (Paris: Gallimard, 1957), p. 175.

4. *Lukàcs et Heidegger* (Paris: Editions Denoël, 1973), pp. 57–89.

5. See Claude Simon, *Orion aveugle* (Geneva: A. Skira, 1970), p. 106.

6. Alain Robbe-Grillet, "Le Sadisme contre la peur," *Le Nouvel Observateur*, no. 310, 19–25 October 1970, p. 49.

7. See Walter Benjamin, *Charles Baudelaire: A Lyric Poet in the Era of High Capitalism*, trans. Harry Zohn (London: NLB, 1973).

8. See Bertolt Brecht, *Brecht on Theatre: The Development of an Aesthetic*, trans. John Willett (London: Methuen, 1964).

9. As quoted by Eagleton in *Marxism and Literary Criticism*, p. 71.

10. As quoted by Katherine K. Passias in "New Novel, New New Novel: An Interview with A. Robbe-Grillet," *Sub-stance* 13 (1976): 133. Parenthetical references to this interview will appear within the text as Passias.

11. Alain Robbe-Grilet, "Order and Its Double: Eroticism and Literature in the Works of the Marquis de Sade," *The Bennington Review* 3 (1969): 5. Parenthetical references to this article will appear within the text as *OD*.

12. Alain Robbe-Grillet, "For a Voluptuous Tomorrow," *Saturday Review*, 20 May 1972, p. 46. Parenthetical references to this article will appear within the text as *FVT*.

13. (Paris: F. Maspero, 1978).

14. See Georg Lukács, *Writer and Critic*, ed. and trans. Arthur Kahn (London: Merlin

Press, 1970) and Vladimir Il'ich Lenin, *Materialism and Empirio-Criticism: Critical Comments on a Reactionary Philosophy* (Moscow: Foreign Languages Publishing House, 1952).

15. See Althusser's "Letter on Art in reply to André Daspre" in *Lenin and Philosophy*, trans. Ben Brewster (London: New Left Books, 1971).

16. Alain Robbe-Grillet, *Pour un nouveau roman* (Paris: Editions de Minuit, 1963), p. 35. Parenthetical references to this edition will appear within the text as *PNR*.

17. Eugene Ionesco, "Ionesco on Politics: How Strange, How Bizarre and What a Coincidence!" *Los Angeles Times*, Part 5, 18 May 1980, p. 2.

18. Alain Robbe-Grillet, *Glissements progressifs du plaisir* (Paris: Editions de Minuit, 1974), p. 14. Parenthetical references to this edition will appear within the text as *GPP*.

19. *Projet pour une révolution à New York* (Paris: Editions de Minuit, 1970), p. 198. Parenthetical references to this edition will appear within the text as *PRNY*.

20. *Minuit* 18 (1976): 2–15.

21. Alain Robbe-Grillet, "Discussion," *Nouveau Roman: Hier, aujourd'hui*, ed. Jean Ricardou and Françoise van Rossum-Guyon (Paris: Union générale d'éditions, 1972), 1:173.

22. Ibid.

23. "There is something very particular in this terrorism: I like it, but I can't stand it." Ibid.

24. "Politique et Nouveau Roman," Ibid., p. 369.

Chapter 3. The Body of the Text

1. *Le Plaisir du texte* (Paris: Editions du Seuil, 1973), p. 105. Parenthetical references to this edition will appear within the text as *PT*.

2. *Capitalisme et schizophrénie: L'anti-Oedipe* (Paris: Editions de Minuit, 1974), p. 138.

3. See "Thematic Generation in Robbe-Grillet's *Projet pour une révolution à New York*," *Twentieth-Century French Fiction* (New Brunswick, N.J.: Rutgers University Press, 1975), pp. 195–96.

4. Ferdinand de Saussure, *Course in General Linguistics* (New York: McGraw Hill, 1966), p. 13. Parenthetical references will appear within the text as *CGL*.

5. Alain Robbe-Grillet, *Projet pour une révolution à New York* (Paris: Editions de Minuit, 1970), pp. 184–85.

6. P. A. Doyle: "Robbe-Grillet makes de Sade seem like Sesame Street. This is a totally disgusting novel, frightfully degenerate, and . . . possesses no redeeming social values." Roger Shattuck: "The great dangers that threaten this kind of fiction are triviality leading to boredom." *Book Review Digest* (1972), p. 1092. *Doxal* system or *Doxology* (from Leibnitz): a speaking attitude adapted to appearances, to opinion, or accepted practice. *Doxa*: public opinion, the voice of the majority, whatever passes for being "natural," the violence of prejudice. See *Roland Barthes* by Roland Barthes (Paris: Editions du Seuil, 1975), p. 51. Parenthetical references will appear within the text as *RB*.

7. Alain Robbe-Grillet, "Sur le choix des générateurs," *Nouveau Roman: Hier, aujourd'hui*, ed. Jean Ricardou and Françoise van Rossum-Guyon (Paris: Union générale d'éditions, 1972), 2:161.

8. Maurice Merleau-Ponty, *Phenomenology of Perception*, trans. Colin Smith (New York: The Humanities Press, 1962), p. 189. Parenthetical references to this edition will appear within the text as *PP*.

9. *The Prison-House of Language: A Critical Account of Structuralism and Russian Formalism* (Princeton, N.J.: Princeton University Press, 1972), p. 58.

10. *Roland Barthes*, by Roland Barthes, p. 67.

11. (Paris: Editions de Minuit, 1976), p. 196. Parenthetical references to this edition will appear within the text as *TCF*.

12. *Minuit* 18 (1976):2–15.

13. Alain Robbe-Grillet, *Souvenirs du triangle d'or* (Paris: Editions de Minuit, 1978).

14. *"To Write: An Intransitive Verb?"* in *The Languages of Criticism and the Sciences of Man: The Structuralist Controversy*, ed. Richard Macksey and Eugenio Donato (Baltimore: The Johns Hopkins University Press, 1970), p. 135.

Chapter 4. *Mirror, Mirror on the Wall . . .*

1. As quoted by André Malraux in *La Tête d'obsidienne* (Paris: Gallimard, 1974), pp. 127–28. Parenthetical references to this edition will appear within the text as *TO*.

2. *Pour un nouveau roman* (Paris: Editions de Minuit, 1963), p. 120. Parenthetical references to this edition will appear within the text as *PNR*.

3. As quoted by E. H. Gombrich in *Art and Illusion* (New York: Random House, 1960), p. 115. Parenthetical references to this edition will appear within the text as *AI*.

4. *Cubism and Twentieth-Century Art* (New York: Harry N. Abrams, 1960), p. 40. For more detail concerning Robbe-Grillet and Cubism see Elly Jaffé-Freem, *Alain Robbe-Grillet et la peinture cubiste* (Amsterdam: J. M. Meulenhoff, 1966). Parenthetical references to this edition will appear within the text as *RGPC*.

5. *Le Récit spéculaire: Essai sur la mise en abyme* (Paris: Editions du Seuil, 1977), p. 52. Parenthetical references to this edition will appear within the text as *RS*.

6. "Un Héritage d'André Gide: La Duplication Intérieure," *Comparative Literature Studies* 8 (1971): 125–42.

7. *Journal, 1889–1939* (Paris: Gallimard, Pléiade ed., 1948), p. 41.

8. *Les Gommes: Profil d'une oeuvre* (Paris: Hatier, 1973), p. 39.

9. *Le Nouveau Roman* (Paris: Seuil, Ecrivains de toujours, 1973), p. 50.

10. Alain Robbe-Grillet, *Le Voyeur* (Paris: Editions de Minuit, 1955), pp. 119–20.

11. Dällenbach, p. 216. Jacques Derrida, *De la grammatologie* (Paris: Editions de Minuit, 1967), p. 434.

12. *Les Mots et les choses* (Paris: Gallimard, 1966), p. 319.

13. Pierre Teilhard de Chardin, *The Phenomenon of Man* (New York: Harper and Brothers, 1959), p. 147.

14. *L'Intérieur et l'extérieur* (Paris: Corti, 1968), p. 233. Parenthetical references to this edition will appear within the text as *IE*.

15. Ibid. and Christine Brooke-Rose, "L'Imagination baroque de Robbe-Grillet," *Revue des Lettres Modernes*, nos. 94–99 (1964): 131.

16. See Ben Stoltzfus, "A Novel of Objective Subjectivity: *Le Voyeur* by Alain Robbe-Grillet," *PMLA* 77 (1962): 499–507.

17. *Dans le labyrinthe* (Paris: Editions de Minuit, 1959), p. 142.

18. Interview with André Bourin, *Nouvelles Littéraires*, 5 December 1957, p. 9.

19. *Topologie d'une cité fantôme* (Paris: Editions de Minuit, 1976), pp. 21, 33.

20. Jacques Leenhardt, "Nouveau roman et société," *Nouveau Roman: Hier, aujourd'hjui*, ed. Jean Ricardou and Françoise van Rossum-Guyon (Paris: Union générale d'éditions, 1972), 1:169.

21. *Raymond Roussel* (Paris: Gallimard, 1963), p. 205.

22. Intertextuality functions in three ways: (a) as a network of references from one work to another by the same author; (b) the text of one author may interlock with the text of other

authors (Ricardou uses the word "abeille" (bee) from a Claude Ollier novel as a generative theme for *La Prise de Constantinople*); (c) the text may use a combination of (a) and (b).

23. *Phénoménologie de l'expérience esthétique* (Paris: Presses universitaires de France, 1951), 1:6.

Chapter 5. A Dialectical Topology

1. "Topology and the French *Nouveau Roman*," *Boundary 2* (1972): 47.

2. "The Theory and Practice of Reading Nouveaux Romans: Robbe-Grillet's *Topologie d'une cité fantôme*," *The Reader in the text*, ed. Susan R. Suleiman and Inge Crosman (Princeton, N.J.: Princeton University Press, 1980), pp. 371–401.

3. "Interview" with Vicki Mistacco, *Diacritics* 6 (1976): 37.

4. *Le Récit spéculaire: Essai sur la mise en abyme* (Paris: Editions du Seuil, 1977), p. 47.

5. "The movement described is thus the lifting of a release, the *Aufhebung* of an *Aufhebung* with which I rediscover in the other whatever I lose from myself." *Glas* (Paris: Editions Galilée, 1974), p. 25.

6. Bruce Morrissette, "Topology and the French *Nouveau Roman*," and "Robbe-Grillet No. 1, 2 . . . x," *Nouveau Roman: Hier, aujourd'hui, vol. 2*, ed. Jean Ricardou and Françoise van Rossum-Guyon *(Paris: Union générale d'éditions, 1972), p. 127; Jacques Leenhardt, Lecture politique du roman: "La Jalousie" d'Alain Robbe-Grillet* (Paris: Editions de Minuit, 1973); Betty T. Rahv, *From Sartre to the New Novel* (Port Washington, N.Y.: Kennikat Press, 1974), p. 108.

7. *Forme et signification* (Paris: Corti, 1962), p. 123.

8. Leenhardt, *Lecture politique du roman;* Robbe-Grillet, "Order and Disorder in Film and Fiction," trans. Bruce Morrissette, *Critical Inquiry* 4 (1977): 1–20.

9. *La Poétique de l'espace* (Paris: Presses universitaires de France, 1967), pp. 18–19.

10. Mircea Eliade, *The Sacred and the Profane: The Nature of Religion*, trans. Willard R. Trask (New York: Harcourt, Brace and World, 1959), p. 43.

11. *Lecture politique du roman*, p. 66.

12. Alain Robbe-Grillet, *Pour un nouveau roman* (Paris: Editions de Minuit, 1963), p. 88.

13. Alain Robbe-Grillet, *La Jalousie* (Paris: Editions de Minuit, 1957), pp. 159–60.

14. "(Début d'un projet de film)," *Minuit* 18 (1976): 2–15. Parenthetical references to "Piège" will appear within the text.

15. *Dans le labyrinthe* (Paris: Editions de Minuit, 1959), p. 11.

16. *Topologie d'une cité fantôme* (Paris: Editions de Minuit, 1976), pp. 95–96. Parenthetical references to this edition will appear within the text as *T*.

17. Robbe-Grillet's collaboration with these four artists is as follows: *Rêves de jeunes filles*, text by Robbe-Grillet, photos by David Hamilton (Paris: Laffont, 1971), *Les Demoiselles d'Hamilton*, text by Robbe-Grillet, photos by David Hamilton (Paris: Laffont, 1972). Construction d'un temple en ruines à la déesse Vanadé, prints by Paul Delvaux, text by Robbe-Grillet (Paris: Le Bateau-Lavoir, 1975), reprinted in *Topologie d'une cité fantôme; La Belle Captive*, text by Robbe-Grillet, illustrations by René Magritte (Paris: Bibliothèque des arts, 1976); *Traces suspectes en surfaces*, text by Robbe-Grillet, original lithographs by Robert Rauschenberg, limited signed edition, 1978; Robbe-Grillet's text corresponds to four chapters in *Topologie d'une cité fantôme*. Some of Rauschenberg's lithographs are printed over Robbe-Grillet's hand-written text.

18. Françoise van Rossum-Guyon, "Conclusions et Perspectives," *Nouveau Roman: Hier, aujourd'hui*, ed. Jean Ricardou and Françoise van Rossum-Guyon. (Paris: Union générale d'éditions, 1972), 1:407.

19. Jean Ricardou, *Pour une théorie du Nouveau Roman* (Paris Editions du Seuil, 1971, p. 214.

20. Alain Robbe-Grillet, "Discussion," *Nouveau Roman: Hier, aujourd'hui*, 2:236.

21. Ibid., p. 165.

22. Sigmund Freud, *A General Introduction to Psycho-Analysis* (New York: Liveright, 1935), p. 141.

23. Michel Foucault, "La Pensée du dehors," *Critique* 229 (June 1966): 525.

Chapter 6. The Labyrinth

1. As quoted by André Gardies in *Alain Robbe-Grillet* (Paris: Seghers, Cinéma d'aujourd'hui, 1972), p. 117.

2. S. H. Hooke, *The Labyrinth* (London: Society for Promoting Christian Knowledge; New York: The Macmillan Company, 1935), p. 42. In addition to its specific meanings in Greek mythology, in anatomy, and in geology, Webster's dictionary defines labyrinth as an intricate combination of passages in which it is difficult to find one's way or to reach the exit; also, as any confusingly intricate state of things or events—an entanglement. William H. Matthews says that labyrinth signifies "a complex problem involving merely time and perseverance for its solution," whereas maze is "reserved for situations fraught, in addition, with the elements of uncertainty and ambiguity, calling for the exercise of the higher mental faculties." William H. Matthews, *Mazes and Labyrinths: A General Account of Their History and Developments* (London: Longmans, Green and Co., 1922), pp. 177–78. Since neither the dictionary nor common usage distinguishes between labyrinth and maze, I will use them interchangeably. Both words will denote either an actual place and/or connote confusion. Parenthetical references to *Mazes and Labyrinths* will appear within the text as *ML*.

3. "Le Labyrinthe, espace significatif," *Cahiers Internationaux de Symbolisme* 9–10 (1966): 29. Parenthetical references to this issue will appear within the text as *CIS*.

4. Jorge Luis Borges, "El Inmortal," *El Aleph* (Buenos Aires: Editorial Losada, 1952), pp. 14–15.

5. *Franz Kafka: Parable and Paradox* (Ithaca, N.Y.: Cornell University Press, 1962), pp. 230–31.

6. *The Phenomenon of Man* (New York: Harper and Brothers, 1959), p. 228. A parenthetical reference to this edition will appear within the text as *PM*.

7. In *Thésée*, André Gide says that the monsters of antiquity have been interiorized, that they devour from within. *Romans, récits, soties* (Paris: Gallimard, Pléiade ed., 1958), pp. 1432–33. Nevertheless, concentration camps are "external monsters" that devour their annual quota of human flesh. See Paul Hofmann, "Horrors of Soviet Dissident Detailed," *International Herald Tribune*, 30 May 1979, p. 2. Mrs. Ida Nudel, a Jewish dissident banished to Siberia because she wanted to emigrate to Israel, is a typical victim of today's bureaucratized terror. She is the only woman in a camp of sixty men, former convicts who, when drunk, attack her at night, brutalize her, and "behave like apes." She shares a sink with other inmates and rats so large she suffers from hallucinations. When not under attack, she is alone in a little room which is her fortress, her bedroom, her kitchen, her toilet, her washroom, and her laundry. Village people are afraid to come near her in the streets lest they be interrogated by the police. She weeps for the meaninglessness of her life. "Kafka, Kafka, where are you?" is Mrs. Nudel's anguished cry that was smuggled out of the Soviet Union on tape by visitors who saw her at the camp. "Even your imagination could not create a situation like this." An invocation to Kafka from a concentration camp in Siberia! What could be more tragic, yet ironic, considering the attacks against Kafka by Marxist critics who allege that Kafka does not address himself to the class struggle in a prose appropriately "realistic." On

the contrary, the realism of Kafka's fiction, by addressing itself to human suffering, nullifies the political objections of commentators such as Lukács.

8. *Borges the Labyrinth Maker*, ed. and trans. Robert Lima (New York: New York University Press, 1965), p. 61.

9. *Dans le labyrinthe* (Paris: Editions de Minuit, 1959), p. 54.

10. *The Sacred and the Profane: The Nature of Religion*, trans. Willard R. Trask (New York: Harcourt, Brace and World, 1959), pp. 23–24. Parenthical references to this edition will appear within the text as *SP*.

11. I am "recuperating" this novel in ways which will offend some commentators, but then the purpose of my study is to show, in part, that reflexive works are "recuperable"; that whereas they may designate themselves as objects, they nevertheless, as Jacques Leenhardt's study of Robbe-Grillet demonstrates, possess levels of meaning that integrate them into the age that produced them. See *Lecture Politique du roman: "La Jalousie" d'Alain Robbe-Grillet* (Paris: Editions de Minuit, 1973).

12. "Le Sadisme contre la peur" (an interview), *Le Nouvel Observateur*, no. 310, 19 October 1970, p. 48.

13. *From Sartre to the New Novel* (Port Washington, N.Y.: Kennikat Press, 1974), p. 142. Parenthical references to this edition will appear within the text as *FSNN*.

14. For an interesting study of Robbe-Grillet's topological dialectic in *Dans le labyrinthe*, see Bruce Morrissette, "Topology and the French Nouveau Roman," *Boundary 2* 1 (Fall 1972): 47.

15. *La Crise du roman français et le nouveau réalisme* (Paris: Nouvelles Editions Debresse, 1968), pp. 260–61.

16. (Paris: Editions de Minuit, 1970), p. 7.

17. (Paris: Editions de Minuit, 1976), p. 201.

18. See John J. Michalczyk, "Recurrent Imagery of the Labyrinth in Robbe-Grillet's Films," *Stanford French Review* 2 (1978): pp. 115–28.

19. (Paris: Editions de Minuit, 1974), p. 34.

20. P. W. Bridgman, "The New Vision of Science," *Harper's*, December 1928–May 1929, pp. 443–51.

21. *L'Oeuvre ouverte*, trans. Chantal Roux de Bézieux (Paris: Editions du Seuil, 1965), p. 30.

22. *S/Z.*, trans. Richard Miller (London: Jonathan Cape, 1975), p. 4.

23. *The Concept of Structuralism: A Critical Analysis* (Berkeley and Los Angeles: The University of California Press, 1975), p. 45.

24. Alain Robbe-Grillet, "Autour du film *L'Immortelle*," *Cahiers internationaux de symbolisme* 9–10 (1965–66): 108.

25. "Linguistic Patterning and Narrative Structure," *Journal of Literary Semantics* 4 (1975): 100.

Chapter 7. Games: Dramatized Play

1. Robbe-Grillet's "nouveau nouveau roman," emphasizing polysemy, generative themes, generative numbers, and the play of language, corresponds, generally speaking, to his work after *Dans le labyrinthe* (1959). His fiction as "theater," however, covers both periods, i.e., the "nouveau roman" and the "nouveau nouveau roman" (1953 to the present). For a useful introduction to "Games and Game Structures in Robbe-Grillet," see Bruce Morrissette's article in *Yale French Studies* 41 (1968): 159–67, a special issue entitled *Game, Play, Literature*.

2. *L'Ecriture et l'expérience des limites* (Paris: Editions du Seuil, 1968), p. 92. Parenthetical references to this edition will appear within the text as *EEL*.

3. *Projet pour une révolution à New York* (Paris: Editions de Minuit, 1970), p. 181.

4. *Pour un nouveau roman* (Paris: Editions de Minuit, 1963), p. 95.

5. *Les Gommes* (Paris: Editions de Minuit, 1953), p. 11. Parenthetical references to this edition will appear within the text as *G*.

6. *Dans le labyrinthe* (Paris: Editions de Minuit, 1959), pp. 202–3.

7. *Topologie d'une cité fantôme* (Paris: Editions de Minuit, 1976), pp. 71–72.

8. *Souvenirs du triangle d'or* (Paris: Editions de Minuit, 1978), p. 21.

9. Kostas Axelos, "Planetary Interlude," *Yale French Studies* 41 (1968): 6–18. Excerpts translated by Sally Hess from the introductory and concluding chapters of *Vers la pensée planétaire* (Paris: Editions de Minuit, 1964). Parenthetical references to this article will appear within the text as *PI*.

10. Alain Robbe-Grillet, "Le Sadisme contre la peur," *Le Nouvel Observateur*, no. 310, 19 October 1970, p. 48.

11. Jean-Paul Sartre, *The Psychology of Imagination* (New York: The Citadel Press, 1961), pp. 270–71.

12. See *Pleasure of the Text*, trans. Richard Miller (New York: Hill and Wang, 1975), p. 37.

13. "Autour du film *L'Immortelle*," *Cahiers internationaux de symbolisme* 9–10 (1966): 122.

14. Alain Robbe-Grillet, "Discussion," *Nouveau Roman: Hier, aujourd'hui*, ed. Jean Ricardou and Françoise van Rossum-Guyon (Paris: Union générale d'éditions, 1972), 1:128. Robbe-Grillet says that "Butor's writing, in the final analysis, is just like the writing of the past, a deciphering of God's work . . . while we, today, in contrast, are writing in an entirely different perspective; our endeavor consists in the creation of man through language as though he had not been created by God." "Discussion," *Nouveau Roman: Hier, aujourd'hui*, ed. Jean Ricardou and Françoise van Rossum-Guyon (Paris: Union générale d'éditions, 1972), 2:280.

15. *Structuralist Poetics* (Ithaca, N.Y.: Cornell University Press, 1975), p. 245.

16. Jacques Derrida, *L'Ecriture et la différence* (Paris: Editions du Seuil, 1967), p. 411.

17. As quoted by Jonathan Culler in *Structuralist Poetics*, p. 247.

18. "The Oasis of Happiness: Toward an Ontology of Play," *Yale French Studies* 41 (1968): 19. Parenthetical references to this article will appear within the text as *OH*.

19. Roger Caillois, *Man, Play, and Games* (New York: Free Press, 1961), pp. 9–10. J. Huizinga, *Homo Ludens* (New York: Roy Publishers, 1950), p. 13. Caillois defines play as free, separate, uncertain, unproductive, regulated, and fictive.

20. Alain Robbe-Grillet, "Après *l'Eden et après*," *Le Nouvel Observateur*, no. 294, 29 June 1970, p. 35. Parenthetical references to this essay will appear within the text as *AEA*.

21. Alain Robbe-Grillet, "For a Voluptuous Tomorrow," trans. Richard Howard, *Saturday Review*, 20 May 1972, p. 46.

22. Alain Robbe-Grillet, "Projet pour une révolution à New York," lecture given at the University of California, Los Angeles, June 1, 1978.

23. As quoted by Kostas Axelos in "Planetary Interlude," p. 7.

24. *Eros and Civilization: A Philosophical Inquiry into Freud* (New York: Vintage, 1955), p. 77.

25. *Le Nouveau Roman* (Paris: Bordas, 1972), p. 132.

26. As quoted by Vincent Therrien in *La Révolution de Gaston Bachelard en critique littéraire* (Paris: Klincksieck, 1970), p. 116.

27. *Proêmes* (Paris: Gallimard, 1965), pp. 227–28.

Bibliography

Works of Alain Robbe-Grillet

In French:

Un Régicide. Paris: Les Editions de Minuit, 1978. Written in 1949. A novel.

Les Gommes. Paris: Les Editions de Minuit, 1953. Written in 1951. Prix Fénéon, 1954. A novel.

Le Voyeur. Paris: Les Editions de Minuit, 1955. Prix des Critiques, 1955. A novel.

La Jalousie. Paris: Les Editions de Minuit, 1957. A novel.

Dans le labyrinthe. Paris: Les Editions de Minuit, 1959. A novel.

L'Année dernière à Marienbad. Paris: Les Editions de Minuit, 1961. Ciné-roman.

Instantanés. Paris: Les Editions de Minuit, 1962. Short stories written between 1954 and 1962.

L'Immortelle. Paris: Les Editions de Minuit, 1963. Ciné-roman.

Pour un nouveau roman. Paris: Les Editions de Minuit, 1963. Critical essays written between 1953 and 1963.

La Maison de rendez-vous. Paris: Les Editions de Minuit, 1965. A novel.

Projet pour une révolution à New York. Paris: Les Editions de Minuit, 1970. A novel.

Rêves de jeunes filles. Paris: Laffont, 1971. Text by Robbe-Grillet, photographs by David Hamilton.

Les Demoiselles d'Hamilton. Paris: Laffont, 1972. Text by Robbe-Grillet, photographs by David Hamilton.

Glissements progressifs du plaisir. Paris: Les Editions de Minuit, 1974. Ciné-roman.

Construction d'un temple en ruines à la déesse Vanadé. Paris: Le Bateau-Lavoir, 1975. Prints by Paul Delvaux, text by Robbe-Grillet.

La Belle Captive. Paris: Bibliothèque des arts, 1976. A novel, with illustrations by René Magritte.

Topologie d'une cité fantôme. Paris: Les Editions de Minuit, 1976. A novel.

Traces suspectes en surfaces. Limited edition of original lithographs by Robert Rauschenberg with a text by Robbe-Grillet, 1978.

Souvenirs du triangle d'or. Paris: Les Éditions de Minuit, 1978. A novel.

Temple aux miroirs. Paris: Seghers, 1979. Text by Robbe-Grillet, photographs by Irina Ionesco.

Le Rendez-vous. New York: Holt, Rinehart, and Winston, 1981. Intermediate-level French textbook; text by Robbe-Grillet; grammatical exercises by Yvone Lenard. Same text as *Djinn.*

Djinn. Un trou rouge entre les pavés disjoints. Paris: Les Editions de Minuit, 1981. A novel.

[For a listing of Robbe-Grillet's book reviews, essays, articles, and interviews not published in volume form see Michel Rybalka, "Bibliographie," *Obliques* Nos. 16–17 (Paris: Editions Borderie, 1978): 263–77.]

In English

The Erasers. Translated by Richard Howard. New York: Grove Press, 1964.

The Voyeur. Translated by Richard Howard. New York: Grove Press, 1958.

Jealousy. Translated by Richard Howard. New York: Grove Press, 1959.

In the Labyrinth. Translated by Richard Howard. New York: Grove Press, 1960.

In the Labyrinth. Translated by Christine Brooke-Rose. London: Calder and Boyars, 1967.

Two Novels by Robbe-Grillet (Jealousy) and (In the Labyrinth). Translated by Richard Howard. New York: Grove Press, 1965.

Last Year at Marienbad. Translated by Richard Howard. New York: Grove Press, 1962.

For a New Novel: Essays on Fiction. Translated by Richard Howard. New York: Grove Press, 1965.

La Maison de Rendez-vous. Translated by Richard Howard. New York: Grove Press, 1966.

Snapshots. Translated by Bruce Morrissette. New York: Grove Press, 1968.

The Immortal One. Translated by A. M. Sheridan Smith. London: Calder and Boyars, 1971.

Project for a Revolution in New York. Translated by Richard Howard. New York: Grove Press, 1972.

Topology of a Phantom City. Translated by J. A. Underwood. New York: Grove Press, 1976.

Djinn. Translated by Yvone Lenard and Walter Wells. New York: Grove
Press, 1982.

Films by Alain Robbe-Grillet

L'Année dernière à Marienbad, 1961. Original screenplay and dialogue by
Alain Robbe-Grillet. Director: Alain Resnais. Producers: Pierre
Courau (Précitel), Raymond Froment (Terrafilm). Distributor:
Cocinor.

L'Immortelle, 1963. Written and directed by Robbe-Grillet. Producers:
Samy Halfon, Michel Fano. Distributor: Cocinor.

Trans-Europ-Express, 1966. Written and directed by Robbe-Grillet. Producer: Samy Halfon. Production: Como Films (Paris). Distributor:
Lux-C.C.F.

L'Homme qui ment, 1968. Written and directed by Robbe-Grillet. Producer: Samy Halfon. Production: Como Films, Lux-C.C.F., Ceskos-
lovensky Film (Bratislava). Distributor: Lux-C.C.F. Best actor prize to
Jean-Louis Trintignant and screenplay prize to Robbe-Grillet at the
1969 Berlin Festival.

L'Eden et après, 1971. Written and directed by Robbe-Grillet. Producer:
Samy Halfon. Production: Como Films (Paris), Ceskoslovenky Film
(Bratislava). Distributor: Plan Films.

N. a pris les dés. A reworking of *L'Eden et après* for French television.
Broadcast on Channel 3 at the end of 1975.

Glissements progressifs du plaisir, 1974. Written and directed by Robbe-
Grillet. Producer: Roger Boublil. Production: Coséfa Films (André Co-
hen and Marcel Sébaoun), S.N.E.T.C. (Henri Boublil). Distributor:
Fox.

Le Jeu avec le feu, 1975. Written and directed by Robbe-Grillet. Producers:
Alain Coiffer, Philippe Ogouz. Production: Arcadie (Paris). Distributor: U.G.C.

La Belle Captive, 1983. Written and directed by Robbe-Grillet. Producer:
Anatole Dauman. Production: Argos Films (Paris).

Film Adaptations of Robbe-Grillet's Novels and Short Stories

1962: *In the Labyrinth*, by Robert Lrikala. 12 minutes. Distributor: Film-
Makers Cooperative, New York.

1969: *Les Gommes*. Franco-Belgian co-production. 90 minutes. Directed by
Lucien Deroisy. Adaptation and screenplay by René Micha.

1972: *La Jalousie*, by Klaus Kieschner for German television.

1975: *Les Deux Chambres distantes et/ou les deux chambres discrètes.* An adaptation of "La Chambre secrète." Directed by Kunihiko Nakagawa (Japan).

1977: *La Plage à distance.* An adaptation of "La Plage." Directed by Kunihiko Nakagawa.

1978: *La Chambre secrète.* Directed by J. F. Urrusti, London International Film School.

Selected Essays and Comments by and Interviews with Robbe-Grillet

"Last Words on 'Last Year,'" Interview with Resnais and Robbe-Grillet. *Films and Filming* 8 (1962): 39–41.

"Le Nouveau Roman remonte à Kafka." Interview with Pierre Mazars. *Figaro Littéraire*, 15 September 1962.

"Autour du film *L'Immortelle.*" Round-table discussion, *Cahiers Internationaux de Symbolisme* Nos. 9–10 (1965–66): 97–125.

"The Man Who Lies: An Interview with Alain Robbe-Grillet," by Tom and Helen Bishop. *Film Festival.* New York: Grove Press, 1969, pp. 41–44, 87–89.

"L'Ordre et son double (érotisme et littérature dans les oeuvres du Marquis de Sade)." *The Bennington Review* 3 (1969): 7–14.

"Après *L'Eden et après.*" *Le Nouvel Observateur*, 29 June 1970, pp. 33–34.

"Je réinvente la mythologie de la civilisation dans laquelle je vis." Interview with Colette Canty. *Le Progrès* (Lyon), 15 October 1970.

"Le Sadisme contre la peur." Interview with Guy Dumur. *Le Nouvel Observateur*, no. 310, 19 October 1970, p. 48.

"For a Voluptuous Tomorrow." Translated by Richard Howard. *Saturday Review*, 20 May 1972, pp. 44–46.

"Sur le choix des générateurs." *Nouveau Roman: Hier, aujourd'hui.* Edited by Jean Ricardou and Françoise van Rossum-Guyon, 2:157–62. Paris: Union générale d'éditions, 1972.

"Le Cinéma selon Robbe-Grillet." In André Gardies, *Alain Robbe-Grillet*, pp. 104–25. Paris: Seghers, Coll. Cinéma d'aujourd'hui, 1972. Also fragments from *Trans-Europ-Express*, *L'Homme qui ment*, and a statement by Robbe-Grillet on *L'Eden et après*, pp. 126–60.

"Glissements progressifs du plaisir." Interview with Jean-Louis Ezine. *Nouvelles Littéraires*, 18 February 1974.

"Le Droit au jeu et à la volupté." *Le Point*, 25 February 1974.

"Alain Robbe-Grillet: Apel à l'intelligence du lecteur." Interview with Jacqueline Piatier. *Le Monde*, 29 March 1974.

"Alain Robbe-Grillet, la provocation constante." Interview with Anne Andreu. *Magazine Littéraire*, no. 87 (April 1974).

"L'Ecriture a-t-elle un sexe?" *Quinzaine Littéraire*, no. 192, 1–30 August 1974.

"Robbe-Grillet: The 'Ironic' Treatment of Eroticism." Interview with Melinda Camber. *The Times*, 29 October 1974.

"Dans son septième film, le chef de file du nouveau roman joue avec le feu: *Robbe-Grillet entre la foudre et l'encens.*" Interview with Pierre Montaigne. *Le Figaro*, 18 February 1975.

"New Novel, New New Novel." Interview with Katherine Passias, *Sub-Stance*, no. 13 (March 1976): 130–35.

"Alain Robbe-Grillet." Interview with Vicki Mistacco. *Diacritics* 6 (1976): 35–43.

"Piège à fourrure (Début d'un projet de film)." *Minuit* no. 18 (1976): 2–15.

"Order and Disorder in Film and Fiction." Translated by Bruce Morrissette, *Critical Inquiry* 4 (1977): 1–20.

"La Cible." *Jasper Johns Catalogue*. Paris: Centre Georges Pompidou, 1978, pp. 8–13.

Special issue of *Obliques* nos. 16–17. Paris: Editions Borderie, 1978. Contains the following articles, excerpts, and letters:

    "Le Réalisme, la psychologie et l'avenir du roman," p. 5.

    "Lettre à François Mauriac: La technique du cageot," p. 5.

    "Scénario de *Trans-Europ-Express*," p. 13.

    "*Trans-Europ-Express*, ciné-roman," p. 21.

    "L'Engagement de l'artiste," p. 41.

    "La Japonaise," p. 43.

    "Quatre jours en Bulgarie," p. 49.

    "Brouillon des premières pages des *Gommes*," p. 74.

    "Lettre à Gérard Bauër," p. 76.

    "Lettre à Emile Henriot," p. 88.

    "L'Ange gardien," p. 93.

    "Brouillon des premières pages de *La Maison de rendez-vous*," p. 132.

    "Moisissures," p. 157.

    "Poèmes," p. 159.

    "*Un Régicide*," p. 161.

    " 'Histoire de rats,' ou La Vertu, c'est ce qui mène au crime," p. 169.

    "Scénario de *l'Homme qui ment*," p. 175.

    "Deux lettres, à André Rousseaux et à Emile Henriot," p. 183.

"Scénario de *l'Eden et après*," p. 185.

"Impressions de Turquie," p. 227.

"La Chambre secrète," p. 231.

"Scénario du *Magicien*," p. 259.

This Special Number of *Obliques* also contains nine reproductions of Robbe-Grillet's paintings, p. 241 (I–VIII), and many color and black-and-white reproductions from his films.

"Fragment Autobiographique Imaginaire," *Minuit* no. 31 (November 1978): 2–8.

"Robbe-Grillet artiste joueur." Interview with Michel Rybalka. *Le Monde*, 22 September 1978.

Selected Secondary Sources: Robbe-Grillet Criticism, "Nouveau (Nouveau) Roman," Film, Marxist, Structuralist, and Play Criticism

Albérès, R. M. "A. Robbe-Grillet et la sacralisation du roman policier." In *Métamorphoses du roman*, pp. 143–51. Paris: Albin Michel, 1972.

Alter, Jean. *La Vision du monde d'Alain Robbe-Grillet*. Geneva: Droz, 1966.

Althusser, Louis. *Lenin and Philosophy*. Translated by Ben Brewster. London: New Left Books, 1971.

Armes, Roy. "Robbe-Grillet in Africa." *London Magazine* 4 (1973): 107–113.

―――. "Robbe-Grillet, Ricardou, and *Last Year at Marienbad*." *Quarterly Review of Film Studies* 5 (1980): 1–17.

―――. *The Films of Alain Robbe-Grillet*. Vol. 6. Purdue University Monographs in Romance Languages. Amsterdam: John Benjamins B.V., 1981.

Astier, Pierre A. G. *La Crise du roman français et le nouveau réalisme*. Paris: Nouvelles Editions Debresse, 1968.

Axelos, Kostas. *Vers la pensée planétaire*. Paris: Les Editions de Minuit, 1964.

Bachelard, Gaston. *La Terre et les rêveries du repos*. Paris: Corti, 1948.

―――. *La Poétique de l'espace*. Paris: Presses universitaires de France, 1967.

Bajomée, Danielle. *Un Nouveau Nouveau Roman*. Liège: Association des Romanistes de l'Université de Liège, 1979.

Baqué, Françoise. *Le Nouveau Roman*. Paris: Bordas, 1972.

Barnes, Hazel E. "The Ins and Outs of Robbe-Grillet." *Chicago Review* 15 (1962): 21–43.

Barrenechea, Ana Maria. *Borges the Labyrinth Maker*. Edited and translated by Robert Lima. New York: New York University Press, 1965.

Barthes, Roland. *Mythologies*. Paris: Editions du Seuil, 1957.

———. *Pleasure of the Text*. Translated by Richard Miller. New York: Hill and Wang, 1975.

———. *Roland Barthes*. Paris: Seuil, "Ecrivains de toujours," 1975.

———. *S/Z*. Translated by Richard Miller. London: Jonathan Cape, 1975.

Bataille, Georges. *La Littérature et le mal*. Paris: Gallimard, 1957.

Baum, Alwin L. "The Metanovel: Robbe-Grillet's Phenomenal *Nouveau Roman*." *Boundary 2* 6 (1977–78): 557–75.

Beaujour, Michel. "The Game of Poetics." *Yale French Studies* 41 (1968): 58–67. Special Issue on "Game, Play, Literature."

Beauvoir, Simone de. *The Marquis de Sade*. With selections from his writings chosen by Paul Dinnage. New York: Grove Press, 1953.

Beckett, Samuel. *Our Exagmination Round His Factification for Incamination of "Work in Progress."* Paris: Shakespeare & Co., 1929.

Benjamin, Walter. *Charles Baudelaire: A Lyric Poet in the Era of High Capitalism*. Translated by Harry Zohn. London: NLB, 1973.

Berkowitz, Janice. "Les Ficelles métanaratives dans *Le Voyeur* de Robbe-Grillet." *Rackam Literary Studies* 8 (1977): 39–47.

Bernal, Olga. *Alain Robbe-Grillet: Le roman de l'absence*. Paris: Gallimard, 1964.

Bettetini, Gianfranco. *The Language and Technique of the Film*. The Hague: Mouton, 1973.

Brecht, Bertolt. *Brecht on Theatre: The Development of an Aesthetic*. Translated by John Willett. London: Methuen, 1964.

Butler, Christopher. *After the Wake: An Essay on the Contemporary Avant-Garde*. Oxford: Clarendon Press, 1980.

Caillois, Roger. *Man, Play, and Games*. New York: Free Press, 1961.

Carrabino, Victor. *The Phenomenological Novel of Alain Robbe-Grillet*. Parma: C.E.M., 1970.

Cassirer, Ernst. *Language and Myth*. Translated by Susanne K. Langer. New York: Harper and Brothers, 1946.

Champigny, Robert. *Pour une esthétique de l'essai*. Paris: Minard, 1967.

Chateau, Dominique, and François Jost. "Robbe-Grillet, le plaisir du glissement." *Ça* 3 (1974): 10–19.

———. *Nouveau Cinéma, nouvelle sémiologie: Essai d'analyse des films d'Alain Robbe-Grillet*. Paris: U.G.E., 10/18, 1979.

Clayton, John J. "Alain Robbe-Grillet: The Aesthetics of Sadomasochism." *Massachusetts Review* 18 (1977): 106–119.

Cohn, Dorrit. "Castles and Anti-castles, or Kafka and Robbe-Grillet." *Novel* 5 (1971): 19–31.

Les Critiques de notre temps et le nouveau roman. Paris: Garnier, 1972. Anthology of critical articles by a variety of writers.

Culler, Jonathan. *Structuralist Poetics.* Ithaca, N.Y.: Cornell University Press, 1975.

Dällenbach, Lucien. *Le Récit spéculaire: Essai sur la mise en abyme.* Paris: Editions du Seuil, 1977.

Deleuze, Gilles and Félix Guattary. *Capitalisme et schizophrénie: L'anti-Oedipe.* Paris: Editions de Minuit, 1972.

Delfosse, Pascale. "*Glissements progressifs du plaisir:* Robbe-Grillet et son 'nouveau langage.'" *Revue Nouvelle* 30 (1974): 85–94.

Deneau, Daniel. "The Interrogation of the Narrator in Robbe-Grillet's *Project for a Revolution in New York.*" *Notes on Contemporary Literature* 6 (1976): 3–10.

———. "Notes on Robbe-Grillet's *La Maison de rendez-vous.*" *Neophilologus* 63 (1979): 521–29.

Derrida, Jacques. *De la grammatologie.* Paris: Editions de Minuit, 1967.

———. *L'Ecriture et la différence.* Paris: Editions du Seuil, 1967.

———. *Glas.* Paris: Editions Galilée, 1974.

Dhaenens, Jacques. "*La Maison de rendez-vous:*" *Pour une philologie sociologique.* Paris: Minard, 1970.

Dufrenne, Mikel. *Phénoménologie de l'expérience esthétique.* Vol. 1. Paris: Presses universitaires de France, 1951.

Durozoi, Gérard. "*Les Gommes*": *Profil d'une oeuvre.* Paris: Hatier, 1973.

Eagleton, Terry. *Marxism and Literary Criticism.* Berkeley and Los Angeles: University of California Press, 1976.

Eco, Umberto. *L'Oeuvre ouverte.* Translated by Chantal Roux de Bézieux. Paris: Aux Editions du Seuil, 1965.

———. *A Theory of Semiotics.* Bloomington, Ind.: Indiana University Press, 1976.

Ehrmann, Jacques. "Homo Ludens Revisited." Translated by Cathy and Phil Lewis. *Yale French Studies* 41 (1968): 31–57. Special Issue on "Game, Play, Literature."

Eliade, Mircea. *The Sacred and the Profane: The Nature of Religion.* Translated by Willard R. Trask. New York: Harcourt, Brace and World, 1959.

Ellis, Zilpha. "Robbe-Grillet's Use of Pun and Related Figures in *La Jalousie.*" *International Fiction Review* 2 (1975): 9–17.

Ellul, Jacques. *The Presence of the Kingdom.* Translated by Olive Wyon. New York: The Seabury Press, 1967.

Fano, Michel. "L'Attitude musicale dans *Glissements Progressifs du plaisir.*" *Ça* 3 (1974): 20–22.

Fink, Eugen. *Le Jeu comme symbole du monde.* Translated by Hans Hildenberg and Alex Lindenberg. Paris: Editions de Minuit, 1966.

Foucault, Michel. *Raymond Roussel.* Paris: Gallimard, 1963.

———. *Les Mots et les choses.* Paris: Gallimard, 1966.

———. "La Pensée du dehors." *Critique* 229 (June 1966): 523–46.

———. *La Volonté de savoir: Histoire de la sexualité* Vol. 1. Paris: Gallimard, 1976.

Galand, René M. "La Dimension sociale dans *La Jalousie* de Robbe-Grillet." *French Review* 39 (1966): 703–8.

Gardies, André. *Alain Robbe-Grillet.* Paris: Seghers, Cinéma d'aujourd'hui, 1972.

———. "Ecriture, image: Texte." *Etudes Littéraires* 6 (1973): 445–55.

———. "Génèse, générique, générateurs, ou la naissance d'une fiction." *Revue d'Esthétique* 4 (1976): 86–120.

Garzilli, Enrico. "Daedalus and the Nouveau Roman." In *Circles without Center.* Cambridge, Mass.: Harvard University Press, 1972, pp. 106–17.

Genette, Gérard. "Vertige fixé." In *Dans le labyrinthe* by Alain Robbe-Grillet. Paris: U. G. E., 10/18, 1964.

———. *Figures III.* Paris: Editions du Seuil, 1973.

George, Richard and Fernande de, eds. *The Structuralists: From Marx to Lévi-Strauss.* New York: Doubleday & Co., Inc., 1972.

Gerhart, Mary Jane. "The Purpose of Meaninglessness in Robbe-Grillet." *Renascence* 23 (1970–71): 79–97.

Goldmann, Lucien. *Pour une sociologie du roman.* Paris: Gallimard, 1964.

———. *Lukàcs et Heidegger.* Paris: Editions Denoël, 1973.

Gombrich, E. H. *Art and Illusion.* New York: Random House, 1960.

Goodstein, Jack. "Pattern and Structure in Robbe-Grillet's *La Maison de rendez-vous.*" *Critique: Studies in Modern Fiction* 14 (1972): 91–99.

Greimas, A. J. *Du Sens: Essais sémiotiques.* Paris: Editions du Seuil, 1970.

——— et al. eds. *Sign, Language, Culture.* The Hague: Mouton, 1970.

Hahn, Otto. "Plan du Labyrinthe de Robbe-Grillet." *Les Temps Modernes* 16 (1960): 150–68.

Heath, Stephen. *The Nouveau Roman: A Study in the Practice of Writing.* Philadelphia: Temple University Press, 1972.

Hooke, S. H. *The Labyrinth.* London: Society for Promoting Christian Knowledge; New York: The Macmillan Company, 1935.

Huizinga, J. *Homo Ludens.* New York: Roy Publishers, 1950.

Husserl, Edmund. *The Paris Lectures.* Translated by Peter Koestenbaum. The Hague: Martinus Nijhoff, 1967.

Ionesco, Eugene. "Ionesco on Politics: How Strange, How Bizarre and What a Coincidence!" *Los Angeles Times*, Part 5, 18 May 1980, p. 2.

Jaffé-Freem, Elly. *Alain Robbe-Grillet et la peinture cubiste.* Amsterdam: J. M. Meulenhoff, 1966.

Jameson, Fredric. *The Prison-House of Language: A Critical Account of Structuralism and Russian Formalism.* Princeton, N.J.: Princeton University Press, 1972.

―――. "Modernism and Its Repressed: Robbe-Grillet as Anti-Colonialist." *Diacritics* 6 (1976): 7–14.

Janvier, Ludovic. *Une Parole exigeante.* Paris: Editions de Minuit, 1964.

Jefferson, Ann. *The Nouveau Roman and the Poetics of Fiction.* Cambridge: Cambridge University Press, 1980.

Johnson, Patricia J. *Camus et Robbe-Grillet: Structure et techniques narratives dans "Le Renégat" de Camus et "Le Voyeur" de Robbe-Grillet.* Paris: Nizet, 1972.

Jost, François. "A propos de *Glissements* de Robbe-Grillet: Ponctuation et parataxe." *Critique* 30 (1974): 326–34.

―――. "Le Je à la recherche de son identité." *Poétique*, no. 24 (1975): 479–87.

―――, ed. "Robbe-Grillet." *Obliques.* Special Issue, Nos. 16–17. Paris: Editions Borderie, 1978.

Laffay, Albert. *Logique du cinéma.* Paris: Masson, 1964.

Leach, David, ed. *Generative Literature and Generative Art.* Fredericton, N.B.: York Press, 1983.

Leenhardt, Jacques. *Lecture politique du roman: "La Jalousie" d'Alain Robbe-Grillet.* Paris: Editions de Minuit, 1973.

Leki, Ilona. *Alain Robbe-Grillet.* Boston: Twayne Publishers, 1983.

Lenin, Vladimir Il'ich. *Materialism and Empirio-Criticism: Critical Comments on a Reactionary Philosophy.* Moscow: Foreign Languages Publishing House, 1952.

Lethcoe, James. "The Structures of Robbe-Grillet's Labyrinth." *French Review* 38 (1965): 497–506.

Lévi-Strauss, Claude. *La Pensée sauvage*. Paris: Plon, 1962.

————. *The Raw and the Cooked*. London: Jonathan Cape, 1964.

Lukács, Georg. *Realism in Our Time*. New York: Harper & Row Publishers, 1964.

————. *Writer and Critic*. Edited and translated by Arthur Kahn. London: Merlin Press, 1970.

Macherey, Pierre. *Pour une théorie de la production littéraire*. Paris: F. Maspéro, 1978.

Macksey, Richard, and Eugenio Donato, eds. *The Languages of Criticism and the Sciences of Man: The Structuralist Controversy*. Baltimore: The Johns Hopkins University Press, 1970.

Malraux, André. *La Tentation de l'Occident*. Paris: Gallimard, 1970.

————. *La Tête d'obsidienne*. Paris: Gallimard, 1974.

Marcuse, Herbert. *Eros and Civilization: A Philosophical Inquiry into Freud*. New York: Vintage, 1955.

Matthews, J. H., ed. *Un Nouveau Roman?* Paris: Minard, 1964. Special Issue of *La Reveue des lettres modernes*. Articles on Robbe-Grillet by Renato Barilli, Christine Brooke-Rose, and Ben Stoltzfus. Reprinted, 1983.

Matthews, William H. *Mazes and Labyrinths: A General Account of Their History and Developments*. London: Longmans, Green and Co., 1922.

Mauriac, François. "La Technique du cageot d'Alain Robbe-Grillet." *Le Figaro littéraire*, 8 November 1956. Reprinted in *Les Critiques de notre temps et le Nouveau Roman*, pp. 41–43. Paris: Garnier, 1972.

Meltzer, Françoise. "Preliminary Excavations of Robbe-Grillet's Phantom City." *Chicago Review* 28 (1976): 41–50.

Mercier, Vivian. *The New Novel: From Queneau to Pinget*. New York: Farrar, Straus and Giroux, 1971.

Merleau-Ponty, Maurice. *Phenomenology of Perception*. Translated by Colin Smith. New York: The Humanities Press, 1962.

Metz, Christian. *Film Language: A Semiotics of the Cinema*. Translated by Michael Taylor. New York: Oxford University Press, 1974.

Micciollo, Henri. *"La Jalousie" d'Alain Robbe-Grillet*. Paris: Hachette, 1973.

Michalczyk, John J. "Structural and Thematic Configurations in Robbe-Grillet's Films." *American Society Legion of Honor Magazine* 48 (1977): 13–44.

————. "Intertextual Assemblage as Fictional Generator: *Topologie d'une cité fantôme*." *International Fiction Review* 5 (1978): 1–14.

————. "Recurrent Imagery of the Labyrinth in Robbe-Grillet's Films." *Stanford French Review* 2 (1978): 115–28.

"Midnight Novelists." *Yale French Studies*. Special Issue. No. 24 (1959).

Articles by René Girard, Bernard Pingaud, Bernard Dort, W. M. Frohock, Germaine Brée, Jacques Guicharnaud, and others.

Miesch, Jean. *Robbe-Grillet*. Paris: Editions Universelle, 1965.

Minogue, Valerie. "The Creator's Game: Some Reflexions on Robbe-Grillet's *Le Voyeur*." *Modern Language Review* 72 (1977): 815–28.

Mistacco, Vicki. "The Theory and Practice of Reading Nouveaux Romans: Robbe-Grillet's *Topologie d'une cité fantôme*." In *The Reader in the Text: Essays on Audience and Interpretation*. Edited by Susan R. Suleiman and Inge Crosman, pp. 371–401. Princeton, N.J.: Princeton University Press, 1980.

Mitry, Jean. Esthétique et psychologie du cinéma. Vol. 1. Paris: Editions universitaires, 1963.

———. "D'un langage sans signes." *Revue d'Esthétique* 2–3 (1967): 139–52.

Moeller, Hans-Bernard. "Literature in the Vicinity of the Film: On German and *nouveau roman* Authors." *Symposium* 28 (1974): 315–35.

Morrissette, Bruce. *Les Romans de Robbe-Grillet*. Paris: Editions de Minuit, 1963.

———. "Aesthetic Response to Novel and Film: Parallels and Differences." *Symposium* 27 (1973): 137–51.

———. "Games and Game Structures in Robbe-Grillet." *Yale French Studies* 41 (1968): 159–67. Special Issue entitled "Game, Play, Literature."

———. "Un Héritage d'André Gide: La duplication intérieure." *Comparative Literature Studies* 8 (1971): 125–42.

———. *The Novels of Robbe-Grillet*. Ithaca, N.Y.: Cornell University Press, 1975.

———. "Post-Modern Generative Fiction: Novel and Film." *Critical Inquiry* 2 (1975): 253–62.

———. "Topology and the French *Nouveau Roman*." *Boundary 2* 1 (1972): 45–57.

———. *Intertextual Assemblage in Robbe-Grillet from Topology to the Golden Triangle*. Fredericton, N.B.: York Press, 1979.

Nouveau Roman: Hier, aujourd'hui. Jean Ricardou and Françoise van Rossum-Guyon, ed. 2 vols. Paris: Union générale d'éditions, 1972.

O'Donnell, Thomas D. "Thematic Generation in Robbe-Grillet's *Projet pour une révolution à New York*." *Twentieth Century French Fiction*. New Brunswick, N.J.: Rutgers University Press, 1975.

Ollier, Claude. "Ce soir à Marienbad." *Nouvelle Revue Française* 9 (1961): 711–19, 906–912.

Panofsky, Erwin. *Meaning in the Visual Arts*. New York: Doubleday & Co. 1955.

Pettit, Philip. *The Concept of Structuralism: A Critical Analysis*. Berkeley and Los Angeles: University of California Press, 1975.

Politzer, Heinz. *Franz Kafka: Parable and Paradox*. Ithaca, N.Y.: Cornell University Press, 1962.

Rahv, Betty T. *From Sartre to the New Novel*. Port Washington, N.Y.: Kennikat Press, 1974.

Ricardou, Jean. *Pour une théorie du Nouveau Roman*. Paris: Editions du Seuil, 1971.

———. *Le Nouveau Roman*. Paris: Editions du Seuil, 1973.

———. *Nouveaux Problèmes du roman*. Paris: Editions du Seuil, 1978.

Ronse, Henri. "Le Labyrinthe, espace significatif," *Cahiers internationaux de symbolisme* 9–10 (1966): 27–43.

Rosenblum, Robert. *Cubism and Twentieth-Century Art*. New York: Harry N. Abrams, 1960.

Roudiez, Leon. *French Fiction Today*. New Brunswick, N.J.: Rutgers University Press, 1972.

Rousset, Jean. *Forme et signification*. Paris: Corti, 1962.

———. *L'Intérieur et l'extérieur: Essais sur la poésie et sur le théâtre au XVIIème siècle*. Paris: Corti, 1968.

Sarraute, Nathalie. *L'Ère du soupçon*. Paris: Gallimard, 1956.

Sartre, Jean-Paul. Pref. *Portrait d'un inconnu*. Nathalie Sarraute. Paris: Gallimard, 1956.

Saussure, Ferdinand de. *Course in General Linguistics*. New York: McGraw-Hill Book Company, 1966.

Sipos, George. "Linguistic Patterning and Narrative Structure." *Journal of Literary Semantics* 4 (1975): 100.

Sollers, Philippe. *L'Ecriture et l'expérience des limites*. Paris: Editions du Seuil, 1968.

Stoltzfus, Ben. "A Novel of Objective Subjectivity: *Le Voyeur* by Alain Robbe-Grillet." *PMLA* 77 (1962): 499–507.

———. *Alain Robbe-Grillet and the French New Novel*. Carbondale: Southern Illinois University Press, 1964.

———. "Camus et Robbe-Grillet: La connivence tragique de *l'Etranger* et du *Voyeur*." *Revue des Lettres Modernes* nos. 94–99 (1964): 153–66. Reprinted, 1983.

———. "Robbe-Grillet, *L'Immortelle*, and the Novel: Reality, Nothingness, and Imagination." *L'Esprit Créateur* 7 (1967): 123–34.

———. "D'Un Langage à l'autre: Les deux Robbe-Grillet." *Etudes cinématographiques*, Nos. 100–103 (1974): 87–104.

———. "Robbe-Grillet: The Reflexive Novel As Process and Poetry." *Symposium* 30 (1976): 343–57.

———. "Un Régicide: A Metaphorical Intrigue." *French Forum* 5 (1980): 269–83.

———. "Dead, Desacralized, and Discontent: Robbe-Grillet's New Man." *Modern Fiction Studies* 27 (1981): 543–53.

———. "The Aesthetics of *Nouveau Roman* and Innovative Fiction." *The International Fiction Review* 10 (1983): 108–16.

———. "Robbe-Grillet's *Djinn:* The Grammar of Subversion." *Degré Second* 8 (1984): 19–26.

Sturdza, Paltin. "Répétition et différence dans *L'Année dernière à Marienbad.*" *Neophilologus* 61 (1977): 48–55.

Sturrock, John. *The French New Novel.* London: Oxford University Press, 1969.

Suleiman, Susan. "Reading Robbe-Grillet: Sadism and Text in *Projet pour une révolution à New York.*" *Romanic Review* 68 (1977): 43–62.

Szanto, George H. *Narrative Consciousness: Structures and Perception in the Fiction of Kafka, Beckett, and Robbe-Grillet.* Austin: University of Texas Press, 1972.

Teilhard de Chardin, Pierre. *The Phenomenon of Man.* New York: Harper and Brothers, 1959.

Todorov, Tzvetan. *Littérature et signification.* Paris: Larousse, 1967.

Towarnicky, Frédéric de. "*L'Homme qui ment:* Procès-verbal." *Cinéma 67,* no. 121 (1967): 57–64.

Van Wert, William U. "Structures of Mobility and Immobility in the Cinema of Alain Robbe-Grillet." *Sub-stance* no. 9 (1974): 79–85.

Vareille, Jean-Claude. "Alain Robbe-Grillet et l'écriture: Délice et supplice." *Critique* no. 381 (1979).

Vidal, Jean-Pierre. *"La Jalousie" de Robbe-Grillet.* Paris: Hachette, 1973.

———. *"Dans le labyrinthe" de Robbe-Grillet.* Paris: Hachette, 1975.

Vise, Stephen S. *Wassily Kandinsky and Arnold Schoenberg: Parallelisms in Form and Meaning.* Ph.D. diss., Washington University 1969. Ann Arbor, Mich.: Music University Microfilms, Inc.

Weiner, Seymour S. "A Look at Techniques and Meanings in Robbe-Grillet's *Le Voyeur.*" *Modern Language Quarterly* 23 (1962): 217–24.

Wollen, Peter. *Signs and Meaning in the Cinema.* London: Martin Secker and Warburg, 1969.

Zants, Emily. *The Aesthetics of the New Novel in France.* Boulder: University of Colorado Press, 1968.

———. "The Relation of Epiphany to Description in the Modern French Novel." *Comparative Literature Studies* 5 (1968): 317–28.

Bibliographical Studies

Alter, Jean. "The New Novel." In *Critical Bibliography of French Literature.* Vol. 6, Part 3. Edited by Douglas W. Alden and Richard A. Brooks, pp. 1472–81. Syracuse, N.Y.: Syracuse University Press, 1980.

Fraizer, Dale Watson. *Alain Robbe-Grillet: An Annotated Bibliography of Critical Studies, 1953–1972.* Metuchen, N.J.: The Scarecrow Press, 1973.

Rybalka, Michel. "Bibliographie." In *Obliques.* Special Robbe-Grillet Issue, nos. 16–17, pp. 263–83. Paris: Editions Borderie, 1978.

———. "Alain Robbe-Grillet." In *Critical Bibliography of French Literature,* Vol. 6, Part 3. Edited by Douglas W. Alden and Richard A. Brooks, pp. 1500–1501. Syracuse, N.Y.: Syracuse University Press, 1980.

Van Wert, William U. *The Film Career of Alain Robbe-Grillet.* Boston: G. K. Hall, 1977.

Index